AF885706

Environmental Constitutionalism: What Impact on Legal Systems?

Le constitutionnalisme environnemental : quel impact sur les systèmes juridiques ?

P.I.E. Peter Lang

Bruxelles · Bern · Berlin · New York · Oxford · Wien

Jochen Sohnle (ed./dir.)

Environmental Constitutionalism: What Impact on Legal Systems?

Le constitutionnalisme environnemental : quel impact sur les systèmes juridiques ?

Préface/Forword: Stéphane Pierré-Caps

EcoPolis
Vol. 32

Le présent ouvrage a été réalisé grâce à l'appui opérationnel de l'équipe de l'IRENEE. Sa publication a bénéficié du soutien financier de l'IRENEE.

Réalisation graphique de la couverture : Nathalie Absalon Saulnier.

Éditions scientifiques internationales
Bruxelles, 2019
1 avenue Maurice, B-1050 Bruxelles, Belgique
www.peterlang.com ; brussels@peterlang.com

Imprimé en Allemagne

ISSN 1377-7238
ISBN 978-2-8076-1242-6
ePDF 978-2-8076-1243-3
ePub 978-2-8076-1244-0
Mobi 978-2-8076-1245-7
DOI 10.3726/b15945
D/2019/5678/31

Information bibliographique publiée par « Die Deutsche Bibliothek »

« Die Deutsche Bibliothek » répertorie cette publication dans la « Deutsche Nationalbibliografie » ; les données bibliographiques détaillées sont disponibles sur le site <http://dnb.ddb.de>.

Bibliographic information published by "Die Deutsche Nationalbibliothek".

"Die Deutsche Nationalbibliothek" lists this publication in the "Deutsche Nationalbibliografie"; detailed bibliographic data is available on the Internet at <http://dnb.d-nb.de>.

Table des matières (Complète)

English version

Version française

Avant-propos
Foreword

Stéphane PIERRÉ-CAPS

Professeur de droit public à l'Université de Lorraine, France
Faculté de droit, sciences économiques et gestion de Nancy
IRENEE/UL (EA 7303)

De quoi le constitutionnalisme environnemental est-il le nom ? La notion, en effet, ne va pas de soi en dépit de l'apparence. L'on peut ainsi comprendre celle-ci, au premier abord, comme exprimant l'insertion du cadre de la vie humaine, l'environnement, dans un processus juridique justifié par un « surcroît de valeur formelle »[1], la Constitution. Le constitutionnalisme environnemental traduirait ainsi l'affirmation d'un constitutionnalisme spécialisé dans l'interaction de l'homme avec la nature, ainsi dédié à la protection constitutionnelle de l'environnement.

C'est un fait que depuis la Conférence des Nations unies sur l'environnement humain[2], une véritable émulation s'est emparée des États quant à la protection constitutionnelle de l'environnement. Les Constitutions de la plupart d'entre eux se réfèrent peu ou prou à l'environnement, souvent même au titre d'un droit public subjectif[3]. Si, en ce sens, la Charte française de l'environnement s'inscrit dans la vocation à l'universalité de la Déclaration des droits de l'homme et du citoyen de 1789, d'autres textes constitutionnels se singularisent par des institutions et mécanismes spécifiques originaux, à l'exemple de la Constitution

---

[1] Xavier Bioy, « L'environnement, nouvel objet du droit constitutionnel ou : qu'est-ce que « constitutionnaliser » ? », *in* : Henry Roussillon, Xavier Bioy, Stéphane Mouton (dir.), *Les nouveaux objets du droit constitutionnel*, Presses de l'Université des Sciences sociales de Toulouse, 2006, p. 26.

[2] Conférence de Stockholm, 5–16 juin 1972.

[3] Michel Prieur, « Promesses et réalisations de la Charte de l'environnement », *Les Nouveaux Cahiers du Conseil constitutionnel*, n° 43, 2014, p. 7–24.

tunisienne de 2014. L'article 129 crée ainsi une autorité constitutionnelle indépendante, dotée de la personnalité juridique et de l'autonomie financière, la « Commission du développement durable et des droits des générations futures », associée au processus législatif[4].

Cet ample mouvement constitutionnel apparaît pour le moins ambivalent : s'agit-il de constitutionnalisation de la protection de l'environnement ou de constitutionnalisation du droit de l'environnement ? Il est certain que le prisme constitutionnel est susceptible d'esquisser « les contours d'une autre notion d'environnement »[5], bien loin de figurer un simple réceptacle d'un droit exogène. Mais cette nouvelle figure constitutionnalisée de l'environnement suscite aussi nombre de questions, qui tiennent tout autant à son contenu même – le rapport de l'humanité et de la nature – qu'à la qualité de la norme qui l'informe, même si l'un et l'autre tendent à se rejoindre pour faire de l'environnement ainsi constitutionnalisé « la manifestation d'un nouveau droit de l'homme »[6]. Encore que ce dernier aspect ne soit pas lui-même exempt d'interrogations : le contentieux constitutionnel de la Charte française de l'environnement, par exemple, est concentré sur le seul article 7 quant au droit à l'information et à la participation en matière environnementale, même si, depuis l'introduction de la Question prioritaire de constitutionnalité, ce contentieux s'est accru de manière significative[7].

Ces incertitudes et questionnements tiennent sans doute au fait qu'il n'existe ni une définition universellement admise, ni une analyse théorique ou normative convaincante de ce que l'on entend par « constitutionnalisme environnemental ». L'on peut, certes, constater que celui-ci se situe au carrefour du droit international et du droit constitutionnel, des droits de l'homme et du droit de l'environnement. Tel auteur peut ainsi y voir tantôt « un patrimoine commun constitutionnalisé », tantôt une norme de *jus cogens*[8] ; tel autre, en une résurgence jusnaturaliste, « la quête

---

4 Elle est « obligatoirement consultée pour les projets de loi relatifs aux questions commerciales, sociales et environnementales, ainsi que pour les plans de développement ». Voir aussi le Préambule et l'article 45.

5 Xavier Bioy, cité, p. 31.

6 Michel Prieur, « Environnement », *in* : Michel Troper, Dominique Chagnollaud (dir.), *Traité international de droit constitutionnel*, Dalloz, 2012, p. 604.

7 Pierre-Yves Gahdoun, « L'ouverture du contentieux constitutionnel à de nouvelles matières », *Les Nouveaux Cahiers du Conseil constitutionnel*, n° 58, 2018, p. 43–57.

8 M. Prieur, respectivement, « Promesses et réalisations de la Charte de l'environnement », cité, p. 15 ; « Environnement », cité, p. 631.

d'un ordre exprimant le juste, tel qu'il se manifeste dans la nature, quête universelle et éternelle »[9].

Dans le même ordre d'idées, les origines internationales du constitutionnalisme environnemental et la mondialisation de la protection de l'environnement conduisent à se demander si l'échelon constitutionnel national est à cet égard le plus pertinent. L'on doit cette interrogation aux tenants du constitutionnalisme global, qui n'ont ainsi pas manqué d'évoquer la possibilité même d'un « constitutionnalisme environnemental global »[10]. Certes, la protection de l'environnement n'a pas encore trouvé une place pleine et entière dans un discours du constitutionnalisme global lui-même sujet à caution : « [...] from a global constitutionalist perspective, it is unclear if there are elements of environmental constitutionalism present in the global environmental regulatory sphere »[11].

La question n'en demeure pas moins posée de l'articulation du constitutionnalisme environnemental national et du constitutionnalisme global, ce dernier demeurant pour l'heure fragmenté et lacunaire, « et dont il faut d'emblée reconnaître qu'il n'a pas l'épaisseur des constitutions nationales »[12]. À défaut de l'existence, pour l'heure, d'un constitutionnalisme environnemental global, il est permis de considérer le droit de l'environnement comme d'un intérêt croissant pour le constitutionnalisme global.

Les contributions ici rassemblées n'ont certes pas pour but de répondre à toutes ces questions. Elles représentent néanmoins un matériau de choix pour qui veut comprendre les enjeux heuristiques du constitutionnalisme environnemental, mais aussi les implications quant à l'articulation des ordres juridiques d'une notion en voie d'autonomisation.

---

9 Jacqueline Morand-Deviller, « La Constitution et l'environnement », *Les Cahiers du Conseil constitutionnel*, n° 13, 2003, p. 122.

10 Pour une première approche en ce sens, voir Louis J. Kotzé, *Global Environmental Constitutionalism in the Anthropocene*, Hart Publishing, 2016, 304 p.

11 Louis J. Kotzé, cité, p. p. 14.

12 Gunther Teubner, « La question constitutionnelle au-delà de l'État-nation : pour une approche sociologique du phénomène constitutionnel », *Revue du droit public*, n° 6, 2017, p. 1610.

Chapter 1

Environmental Constitutionalism – A Multidimensional Issue

I) The Ideological Dimension of the Impact
II) The Pragmatic Dimension of the Impact
III) The Comparative Dimension of the Impact
IV) The International Dimension of the Impact

Chapitre 1

Le constitutionnalisme environnemental – une notion multidimensionnelle

I) La dimension idéologique de l'impact
II) La dimension pragmatique de l'impact
III) La dimension comparative de l'impact
IV) La dimension internationale de l'impact

Jochen SOHNLE

Professor of Public Law
Nancy Faculty of Law, Economics and Management, France
IRENEE/UL (EA 7303)

Abstract: This introductory contribution advances the argument that environmental constitutionalism reflects at least four dimensions or approaches. The first approach is founded on ideological doctrines, such as liberalism, environmentalism, which lead to environmental protection through constitutional provisions. The purpose of the second approach is the pragmatic and more neutral study of how environmental protection norms are fixed in a Constitution as a formal instrument of domestic law and the effects of these norms on case law and on other sources of law. In a third approach, environmental constitutionalism aims to enhance comparative law methods leading ultimately to the establishment of general principles that protect the environment. A fourth approach implements techniques that enable the identification of general principles of international public law built on a foundation of a representative number of domestic constitutional provisions concerning environmental protection and designed to be applied, through a feedback effect, to other domestic legal systems worldwide.

Sommaire : Cette contribution introductive propose de saisir la notion de constitutionnalisme environnemental en l'appréhendant à travers quatre dimensions. La première dimension reflète des idéologies (libéralisme, écologisme) qui sont fixées dans des dispositions constitutionnelles protectrices de l'environnement. La deuxième dimension se présente de manière pragmatique et plus neutre en ce qu'elle se focalise sur le droit constitutionnel de l'environnement mis en œuvre par la jurisprudence et d'autres branches juridiques spécialisées. La troisième dimension du constitutionnalisme environnemental vise à valoriser les méthodes du droit comparé qui permettent notamment de construire des principes généraux du droit protecteurs de l'environnement. Enfin, une quatrième dimension mobilise les techniques du droit international public pour dégager des principes généraux du droit international à partir de dispositions constitutionnelles protectrices de l'environnement dans un nombre de pays suffisamment représentatif. Ceux-ci seront appliqués, par un retour des choses, à d'autres ordres juridiques nationaux et cela à l'échelle mondiale.

While the purpose of environmental constitutionalism can be traced as far back as the late 19th century[13], the expression 'environmental

---

[13] For example the 'Forever Wild' mandate from 1894 in the New York Constitution, see James R. May, "Subnational Environmental Constitutionalism and Reform in New York State", *Widener Law Review*, Vol. 38, 2017, p. 121–150, at 121. See on the national level the German Weimar Constitution of 1919, Article 150: "The monuments of art, history and nature as well as landscape shall enjoy the protection and the stewardship of the state." (*Die Denkmäler der Kunst, der Geschichte und der Natur sowie die Landschaft genießen den Schutz und die Pflege des Staates.*) In general,

constitutionalism' is more recent[14]. The many nouns with "–ism" seem to be peculiar to the English tongue. Indeed, the generous use of "–isms" is quite astonishing for a non-native speaker, even if many languages see it as from deriving from Ancient Greek, Latin and French (–ισμός, –ismus, –isme). In 2015, the word of the year chosen by Merriam-Webster was precisely the suffix "–ism"[15]! It suggests in particular an adherence to a system (stoicism, altruism), a condition based on excess of something (alcoholism), a characteristic feature or trait (colloquialism), or a distinctive doctrine, cause, or theory[16]. Later in this introduction, emphasis will be placed on this ideological dimension of 'environmental constitutionalism', which is equally present in French (at least in the word *constitutionnalisme*).

More precisely, the topic of this book is the impact of environmental constitutionalism on legal systems. The word 'impact' is used in the broad sense of a significant or major effect[17]. In modern French, this figurative meaning seems to be borrowed from English[18] and is also used in the French version of the book title. The impact will be discussed and assessed relative to 'legal systems', whose meaning in different languages is the same, especially in English and in French. In short, it can be defined as a coherent interconnected cluster of rules (*faisceau de règles*)[19]. In comparison to other conceptual domains (for example natural science, economics), legal systems establish a fictitious world of

---

in the absence of explicit environmental protection provisions, old constitutional provisions on landscape protection and culture heritage are becoming interpreted in an environmental sense.

14 James R. May, Erin Daly, *Judicial Handbook on Environmental Constitutionalism*, United Nations Environment Programme, Kenya, March 2017, p. 1; James R. May, Erin Daly, *Global Environmental Constitutionalism*, Cambridge University Press, 2015, p. 1.

15 Online: https://www.merriam-webster.com/words-at-play/word-of-the-year-2015/-ism.

16 *Ibid.*

17 Latin: *impactum, impigere*. See *Merriam-Webster Dictionary online*, v° *Impact*, noun: 1a: an impinging or striking especially of one body against another; 1b: a forceful contact or onset; also: the impetus communicated in or as if in such a contact; 2: the force of impression of one thing on another: a significant or major effect, online: https://www.merriam-webster.com/dictionary/impact.

18 *Petit Robert*, Paris, 2013, v° *impact*, meaning No. 2: effet, influence (emploi critiqué).

19 Gérard Cornu (dir.), *Vocabulaire juridique*, 10e éd., PUF, 2014, v° *système, système juridique*. There is the alternative synonymous term of "ordre normatif", deriving from Latin (*ordo, ordinis*) and defined as a coherent set of legal rules, provided with a separate existence and an autonomous internal organization, *ibid.* v° *ordre*.

their own[20]. Legal systems can be country-specific (French legal system, US legal system)[21] or have within-country variations (federal rules v. state rules, in federations[22]; private law v. public law, in civil law countries). There are even systemic specificities within the very scope of public law (constitutional law, administrative law, etc.) or private law (civil law, trade law, etc.).

There are at least four dimensions of the impacts of environmental constitutionalism on legal orders: they can be ideological (I), pragmatic (II), comparative (III), and international (IV).

I) The Ideological Dimension of the Impact

Ideologies reflect different perceptions of society[23], most of which adopt a critical point of view[24]. In this regard, it is useful to consider environmental constitutionalism as a dimension of ideologies.

For French constitutional law and political science scholars, referring to *constitutionnalisme* has an ideological undertone. It is thought of as an element of the broader political liberalism movement, promoted especially in the Western world by John Locke, Montesquieu and Benjamin Constant. In this context, a Constitution must comply with three key criteria in order to limit political power: the Constitution needs to be written[25], it must provide for separation of powers and it

---

20 Jochen Sohnle, "La représentation de la nature devant le juge : plaidoyer pour une épistémologie juridique du fictif", *in*: Marie-Pierre Camproux Duffrène, Jochen Sohnle (eds.), *La représentation de la nature devant le juge: approches comparative et prospective*, Les Éditions en environnement VertigO, 2015, p. 329–363 and online: https://journals.openedition.org/vertigo/16343.

21 Kenneth Robert Redden, Linda L. Schleuter, *Modern Legal Systems Cyclopedia*, Buffalo, William S. Hein & Co., 1988, 10 Vols.

22 Toni Jaeger-Fine, *American Legal Systems: A Resource and Reference Guide*, LexisNexis, 2nd ed., 2015.

23 For details, see Jochen Sohnle, "Idées, idéalisme et idéologie(s) dans la doctrine du droit international de l'environnement", *Revue juridique de l'environnement (RJE)* 2016, numéro spécial: *La doctrine en droit de l'environnement*, p. 133–160.

24 Otfried Höffe, *Lexikon der Ethik*, C.H. Beck, 1986, v° Ideologie; *Petit Robert* 2013, v° idéologie (second meaning).

25 Pierre Pactet, *Institutions politiques – Droit constitutionnel*, Armand Colin, 2000, p. 65–66; Charles Debbasch, Jacques Bourdon, Jean-Marie Pontier, Jean-Claude Ricci, *Droit constitutionnel et institutions politiques*, Economica, 2001, p. 212–214; Olivier Duhamel, Guillaume Tusseau, *Droit constitutionnel et institutions politiques*, Seuil, 2016, p. 55, 69, 85.

has to enshrine individual rights and liberties[26]. Thus, for our purpose, an important nexus is established with human rights law. The US Constitution and the first French constitutional instruments are taken as the starting points, becoming models for their respective legal systems as well as for other systems, such as, for example Germany through the *Konstitutionalismus* movement[27]: A state with a written and liberal Constitution was called constitutional State or State based on the rule of law (*Rechtsstaat*)[28]. By this assimilation, a conceptual link is established between liberal constitutionalism and the German rule of law doctrine (*Rechtsstaatstheorie*)[29]. The German political language of the 19th century distinguishes two words (both of them are translated into English as "constitution"): *Verfassung*, which is the customary organization of a (German) state[30] and *Konstitution*, which refers to the liberal meaning of constitutionalism based on a written document, following the model advanced by the founders of the United States of America and the initiators of the French revolution[31].

---

26 All these requirements can be found in Article 16 of the French Declaration of Human and Civic Rights of 26 August 1789: "Any society in which no provision is made for guaranteeing rights or for the separation of powers, has no Constitution." (http://www.conseil-constitutionnel.fr/conseil-constitutionnel/english/constitution/declaration-of-human-and-civic-rights-of-26-august-1789.105305.html). In addition, from a more modern perspective, a constitution has to satisfy three requirements: 1) It has to be the highest ranked legal instrument. 2) The amendment procedure has to be more difficult than the enactment of normal statutory law. 3) There is a need of constitutional review, conveniently by a judicial body. See Jean-Claude Cabanne, *Introduction à l'étude du droit constitutionnel et de la science politique*, Privat, 1981, p. 38, 41–56.

27 Hartmut Maurer, *Staatsrecht I – Grundlagen, Verfassungsorgane, Staatsfunktionen*, 2nd ed., C.H. Beck, 2001, paras. 4, 45. See also on the link with the works of Immanuel Kant: Ernst Cassirer, *Die Idee der Republikanischen Verfassung, Rede zur Verfassungsfeier am 11. August 1928*, Friedrichsen/De Gruyter, 1929, English translation online by Seth Berk, *The Idea of a Republican Constitution* https://onlinelibrary.wiley.com/doi/pdf/10.1111/phil.12175.

28 Jean-Claude Cabanne, cited, p. 37–38.

29 Ernst-Wolfgang Böckenförde, *Recht, Staat, Freiheit*, Suhrkamp, 1991, p. 143–169 ; Jean-Claude Cabanne, cited, p. 38; Olivier Duhamel, Guillaume Tusseau, cited, p. 539–542.

30 See German Confederal Act (*Deutsche Bundesakte*), Vienna, 8 June 1815, Article 13.

31 The German language uses in this context the apparent pleonasm "konstitutionnelle Verfassung", see Hartmut Maurer, cited, paras. 45, 47. See also, Dietmar Willoweit, *Deutsche Verfassungsgeschichte*, C.H. Beck, 2001, p. 243–244.

But what are the consequences of this ideological evolution for environmental constitutionalism? Is environmental constitutionalism a part of political liberalism? Indeed, an initial analysis leads to a positive response to the latter question. However, this response must be qualified in a second step since there is at least one further ideological meaning of environmental constitutionalism: political environmentalism. In a simplified, but relevant sense, liberalism and environmentalism can be presented as historically opposite, but nowadays combined ideologies.

In France, the pioneering reference works on environmental law published by Alexandre Kiss emphasize the nexus between human rights and environmental protection, both having to be enshrined in a constitutional instrument[32]. There is also an obvious link between political liberalism and constitutional environmental protection in the German writings on an environmental state, since such a state is based on checks and balances and simultaneously bound by objectives of environmental protection (*Umweltstaat, ökologischer Rechtsstaat*)[33]. The contributions of Michael Kloepfer and Klaus Bosselmann can, in particular, be taken as the first demonstrations of environmental constitutionalism even if the discussion is focused on environmental State policies to be enshrined in the German constitution[34]. Concepts like rule of law, separation of powers, justice and human rights

---

[32] Alexandre Kiss, "Peut-on définir le droit de l'homme à l'environnement?", *RJE*, No. 1, 1976, p. 15–18, at 15–17; Alexandre Kiss, "Définition et nature juridique d'un droit de l'homme à l'environnement", *in*: Pascale Kromarek (ed.), *Environnement et droit de l'homme*, UNESCO, 1987, p. 13–28, see also the appendix with constitutional environmental provisions worldwide, online: http://unesdoc.unesco.org/images/0007/000798/079839fo.pdf; Alexandre Kiss, "Une nouvelle lecture du droit de l'environnement ?", *in*: Alexandre Kiss (ed.), *L'écologie et la loi : le statut juridique de l'environnement*, L'Harmattan, 1989, p. 378–379.

[33] Michael Kloepfer (ed.), *Umweltstaat*, Springer, 1989; Klaus Bosselmann, *Im Namen der Natur. Der Weg zum ökologischen Rechtsstaat*, Scherz, 1992, especially p. 351; Michael Kloepfer (ed.), *Umweltstaat als Zukunft. Juristische, ökonomische und philosophische Aspekte. Ergebnisse des Ladenburger Kollegs Umweltstaat*, Economica, 1994; Christian Calliess, *Rechtsstaat und Umweltstaat: Zugleich ein Beitrag zur Grundrechtsdogmatik im Rahmen mehrpoliger Verfassungsrechtsverhältnisse*, Mohr Siebeck, 2001.

[34] Hasso Hofmann, "Die Aufgaben des modernen Staates und der Umweltschutz – Vom Rechts- und Kulturstaat über den Sozialstaat zum Industrie- und Umweltstaat", *in*: Michael Kloepfer, (ed.), *op. cit.*, p. 2–11. Indeed, the German Constitution (Basic Law) does not contain a distinct chapter addressing environmental protection. It is set forth as a constitutional principle and policy objective, in Article 20a: The state

are still very present in current writings on global environmental constitutionalism[35]. In Canada, David R. Boyd has also highlighted the link between constitutions, human rights, and the environment[36].

The other ideological movement that appears to be relevant is environmentalism, which can be defined as a political and ethical movement that seeks to improve and protect the quality of the natural environment[37]. In this connection, environmental constitutionalism is perceived as 'constitutional environmentalism' or, in other words, ethical ecological claims incorporated into the constitution. 'Green' ideology is quite present in writings about environmental law[38], as well as

"shall protect the natural foundations of life" (*natürliche Lebensgrundlagen*). See Jan Hoffmann, "The Meaning of 'Environment' in the German Legal Order", *Wroclaw Review of Law, Administration & Economics*, Vol. 4, 2014, p. 54–60, at 58. On environmental state policies (*Staatszielbestimmung Umweltschutz*): Werner Hoppe, Martin Beckmann, Petra Kauch, *Umweltrecht*, C.H. Beck, 2000, p. 90–99.

35 Klaus Bosselmann, "Global Environmental Constitutionalism: Mapping The Terrain", *Widener Law Review*, Vol. 21, 2015, p. 171–185, at 172. The question asked is whether global environmental constitutionalism has become a legitimate paradigm: Brian J. Gareau, "Global Environmental Constitutionalism", *Boston College Environmental Affairs Law Review*, Vol. 40, 2013, p. 403–408, at 408.

36 David R. Boyd, *The Environmental Rights Revolution: A Global Study of Constitutions, Human Rights, and the Environment*, University of British Columbia Press, 2012 (on the classical liberal approach, see p. 68).

37 Lorraine Elliott, *Environmentalism*, *in*: *Encyclopedia britannica*, online : https://www.britannica.com/topic/environmentalism: "Political and ethical movement that seeks to improve and protect the quality of the natural environment through changes to environmentally harmful human activities; through the adoption of forms of political, economic, and social organization that are thought to be necessary for, or at least conducive to, the benign treatment of the environment by humans; and through a reassessment of humanity's relationship with nature. In various ways, environmentalism claims that living things other than humans, and the natural environment as a whole, are deserving of consideration in reasoning about the morality of political, economic, and social policies. For discussion of environmental statutes and regulations, including international conventions, see also environmental law."

38 Marino Revedin, "L'écologie entre idéologie et méthodologie juridique", *in*: Marguerite Boutelet, Jean-Claude Fritz (eds.), *L'ordre public écologique – Towards an Ecological Public Order*, Bruylant, 2005, p. 31–45, at 34; Anne Cadoret, Jérôme Fromageau *et al.*, *Protection de la nature, histoire et idéologie: de la nature à l'environnement*, L'Harmattan, 1985; Michel Prieur, "L'environnement est entré dans la Constitution", *RJE*, numéro spécial, 2005, p. 25–31, at 27; Jochen Sohnle, "Idées, idéalisme et idéologie(s)", cited, *RJE*, numéro spécial, 2016, p. 138–144.

among authors dealing with global environmental constitutionalism[39]. Indeed, environmental values are constructed by philosophers[40] and used, consequently, by legal scholars[41]. Environmental values can be integrated indirectly through constitutional interpretation and construction conducted by judges or scholars[42] or directly, through explicit constitutional provisions.

In short, environmental constitutionalism can be considered as the combination of liberal and green ideologies protecting environmental values through constitutional provisions. As a result, the ideological dimension of our subject appears as 'constitutional environmentalism'.

II) The Pragmatic Dimension of the Impact

The pragmatic[43] dimension is focused on constitutional provisions concerning environmental protection. Indeed, the enshrinement of environmental provisions in a Constitution is not self-evident: before the 1970s, environmental protection was mainly the aim of other

---

39 Klaus Bosselmann, "Global Environmental Constitutionalism: Mapping The Terrain", *Widener Law Review*, Vol. 21, 2015, p. 171–185, at 178.

40 A modern value philosophy has been (re)introduced since the early 20th century, see Max Scheler, *Der Formalismus in der Ethik und die materiale Wertethik: Neuer Versuch der Grundlegung eines ethischen Personalismus*, 1913–1916, new edition by Christian Bermes, Meiner, 2014; Elisabeth Anscombe, "Modern Moral Philosophy", *Philosophy 33*, No. 124, January 1958, p. 1–16 (online: https://www.pitt.edu/~mthompso/readings/mmp.pdf). These concepts have been extended to environmental and animal protection by Holmes Rolston, III, *Environmental Ethics, Duties to and Values in The Natural World*, Temple University Press, 1988 and Tom Reagan, *The Case for Animal Rights*, Berkeley, 1983, new edition: University of California, 2004. See also: Andreas Brenner, *UmweltEthik*, Königshausen & Neumann, 2014, p. 62–68; Gérald Hess, *Éthiques de la nature*, PUF, 2013, p. 61–84.

41 Alexandre Kiss, "Une nouvelle lecture du droit de l'environnement ?", *in*: Alexandre Kiss (ed.), *L'écologie et la loi : le statut juridique de l'environnement*, cited, p. 383; James R. May, Erin Daly, *Global Environmental Constitutionalism*, cited, p. 9, 10, 25, 29, 32; James R. May, Erin Daly, *Judicial Handbook on Environmental Constitutionalism*, cited, p. 5, 9.

42 Thomas C. Marks Jr, John F. Cooper, *State Constitutional Law*, West, 2003, p. 31, 120, 285.

43 *Merriam-Webster Dictionary online*, v° pragmatic, less commonly pragmatical: meaning No. 2: "relating to matters of fact or practical affairs often to the exclusion of intellectual or artistic matters: practical as opposed to idealistic".

legal branches: civil law, administrative law, criminal law, EU law and international law[44]. Only more recently, has environmental constitutionalism become a "phenomenon"[45], evidenced by observable constitutional provisions and linked judicial cases, without regards to ethical or political judgments[46].

In this vein, James R. May and Erin Daly argue in their treatise on global environmental constitutionalism that environmental constitutionalism "embodies the recognition that the environment is a proper subject for protection in constitutional texts and for the vindication by constitutional courts worldwide"[47]. This is also the position of Louis J. Kotzé who confirms: "Where environmental care is couched in constitutionalist language, it is termed environmental constitutionalism"[48]. Within this conception, it is possible to identify more precise subdivisions such as the distinction between fundamental environmental constitutionalism which involves textual constitutional provisions protecting fundamental substantive or procedural citizen rights, on one side, and structural environmental constitutionalism, which is the allocation of environmental regulatory authority across levels or branches of government within particular nations, particularly relevant in federal systems, on the other side[49]. In this context, the specificities of federal environmental constitutionalism, for example in

---

44 Alexandre Kiss, "Introduction", *in*: Alexandre Kiss (ed.), *L'écologie et la loi*, cited, p. 9–10 (constitutional law is not mentioned).

45 See the beginning of the book, James R. May, Erin Daly, *Global Environmental Constitutionalism,* cited, p. 1: "Environmental constitutionalism is a relatively recent phenomenon at the confluence of constitutional law, international law, human rights, and environmental law".

46 *The Columbia Encyclopedia* (6th ed.), The Columbia University Press, Online: http://www.encyclopedia.com/reference/encyclopedias-almanacs-transcripts-and-maps/phenomenon, v° phenomenon: "[…] phenomena were considered the observed facts and were contrasted with the theories used to explain them. Modern philosophers have used 'phenomenon' to designate what is apprehended before judgment is applied. For Immanuel Kant a phenomenon was the object of experience and was the opposite of a noumenon, the thing-in-itself, to which Kant's categories did not apply".

47 James R. May, Erin Daly, *Global Environmental Constitutionalism,* cited, p. 1 (second sentence of the book, with references to other works of the same authors).

48 Louis J. Kotzé, "Arguing Global Environmental Constitutionalism", *Transnational Environmental Law,* 2012, p. 199–233, at 208.

49 Blake Hudson, "Structural Environmental Constitutionalism", *Widener Law Review,* Vol. 21, 2015, p. 201–216, at 201–202, 206–210.

the US[50], India, Brazil, Germany[51], and Switzerland, or of environmental constitutionalism in countries with strong sub-national regions[52], can be distinguished from unitary environmental constitutionalism, of which the best illustration is France[53]. In unitary countries, environmental constitutional amendments are highly effective, especially when they are applied by the judiciary. In this regard, Nicolas Huten and Marie-Anne Cohendet have written that, after a long sleep, France woke up with a fanfare[54]. Indeed, in this country, courts were slow to implement the provisions of the Environmental Charter, but now that they have turned their attention to it, they have developed quite a substantial body of law on environmental constitutionalism[55].

In the pragmatic sense, environmental constitutionalism is synonymous with environmental constitutional law. The latter term is indeed used in handbooks on constitutional law[56], political and state law[57] and on

50 James R. May, "Subnational Environmental Constitutionalism and Reform in New York State", cited, p. 121–150.

51 Werner Hoppe, Martin Beckmann, Petra Kauch, *Umweltrecht*, cited, p. 122–124; Jochen Sohnle, "La subsidiarité environnementale en République fédérale d'Allemagne et aux États-Unis d'Amérique: le retour en force de l'échelon fédéré", *in*: Marie-Anne Cohendet (ed.), *Droit constitutionnel de l'environnement, regards croisés*, forthcoming.

52 See for Italy: Peccolo Gianpaolo, "Le droit à l'environnement dans la Constitution italienne", *RJE*, 1994, p. 335–338; for Spain: Luis López Guerra *et al.*, *Derecho Constitucional*, Vol. II, Tirant Lo Blanch, 2003, p. 323–339, at 330.

53 Jochen Sohnle, "Judicial Implementation of Environmental Constitutionalism in France – A Fertile Ground from the Charter of the Environment", *in*: Erin Daly, James R. May (eds.), *Implementing Environmental Constitutionalism – Current Global Challenges*, Cambridge University Press, 2018, p. 159–179.

54 Nicolas Huten, Marie-Anne Cohendet, "La charte cinq ans après: chronique d'un réveil en fanfare", *RJE*, 2010/1, p. 37–60.

55 Blake Hudson, "Structural Environmental Constitutionalism", *Widener Law Review*, Vol. 21, 2015, p. 201–216, at 210–212; Jochen Sohnle, "Judicial Implementation of Environmental Constitutionalism in France – A Fertile Ground from the Charter of the Environment", *in*: Erin Daly, James R. May (eds.), cited, p. 165–176.

56 In France, very few handbooks deal more detailed with the aspect of environmental constitutional law, in principle only the book of Marie-Anne Cohendet, *Droit constitutionnel*, coll. Cours, LGDJ-Lextenso, 2015, paras. 1643–1647.

57 Hartmut Maurer, *Staatsrecht I*, C.H. Beck, 2001, p. 187 (No. 6, 13). In federations, the works on the law of the federated states have to be added: for example Thomas C. Marks Jr, John F. Cooper, *State Constitutional Law*, West, 2003, p. 31, 120, 285;

environmental law (German: *Umweltverfassungsrecht*[58]; French: *droit constitutionnel de l'environnement*[59]), especially when they are written in other languages than English, where the use of "–isms" is generally more restrained. Some books on environmental law focus only on one aspect such as environmental protection in a federation[60].

Thus, from a pragmatic point of view, environmental constitutionalism means (simply) the integration of environmental norms in the constitution. However, the linked case law and the implementation of constitutional provisions through statutes and regulations are also relevant. This dimension of environmental constitutionalism can be loosely described as a system of norms established within 'environmental constitutional law'.

III) The Comparative Dimension of the Impact

In France, students typically discover constitutional law in a comparative context, as the comparative approach is more developed in this field than in other legal disciplines[61]. Moreover, as shown above (*supra* I), ideological constitutionalism as well is a part of a global tendency[62]. And

---

Reinhard Hendler, Friedhelm Hufen, Siegfried Jutzi, *Landesrecht Rheinland-Pfalz*, Nomos, 2012, p. 331–333.

58 Werner Hoppe, Martin Beckmann, Petra Kauch, *Umweltrecht*, cited, 2000, p. 89–124; Reiner Schmidt, Wolfgang Kahl, Klaus Ferdinand Gärditz, *Umweltrecht*, C.H. Beck, 2017, p. 56–87.

59 Later in her book on constitutional law (cited), Marie-Anne Cohendet uses the expression 'comparative environmental constitutional law' (*droit constitutionnel comparé de l'environnement*). However, in the French leading handbook on environmental law, there is no special chapter on this topic. The environmental Charter is only mentioned beside developments on other topics, for example on principles or the constitutional right to a healthy environment (Michel Prieur, with the collaboration of Julien Bétaille, Marie-Anne Cohendet, Hubert Delzangles, Jessica Makowiak, Pascale Steichen, *Droit de l'environnement*, Dalloz, 2016, p. 15–16). In other books, more detailed developments can be found on constitutional environmental law, for example: Agathe Van Lang, *Droit de l'environnement*, PUF, Thémis, 2016, paras. 43, 178–185; Eric Naim-Gesbert, *Droit général de l'environnement*, LexisNexis, 2011, p. 53–59.

60 Daniel A. Farber, *Environmental Law in a nutshell*, West, 2014, p. 57–92.

61 This approach can be found in all standard French handbooks addressing first year constitutional law students. For example: Vlad Constantinesco, Stéphane Pierré-Caps, *Droit constitutionnel*, PUF, thémis, 2016, p. 35 *et seq.*

62 See also: Hartmut Maurer, cited, para. 5.

since environmental situations like pollution or animal migration cannot be stopped at political borders through the mere authority of law[63], the scope of environmental constitutionalism 'naturally' transcends national and international boundaries. In contrast to general constitutionalism, environmental constitutionalism is not only a Western, but also a global phenomenon[64] and scholars have a worldwide perspective[65]. However, constitutional law is a part of domestic law and not international law. As a consequence, its transnational effect has to be addressed primarily by methods of comparative law. The leading work published by James R. May and Erin Daly adopts such a global approach: Their book "deploys principles of comparative constitutionalism to examine whether, and the extent to which, global environmental constitutionalism is occurring, and why"[66]. Our book, like other publications in progress[67], aims, with its diverse contributions, to continue this work, departing, through this Introduction, for the first time from a uniquely civil law[68] and French perspective.

There are many ways of comparing legal systems, whether across international boundaries or across different fields within a single legal system. In this book, readers will find contributions that consider the influence of French environmental constitutionalism on administrative law (contribution of Simon Jolivet) and on corporate law (contribution of Olivier Cachard). Environmental law, in particular, demands interdisciplinary analysis. Such a transsystemic comparison will indeed be conducted by one of our contributors (Samuel Ferey), who examines the environmental economy.

---

63 My mentor and thesis supervisor, Alexandre Charles Kiss, in its classes used a nice French expression: *La pollution se moque des frontières* (Pollution doesn't care about borders). See also: Alexandre Kiss, "Introduction", *in*: Alexandre Kiss (ed.), *L'écologie et la loi*, cited, p. 8.

64 James R. May, Erin Daly, *Global Environmental Constitutionalism,* cited.

65 Alexandre Kiss, "Une nouvelle lecture du droit de l'environnement ?", *in*: Alexandre Kiss (ed.), *L'écologie et la loi*, cited, p. 366–367, 378–379; Jacqueline Morand-Deviller, "L'environnement dans les constitutions étrangères", *Les Nouveaux Cahiers du Conseil constitutionnel*, No. 43, 2014/2, p. 83–95; David R. Boyd, *The Environmental Rights Revolution,* cited; Michel Prieur *et al.*, *Droit de l'environnement*, cited, p. 15–16.

66 James R. May, Erin Daly, *Global Environmental Constitutionalism*, cited, p. 3.

67 For example: Marie-Anne Cohendet (ed.), *Droit constitutionnel de l'environnement, regards croisés,* Mare et Martin, forthcoming.

68 As to the difference between civil law systems and common law systems, David R. Boyd highlights that the latter are less open to incorporation of environmental

Among the strictly legal comparative methods, three are relevant for us[69]. The first method consists in a comprehensive presentation of a legal issue by referring to a single law system (country study). In this respect, our book offers several studies on selected, particularly representative countries, within Europe (France: Marie-Anne Cohendet, Germany: Alexander Proelß, Switzerland: Anne-Christine Favre) and beyond Europe (general survey: James R. May and Erin Daly, India: Gitanjali Nain Gill, Brazil: Letícia Albuquerque) each dealing with some particularly pertinent topics in the field of environmental constitutionalism in those countries.

The second method compares legal functions. Its goal is to check functional equivalencies among rules, regimes, and institutions produced by two or more law systems, especially when they are conceptually distinct or when different languages are involved. Thus, translation is a big challenge[70] as became evident from the first few lines of this Introduction. At its best, functional comparisons consist in creating meta-conceptual terms and principles, following the method of *tertium comparationis*. Such general terms (for example legal standing, *intérêt pour agir*) and principles are situated outside or above concrete legal systems. This approach can be extremely useful in the field of comparative environmental constitutionalism and can be found in all the contributions of this book.

By integrating the previous two methods, the third method establishes a frame of reference that can affect domestic legal systems, for example, through model legislation, harmonized and uniform law instruments, or principles developed by judges or scholars. In this connection, Louis J. Kotzé suggests that global environmental constitutionalism provides for paradigm-shifting reforms worldwide[71]. German authors have also observed a global trend toward the concept of the environmental

---

protection provisions in their constitutions than the former. David R. Boyd, *The Environmental Rights Revolution,* cited, p. 51, 283–284.

69 Jens-Peter Schneider, *Verwaltungsrecht in Europa*, Bd. 1 *(England u. Wales, Spanien, Niederlande*), Universitätsverlag Osnabrück, 2007, “Introduction”, p. 30–31 (on the following three methods).

70 In general, a choice should be made between 1) literal translation (care has to be taken with false cognates, especially between English and French), 2) keeping the foreign term after explaining its meaning, or 3) finding for the foreign term the functional corresponding in the language to whom the study is addressed.

71 Louis J. Kotzé, “Arguing Global Environmental Constitutionalism”, *Transnational Environmental Law*, 2012, p. 199.

state (*Umweltstaat*)[72]. In this manner, comparative environmental constitutionalism contributes to the worldwide development of domestic constitutional provisions and related case law in order to promote the best environmental practices among nations[73]. On the regional level, this can be found in European Union (EU) law where general principles developed by the European courts have evolved in parallel with written legal sources (EU treaties, regulations, directives). In the field of environmental constitutionalism and EU law, this book provides a fine illustration in the contribution of Sven Kaufmann.

These various methods of comparative law facilitate the identification of general principles of environmental constitutionalism. These principles have special relevance in international law.

IV) The International Dimension of the Impact

Environmental constitutionalism is relevant to public international law[74], as the previous discussion about comparative methods suggests. Indeed, any comparative research can lead to ascertain "general principles of law recognized by civilized nations", according to the Statute of the International Court of Justice (Article 38, para. 1c), or, as it is presently described, 'general principles of international law'. This means that when there is a sufficient level of certainty about a principle, due to its incorporation in a representative number of domestic legal systems (for example the precautionary principle), the principle enters into the sphere of international law[75]. It becomes, as a general principle, an autonomous (non-written) source of international law, similar to treaty law, customary law and unilateral commitments. This phenomenon is sometimes neglected in writings on environmental constitutionalism that adopt

---

72 Martin Jänecke, "Möglichkeiten und Probleme von Umweltintegration, Auf dem Weg zum Umweltstaat", *ÖkologischesWirtschaften*, No. 2, 2006, p. 33- 38, at 35.

73 James R. May, Erin Daly, *Global Environmental Constitutionalism*, cited, p. 4, 5.

74 Klaus Bosselmann, "Global Environmental Constitutionalism: Mapping The Terrain", *Widener Law Review*, Vol. 21, 2015, p. 171–185, at 171–173, 182–184.

75 Alexandre Kiss, Dinah Shelton, *International Environmental Law*, Transnational Publishers, 2000, p. 43–45; Ian Brownlie, *Principles of Public Intenational Law*, Clarendon Press Oxford, 1966, p. 12–16; Lassa Francis Lawrence Oppenheim, Hersch Lauterpacht, *International Law – A Treatise*, Vol. I, *Peace*, Longmans, Green and Co, 1958, p. 29–31; Paul Reuter, *Droit international public*, PUF, (first

a common law perspective[76]. Indeed, unlike civil law systems, where general principles must be recognized under international law before being capable of applying to another domestic law system, common law systems are less dependent on international law and there is more permeability between common law systems[77].

The fact that the term 'principle" has multiple meanings among jurists is in this context misleading[78]. First, the term 'in principle' is used to express a rule and as an opposition to possible exceptions. A principle – such as the principle of prevention – might also be an unaccomplished normative standard, without precise legal conditions and effects[79]. Such a principle is meant to become a binding rule, through application and adoption by judges and legislators. In this regard, many non-binding international instruments such as declarations use principles instead of articles, which are normally associated with binding treaties. The principles of the Rio Declaration are an example of this kind of so-called

edition: 1958) 1993, p. 117–119; Albert Bleckmann, *Grundprobleme und Methoden des Völkerrechts*, Alber, 1982, p. 135–149; Pierre-Marie Dupuy, *Droit international public*, Dalloz, 1995, No. 323, p. 259 ; Patrick Daillier, Mathias Forteau, Alain Pellet, *Droit international public*, LGDJ, 2009, p. 380–386; Pierre-Marie Dupuy, Yann Kerbrat, *Droit international public*, Dalloz, 2016, No. 335, p. 371.

76 For example, James R. May and Erin Daly quote as international sources of law only treaties (*Global Environmental Constitutionalism,* cited, p. 21) and customary international law (p. 24). Principles are not considered under the category of general principles of international law, but in their meaning as more or less accomplished norms in domestic constitutional law (p. 3) or referred to together with values ("common set of environmental principles and values derived from international agreements and conventions", p. 6, see also p. 32). See also David R. Boyd, *The Environmental Rights Revolution,* cited, p. 80–92.

77 In this connection, James R. May and Erin Daly come closer to the meaning of principle as a source of law when they find that "environmental constitutionalism has given rise to borrowing from national and transnational common law and other general principles of environmental law, some of which have been codified at the national level, while others remain subject to development and elucidation by constitutional courts" (*Global Environmental Constitutionalism,* cited, p. 8).

78 Jochen Sohnle, "Le paradigme postpositiviste ou révélation d'une méthode spécifique dans l'application du droit international de l'environnement", *Revue européenne de droit de l'environnement*, 1998, p. 455, online: https://www.persee.fr/doc/reden_1283-8446_1998_num_2_4_1066?q=Jochen+Sohnle; Jochen Sohnle, *Idées, idéalisme et idéologie(s)*, cited, *RJE*, numéro spécial, 2016, p. 139–140.

79 In the sense of an unaccomplished norm. See Ronald Dworkin, *Taking rights seriously*, Bloomsbury, 1977, 1997, p. 38–48. See also: Karl Engisch, *Einführung in das juristische Denken*, Kohlhammer, 1983, p. 155–160.

soft law[80]. Sometimes the term 'principle' is also used (in a way that is very much open to criticism) in a non-specific manner or even as a synonym of a legally perfect 'rule'. This happens especially when the term is used without any further explanation by a legal instrument like a statute, constitution, treaty. Without claiming to give an exhaustive account[81], a last meaning refers to one of the sources of law and brings us back to the general principles of international law[82]. Indeed, the most essential contribution of books and treatises on international environmental law since 1975, when Alexandre Kiss published the first handbook in this field in Spanish[83] is to identify general environmental principles[84].

Another question is whether these international principles have a *jus cogens* (peremptory) character. From a strictly formal point of view, only

80 International law can be soft because of the vagueness of its normative standards (substantative soft law = principles) or because of the not binding nature of the legal instrument (formal soft law). See Ryuichi Ida, "Formation des normes internationales dans un monde en mutation: critique de la notion de soft law", *in*: Collectif, *Mélanges M. Virally*, Pedone, 1991, p. 333–340.

81 From the epistemological point of view, it has also the meaning of a logical fundament or axiom of a system (see the double meaning in Spanish: *en el principio* ("in principle" and "in the beginning").

82 Principles as a source of law are also found in domestic law, even on the constitutional level, for example in French law as fundamental principles recognized by the laws of the Republic (*principes fondamentaux reconnus par les lois de la République*).

83 Alexandre Kiss, *Los principios generales del derecho del medio ambiente*, Cuadernos de la Cátedra 'J.B. Scott' Universidad de Valladolid, 1975, see especially p. 10, 23–25, 111. On this first book, see Tullio Treves, "Alexandre-Charles Kiss and the Law of the Environment", *Iustum Aequum Salutare* V. 2009/1, p. 9–14, at 10, online: http://ias.jak.ppke.hu/hir/ias/20091sz/02.pdf.

84 Alexandre Kiss, *Droit international de l'environnement*, Pedone, 1989, p. 60, 67–103; Alexandre Kiss, Dinah Shelton, *International Environmental Law*, Transnational Publishers, (first edition: 1991), 2004, p. 86–88, 203–204; Patricia Birnie, Alan Boyle, Catherine Redgwell, *International Law & the Environment*, Oxford University Press (first edition 1992), 2009, p. 26–28, 38 ; Philippe Sands, Jacqueline Peel, with Adriana Fabra and Ruth Mackenzie, *Principles of International Environmental Law*, Cambridge University Press (first edition: 1995), 2018, p. 197–650; Jean-Marc Lavieille, Hubert Delzangles, Catherine Le Bris, *Droit international de l'environnement*, Ellipses, (first edition: 1998) 2018, p. 141–190; Raphaël Romi, with Thomas Dubreuil, Sandrine Rousseau and Mary Sancy, *Droit international et européen de l'environnement*, Montchrestien, (first edition: 2005) 2013, p. 41–78; Jean-Maurice Arbour, Sophie Lavallée, Jochen Sohnle, Hélène Trudeau, *Droit international de l'environnement*, Éditions Yvon Blais (first edition: 2006) – Thomson Reuters, 2016, p. 105–178; Lakshman D. Guruswamy, Mariah Zebrowski Leach, *International Environmental Law in a Nutshell*, West, 2012, p. 21–22; Pierre-Marie Dupuy, Jorge Enrique Vinuales, *Introduction au droit*

peremptory norms of international law can be compared to substantive domestic constitutional provisions[85] since international law generally ignores constitutions, within the meaning discussed above (*supra* I) – even if there was a vain attempt, within the European Union, to name the founding international treaty "a Constitution for Europe"[86]. However, the distinction in international law between *jus cogens* and *jus dispositivum* becomes less relevant when international law as a whole is opposed to domestic law. Indeed, most constitutions consider international law as a whole as a source of domestic law and frequently even as a source superior to domestic law (such as statutes, regulations, case law and even sometimes constitutional law)[87]. Insofar as domestic law incorporates international law, there is an evolution in Europe that could lead to some kind of "European Constitution"[88]. Establishing general principles of international environmental law is thus a legally sound way to spread environmental rights and duties throughout the world. The most constructive contribution of the comparative dimension of environmental constitutionalism is, through its methods, to identify such general environmental principles.

In summary, environmental constitutionalism reflects at least four dimensions. The first aspect of environmental constitutionalism is

---

international de l'environnement, Bruylant, 2015, p. 80–81; Jean-Pierre Beurier, *Droit international de l'environnement*, Pedone, 2017, p. 129–174; Alexander Proelss (ed.), *Internationales Umweltrecht*, De Gruyter, 2017, p. 69–103. See also for articles: Alexandre Kiss, "Émergence de principes généraux du droit international et d'une politique internationale de l'environnement", *in*: Ivo Rens (ed.), *Le droit international face à l'éthique et à la politique de l'environnement*, Sebes, 1996, p. 19–35; Alexandre Kiss, "Les principes généraux du droit international de l'environnement sont-ils reflétés par le Code de l'environnement?", *RJE*, numéro spécial, 2002, p. 15–20; Jochen Sohnle, "Le paradigme postpositiviste", cited, *Revue européenne de droit de l'environnement* 1998, p. 455; Jochen Sohnle, "Idées, idéalisme et idéologie(s)", cited, *RJE*, numéro spécial 2016, p. 139–140.

85 Alexandre Kiss, "Une nouvelle lecture du droit de l'environnement ?", *in*: Alexandre Kiss (ed.), *L'écologie et la loi,* cited, p. 379, 386.

86 This unsuccessful "constitution" would have remained a treaty in character since amendments would have required unanimous intergovernmental agreement. See, Thomas O. Hueglin, Alan Fenna, *Comparative Federalism, A Systematic Inquiry*, Broadview Press, 2005, p. 15–16.

87 See on this point: James R. May, Erin Daly, *Global Environmental Constitutionalism,* cited, p. 27, 31.

88 Constance Grewe, Hélène Ruiz Fabri, *Droits constitutionnels européens,* PUF, 1995, see the chapter on "La limitation par le droit international : l'émergence d'une Constitution européenne ?", p. 101–133.

based on certain ideological doctrines (such as political liberalism or environmentalism), which leads to environmental protection through constitutional provisions. The purpose of the second dimension is the practical study of the impact of environmental constitutional norms on case law, legislation, and regulation and in other areas of law within a domestic system. In a third dimension, environmental constitutionalism aims to enhance comparative law methods, ultimately leading to the identification of general environmental principles. Finally, in a fourth dimension, environmental constitutionalism indicates general principles of international environmental law, which in turn influence domestic and regional legal systems worldwide. In short, *environmental constitutionalism can be characterized as constitutional environmentalism, environmental constitutional law, and general environmental principles developed through comparative and international law methods.*

This is how environmental constitutionalism impacts legal systems in a general manner. But how, more concretely, does environmental constitutionalism impact legal systems? This question is the focus of the contributions in this book.

*****

The book is presented in two parts. In the first part, the contributors focus on the impact of environmental constitutionalism *within* constitutional law. In the second part, they examine environmental constitutionalism's impact *beyond* constitutional law.

In Part 1, the first set of papers falls within what was called earlier in this introduction 'country studies' of environmental constitutionalism. They are introduced by James R. May and Erin Daly, from the United States of America, who provide an overview of comparative environmental constitutionalism (chapter 2). Among the leading specialists, they are perfectly placed to trace the evolution of this topic through six trends. Marie-Anne Cohendet, as a French representative of the subject, examines whether the French Charter on the Environment is a model of environmental constitutionalism (chapter 3). A German perspective is provided by Alexander Proelß in a contribution on the legal nature, scope, and content of the principle of environmental protection in constitutional law (chapter 4). It is noteworthy that, as indicated in the introductory analysis (*supra* II), Proelß uses, in title of his paper, the term "environmental constitutional law." A last European contribution on environmental constitutionalism in domestic law systems is furnished by Anne-Christine Favre from Switzerland who presents some of the most pertinent issues in her country (chapter 5). Then, outside of Europe, Gitanjali Nain Gill sets out environmental constitutionalism in India. She concentrates on its judicial recognition and application (chapter 6). Letícia Albuquerque from Brazil shows us that, although animal protection is a part of environmental constitutional law in Brazil, it is nonetheless vulnerable to legal regression (chapter 7).

In Part 2 of the book, impact of environmental constitutionalism is considered beyond constitutional law, starting with the example of the French legal system. Since constitutional provisions are the highest ranking legal norms in a domestic legal system, the other norms should comply with them. Indeed, the impact of environmental constitutionalism on special legal branches other than constitutional law becomes apparent, especially if there are, unlike in the US system, different court systems. The *Conseil constitutionnel* is the court checking the conformity of French statutory law with constitutional law. Marie-Anne Cohendet's contribution in Part 1 describes this. Moreover, in France, the *Conseil d'État* is the highest court that ensures conformity of administrative (executive) rules with statutes. In addition, the *Cour de cassation* is the top judicial body ensuring that acts of private law are consistent with statutory law. In this regard, environmental constitutionalism has a very practical impact within French law. Simon Jolivet explains how administrative law follows the requirements of the Charter on the Environment, especially through the case law of the *Conseil d'État* developed the last few years (chapter 8). Olivier Cachard focuses on a very specific, but very sensitive aspect of private law. He deals with the ambiguous role of the state as a shareholder in the field of corporate law and examines how state activities can be consistent with the precautionary principle codified in the Environmental Charter (chapter 9). Samuel Ferey is an economist and the only non-legal contributor. He provides a practical outsider's perspective on (French) environmental constitutionalism by analyzing how compensation methods for environmental harm comply with the polluter-pays-principle under the Environmental Charter (chapter 10).

The final chapter of the book is an original contribution by Sven Kaufmann who takes a regional perspective. The European Union is an international organization that obviously has no Constitution in the sense given earlier (*supra* I). Kaufmann explores the relationship between environmental constitutionalism and EU Law. Indeed, the European Union treaties, with their environmental related provisions, act, in a functional sense, as a Constitution and take precedence over EU regulations and directives. Thus, EU law is an illustration of functional environmental constitutionalism.

The contributions of our experts are written either in French or in English. This is a perfect reflection of the international and comparative dimension of the topic and the increasing interest in environmental constitutionalism in Europe and worldwide.

As scientific director of this project performed within the *Institut de Recherches sur l'Évolution de la Nation Et de l'État* (IRENEE (EA 7303), Nancy/Metz, Université de Lorraine, France), I warmly thank all the contributors for having agreed to provide their expertise in this field. I am also very grateful to the staff members of the IRENEE, Ludivine Starck, Nathalie Absalon, Marjorie de Bortoli and Hélène Viriot for the organization of the conference (September 2017) and the editorial work on this book. I thank also Stéphane Pierré-Caps, former director of the IRENEE, and Christophe Fardet, current director, for having encouraged the project and the publication of this book. And my very special thanks go to my colleague, Erin Daly for her invaluable advice on and review of my writing in English.

Jochen Sohnle, Nancy, January 2019

Part 1) Impact of Environmental Constitutionalism within Constitutional Law

The papers in this part are country studies of environmental constitutionalism. James R. May and Erin Daly provide an overview of comparative environmental constitutionalism (chapter 2). Marie-Anne Cohendet examines the French case under the Charter on the Environment (chapter 3). A German perspective is adopted by Alexander Proelß (chapter 4). Anne-Christine Favre furnishes a contribution on Switzerland (chapter 5). Two papers consider the situation outside Europe: Gitanjali Nain Gill sets out environmental constitutionalism in India (chapter 6); Letícia Albuquerque focuses on an aspect of environmental constitutional law in Brazil through a study on animal protection (chapter 7).

Partie 1) L'impact du constitutionnalisme environnemental sur le droit constitutionnel

Les contributions de cette première partie sont des études de pays sur le constitutionnalisme environnemental. James R. May and Erin Daly fournissent un aperçu général du constitutionnalisme environnemental comparé (chapitre 2). Marie-Anne Cohendet examine la situation française au regard de la Charte de l'environnement (chapitre 3). La perspective allemande est donnée par Alexander Proelß (chapitre 4). Anne-Christine Favre traite la situation en Suisse (chapitre 5). Deux contributions présentent la problématique dans des pays non européens : le regard de Gitanjali Nain Gill porte sur le constitutionnalisme environnemental en Inde (chapitre 6) ; Letícia Albuquerque se focalise sur un aspect du droit constitutionnel de l'environnement au Brésil à travers une étude sur la protection des animaux (chapitre 7).

Chapter 2

Six Trends in Global Environmental Constitutionalism

Chapitre 2

Six tendances dans le constitutionnalisme environnemental mondial

James R. MAY & Erin DALY

Professors of Law, co-Founders of the Dignity Rights Project, and co-Directors of the Environmental Rights Institute, Widener University Delaware Law School, USA

Abstract: Global environmental constitutionalism explores the constitutional incorporation, implementation, and jurisprudence of rights, duties, procedures, policies and other provisions to promote environmental protection. This contribution addresses six important trends in global environmental constitutionalism. The first is the textual incorporation and judicial engagement of climate change. Second is the notion that nature itself has rights, and legal personality to protect itself. Third is the emergence of constitutional dignity rights as means for advancing environmental rights. Fourth is the reflection of sustainability in many constitutions. Fifth is the increasing role of environmental constitutionalism at the subnational level. Last is the growing constitutional incorporation of rights to information, participation, and access in environmental matters.

Sommaire : Le constitutionnalisme environnemental mondial s'entend comme l'intégration dans la Constitution et la mise en œuvre législative et judiciaire de droits, devoirs, procédures, politiques et d'autres dispositifs qui visent à promouvoir la protection de l'environnement. La présente contribution s'intéresse à six tendances importantes qui s'observent dans ce contexte. Il s'agit (1) de l'intégration constitutionnelle et de la prise en compte judiciaire du changement climatique, (2) de la valorisation de la notion de nature investie de droits et d'une personnalité juridique, (3) de l'émergence de droits constitutionnels de dignité comme moyens du progrès des droits environnementaux, (4) de la consécration constitutionnelle de la durabilité, (5) de l'augmentation du rôle du constitutionnalisme environnemental au niveau infraétatique et (6) d'une intégration croissante de droits environnementaux liés à l'information, la participation et l'accès à la justice.

I) Introduction

Global environmental constitutionalism is a relatively recent phenomenon at the confluence of constitutional law, international law, human rights, and environmental law. It embodies the recognition that the environment is a proper subject for protection in constitutional texts and for vindication by constitutional courts worldwide. Global environmental constitutionalism explores the constitutional incorporation, implementation, and jurisprudence of environmental rights, duties, procedures, policies and other provisions to promote environmental protection[89]. This chapter recounts six important trends in global environmental constitutionalism, including those involving climate change, rights of nature, dignity rights, sustainability, subnational developments, and procedural rights in environmental matters.

Environmental constitutionalism arguably began in 1971, when voters in the State of Pennsylvania in the United States resoundingly passed a referendum to amend the state Constitution to incorporate what may be the world's first environmental rights provision, coupled with another requiring that the government hold natural resources in public trust for present and future generations.

Since then, the field has grown significantly. The constitutions of about three-quarters of nations worldwide address environmental matters in some fashion, some by committing to environmental stewardship, others by recognizing a basic right to a quality environment, and still others by ensuring a right to information, participation, and justice in environmental matters[90].

The most common form of constitutional environmental protection is the recognition of a personal right to a quality environment. While the exact

---

[89] See generally, James R. May, Erin Daly, *Global Judicial Handbook on Envionmental Constitutionalism*, United Nations Environment Programme (UNEP), Kenya, March 2018; Erin Daly, James R. May, *Companion to Global Judicial Handbook on Environmental Constitutionalism: Selected Cases and Material*, UNEP, Kenya, March 2018; Louis J. Kotzé, *Global Environmental Constitutionalism in the Anthropocene*, Hart Publishing, Oxford, 2016; James R. May, Erin Daly, *Global Environmental Constitutionalism*, Cambridge University Press, 2015; James R. May, "Symposium on Global Environmental Constitutionalism: An Introduction and Overview", *Widener Law Review*, Vol. 21, 2015, p. 139; Stephen Turner, *Substantive Environmental Rights*, Kluwer Law International, 2008; Louis J. Kotzé, "The Conceptual Contours of Environmental Constitutionalism", *Widener Law Review*, Vol. 21, 2015, p. 187; Erin Daly, James May, "Comparative Environmental Constitutionalism", *Jindal Global Law Review*, Vol. 6, 2015, p. 10; David Boyd, *The Environment Rights Revolution*, UBC Press, 2011, p. 226; Richard P. Hiskes, *The Human Right to a Green Future: Environmental Rights and Intergenerational Justice*, Cambridge University Press, 2009; See generally James R. May, "Constituting Fundamental Environmental Rights Worldwide", *Pace Environmental Law Review*, Vol. 23, 2006, p. 113.

[90] James R. May, Erin Daly, *Global Environmental Constitutionalism*, cited. See generally, *Environmental Rights Map*, available at http://envirorightsmap.org.

number is open for discussion, at least 85 national constitutions, as well as many subnational constitutions, explicitly recognize that individuals are entitled to a substantive right to a quality environment, including rights to an 'adequate', 'clean', 'healthy', 'productive', 'harmonious' or 'sustainable' environment. A dozen or so more recognize such substantive rights as an implicit component of other social and cultural rights, such as life, dignity or health. A few constitutions address specific environmental endowments including water, flora, and fauna, while others define the environment in certain ways, including as a public trust or in terms of sustainable development[91]. It has also inspired considerations of constitutional reform at the subnational level in several countries[92].

Environmental constitutionalism has provided new causes of action and stretched existing environmental rights into new forms[93]. It has also served to promote human and environmental rights[94], procedural guarantees[95], remedies[96], and judicial engagement aimed at protecting the natural environment[97]. Environmental constitutionalism has also animated international considerations about inherent rights to a healthy

---

91 James R. May, Erin Daly, *Global Environmental Constitutionalism*, cited.

92 See, e.g., Maya Van Rossum, *The Green Amendment: Securing our Right to a Healthy Environment*, Disruption Books, 2017; James R. May, Kenneth T. Kristl, John C. Dernbach, *Pennsylvania Environmental Defense Foundation v. Commonwealth of Pennsylvania: Recognition of Environmental Rights for Pennsylvania Citizens, Ruthers University Law Review*, Vol. 70, 2018; James R. May, "Subnational Environmental Constitutionalism and Reform in New York State", *Pace Law Review*, 38/2017, p. 121.

93 See generally, James R. May, Erin Daly (eds.), *Environmental Constitutionalism*, Edward Elgar Publishing, 2016.

94 See generally, John H. Knox, Ramin Pejan, *The Human Right to a Healthy Environment*, Cambridge University Press, 2018; Stephen Turner, *A Global Environmental Right*, Routledge, 2018; James R. May, Erin Daly, "New Directions in Earth Rights, Environmental Rights and Human Rights: Six Facets of Constitutionally Embedded Environmental Rights Worldwide", *IUCN Academy of Environment Law E-Journal*, Vol. 1, 2011, posted Feb. 22, 2011; Stephen Turner, *Substantive Environmental Rights*, cited; Tim Hayward, *Constitutional Environmental Rights*, Oxford University Press, 2005.

95 James R. May, "Constitutional Directions in Procedural Environmental Rights", *Journal of Environmental Law and Litigation*, Vol. 28, 2013, p. 101.

96 James R. May, Erin Daly, "Constitutional Environmental Rights and Liabilities", *Environmental Liability*, Vol. 20, 2012/3, p. 75, online: http://www.lawtext.com/lawtextweb/default.jsp?PageID=2&PublicationID=4&pubSection=4#12.

97 James R. May, Erin Daly, "Vindicating Fundamental Environmental Rights Worldwide, Symposium: The Confluence of Human Rights and the Environment", *Oregon Review of International Law*, Vol. 11, 2010, p. 365.

planet, including the United Nations mandate on human rights and the environment and the appointment of a special rapporteur, culminating in Framework Principles on Human Rights and the Environment and more recent calls for the United Nations to recognize the human right to a healthy environment[98]. Environmental constitutionalism also has normative spillover effects, including lower greenhouse gas emissions[99].

Global environmental constitutionalism is likely to continue to spread in influence. It is the product of several global political and legal trends that have gathered strength in the last few decades. First, the spread of constitutionalism in the post-colonial period of the 1960s and 1970s, and then in the post-communist period in the 1990s, created a global norm of constitution-making. In the new millennium, the practice of adopting and amending constitutions has continued apace, spreading most recently in parts of the Arab world[100]. As a result, legal traditions in all regions of the world have seen new or dramatically amended constitutions adopted in the last few decades. For the most part, this has produced longer constitutions with more elaborate provisions, drawing from both civil and political and socio-economic lists of rights, often in intermingled and undifferentiated ways.

At the same time, growing global consciousness of environmentalism in tandem with increasing threats to social and environmental sustainability and climate change have contributed to the greening of constitutions. The frequent high-profile global summits on environmental matters in Stockholm (1972), Rio (1992), Kyoto (1997), Johannesburg (2002), Rio again (2012), and Paris (2015), among dozens of others, seem to have influenced drafters of domestic constitutions, who have included sustainable development, climate change, biodiversity, protection of waters, and other environmental matters within their constitutional texts.

---

98 *Report of the Special Rapporteur on the issue of human rights obligations relating to the enjoyment of a safe, clean, healthy and sustainable environment: Framework Principles*, UN Doc. A/HRC/37/59 (January 24, 2018). For a discussion of the mandate and its outcomes, see generally, John H. Knox, "The United Nations Mandate on Human Rights and the Environment", *in*: James R. May, Erin Daly (eds.), *Encyclopedia of Human Rights and the Environment: Indivisibility, Dignity and Legality*, forthcoming (2019).

99 See David Boyd, *The Environment Rights Revolution*, cited, p. 226, 273.

100 Andrea Pin, *The Arab Road to Dignity: The Goal of the Arab Spring*, Kellogg Institute for International Studies, 2016.

Here we address six important trends in global environmental constitutionalism. The first is the textual incorporation and judicial engagement of climate change (II). Second is the notion that nature itself has rights and legal personality to protect itself (III). Third is the emergence of constitutional dignity rights as means of advancing environmental rights (IV). Fourth is the reflection of sustainability in many constitutions (V). Fifth is the increasing role of environmental constitutionalism at the subnational level (VI). Last is the growing constitutional incorporation of rights to information, participation, and access in environmental matters (VII). Each of these developments underscores the emerging importance of global environmental constitutionalism.

II) Climate Constitutionalism

Constitutional engagement of climate change[101] has made substantial progress of late, first by the express incorporation of climate change provisions into constitutional text, and second by interpreting other express constitutional rights as impliedly encompassing obligations to address climate change. These trends likely reflect an emerging worldwide phase in constitutional litigation regarding the climate[102].

As of this writing, at least seven countries have incorporated climate change into their domestic constitutions. The Dominican Republic may have been the first to make a constitutional commitment to address climate change in 1998, followed by Venezuela the following year. The last decade has seen many more instances. Ecuador amended its Constitution in 2008 to adopt comprehensive climate mitigation measures, limit greenhouse gas emissions and deforestation, and promote the use of renewable energy. In 2013, Viet Nam amended its Constitution to ensure that the government "takes initiative in prevention and resistance against natural calamities and response to climate change". Tunisia – which stands to lose up to one-third of its land to climate change – entered the canon of climate constitutionalism in 2014, guaranteeing

---

[101] This section is largely adopted from "Climate Constitutionalism in the Courts", *in*: Jordi Jaria I Manzano *et al.* (eds.), *Climate Constitutionalism*, Edward Elgar Pub., forthcoming (2019); and, James R. May, Erin Daly, *Global Environmental Constitutionalism*, cited.

[102] See generally, Jordi Jaria-Manzano, Susana Borràs (eds.), *Global Climate Constitutionalism*, forthcoming.

the "right to participate in the protection of the climate". The Preamble to Cote d'Ivoire's 2016 Constitution now provides for the government's express "commitment to […] contributing to climate protection"[103]. And most recently, Thailand amended its Constitution in 2017 to provide for protection of water resources under threat from climate change.

There is also a growing body of jurisprudence from international and regional courts and tribunals surrounding climate change worldwide[104], including a recent decision that recognizes climate change's disproportionate impact on vulnerable persons from the Inter-American Court on Human Rights[105]. Yet almost none of it yet involves express provisions about climate change; an advisory opinion from Ecuador upholding the constitutionality of a bilateral agreement between Ecuador and Peru seems to be an outlier. Yet an increasing number of courts have turned to other constitutional rights – including environmental rights, as well as the right to life, health or dignity – to advance climate justice.

A leading example stems from the Constitutional Court of Colombia, which in 2018 issued a landmark decision involving the need to protect the Amazon rainforest as a palliative against climate change. In that case, 25 plaintiffs between the ages of 7 and 26 sought individualized constitutional protection against the government's failure to protect against deforestation in the Colombian Amazon (an area roughly the size of Germany and the U.K. combined), which was increasing at the alarming rate of 44% between 2015 and 2016. The nation's most senior judge, following a 2016 judgment which had recognized the juridical personality of the Rio Atrato – Colombia's largest river – reasoned that because the Amazonian ecosystem is vital for the future of the globe, the Colombian Amazon, too, enjoys legal rights to protection, conservation, maintenance, and restoration from the State. Following the Rio Atrato case, the Court based its ruling on "many clauses" of the Colombian Constitution which, collectively, make it an "Ecological Constitution" or a "Green Constitution"[106].

---

[103] Côte d'Ivoire (2016), Preamble: "Express our commitment to […] contributing to climate protection and to maintaining a healthy environment for future generations".

[104] See generally, Michael Burger, Justin Gundlach, *The Status of Climate Change Litigation: A Global Review*, UNEP, Kenya, 2017.

[105] Inter-American Court of Human Rights, Advisory Opinion OC-23/17 of 15 November 2017 (published on 7 February 2018), para. 47.

[106] Corte Suprema de Justicia (Colombia), STC4360-2018, at 27.

In countries where the text of the Constitution is not as green, courts have looked elsewhere to advance climate justice – often in the rights of life and dignity, exemplified by three recent cases. First, in 2018's *Ashgar Leghari v. Federation of Pakistan*, the Lahore High Court inovoked continuing mandamus jurisdiction to assess the work of the Climate Change Commission (CCC) it had established pursuant to a ruling in 2015 to implement climate change mitigation and adaptation plans to fulfill constitutional rights to life and dignity. In the 2018 decision, the Court reviewed at some length the threats of climate change in Pakistan, considering its effects on water resources as well as forestry and agriculture, among other things but found that the Commission had been the driving force in sensitizing the Governments and other stakeholders regarding the gravity and importance of climate change and had accomplished 66 percent of the goals assigned to it. The Court then dissolved the CCC and established a Standing Committee to act, on an ongoing basis, as a link between the Court and the Executive and to render assistance to the government to further implementation[107].

Second, in a 2017 case, an Irish environmental organization challenged a permit issued by the Fingal County Council authorizing an expansion of the Dublin Airport. The plaintiffs argued that the permit violated statutory and regulatory requirements, as well as Ireland's obligations relating to climate change. The Irish High Court, finding no standing, nonetheless issued an opinion of nearly 300 pages in which found that "an unenumerated personal constitutional right to an environment that is consistent with the human dignity and well-being of citizens at large" exists in the Irish Constitution, whose Article 40.3.1, "guarantees in its laws to respect, and, as far as practicable, by its laws to defend and vindicate the personal rights of the citizen"[108].

Last, the court in *Gbemre v. Shell Petroleum Development Company Nigeria*, heard a claim by farmers to address natural gas flaring and climate change in a constitutional right to dignity. It held that the petroleum developers' flaring of 'waste' natural gas in the Niger Delta without the preparation of an environmental impact statement abridged

[107] *Ashgar Leghari v. Federation of Pakistan* (Lahore High Court, Pakistan, 2018).

[108] *Merriman & ors -v- Fingal County Council & ors*; *Friends of the Irish Environment Clg -v- Fingal County Council & ors Neutral Citation*: [2017] IEHC 695 at 292, citing Constitution of Ireland (Bunreacht Na Héireann), Art. 40.3.1.

the community plaintiffs' constitutionally guaranteed right to dignity and the right to a clean, poison-free, pollution-free healthy environment[109].

Constitutional rights to health and welfare can also be used to advance climate justice. The leading case so far is *Urgenda Foundation v. Kingdom of the Netherlands*, where a trial court ordered the federal government to reduce greenhouse gas emissions and to mitigate the effects of climate change as a means of fulfilling constitutionally recognized rights to health and welfare[110].

Oblique notions of 'due process' may form the basis for a constitutional claim to address climate change. Deprivation of due process can have substantive or procedural dimensions. On the substantive side, the leading case is *Juliana v. United States*, in which a federal trial court held that the plaintiffs had a legally cognizable cause of action to assert that the U.S. government's collective actions and inactions concerning greenhouse gas emissions deprived them of a "right to a stable climate" under the Due Process Clause of the 5th Amendment[111].

Some courts have turned to constitutionally-entrenched environmental rights provisions to resolve climate justice-based claims. For example, in *Earthlife Africa Johannesburg v Minister of Environmental Affairs* (2017), an ENGO appealed the issuance of a permit to build a large coal-fired power station without having considered the climate change impacts. The Court held that even in the absence of an express obligation to consider climate change, the ministry is nonetheless required to consider all the relevant issues, including climate change and to do so before, and not after, the permit is issued[112].

III) Rights of Nature

Another significant trend in environmental constitutionalism[113] in some regions is the recognition of nature as a bearer of judicially

[109] Nigeria, *Gbemre v Shell Petroleum Development Company Nigeria Limited and Others* (2005), AHRLR 151 (NgHC 2005).

[110] *Urgenda Foundation v. The State of the Netherlands*, C/09/456689/HA ZA 13-1396 (24 June 2015).

[111] *Juliana v. U.S.*, No. 6:15-cv-1517-TC (D.Ct. Or., 2016).

[112] *Earthlife Africa Johannesburg and Another v Minister of Energy and Others* (19529/2015) [2017] ZAWCHC 50; [2017] 3 All SA 187 (WCC); 2017 (5) SA 227 (WCC) (26 April 2017).

[113] This section is largely adopted from James R. May, Erin Daly, *Global Environmental Constitutionalism*, cited; and, Erin Daly, "First vindication of constitutional rights

cognizable rights. This one is more recent but its implications have the potential to be more profound. There are two forms of the recognition of the rights of nature – one more narrow than the other – but in either form and in every country where it has been accepted, the idea that nature has rights represents a paradigmatic shift in thinking about the world, and the relationship of human beings to the world.

Ecuador's was the first Constitution to give nature itself rights. In a chapter dedicated exclusively to Rights of Nature, the Constitution explains that "Nature, or Pacha Mama, where life is reproduced and occurs, has the right to integral respect for its existence and for the maintenance and regeneration of its life cycles, structure, functions and evolutionary processes". This language is essential for several reasons. First, it identifies the rights holder as "nature" or "mother earth" thus evincing a concern for the integrity of nature's ecoystems, rather than any individual element thereof in isolation. Second, it identifies the specific rights that nature has: to respect for its existence and to respect for the maintenance and regeneration of its life cycles, structure, functions and evolutionary processes. (By contrast, when corporations or animals are recognized as rights bearers, the rights they bear are human rights).

Since shortly after its adoption, a series of cases in Ecuador recognized the rights of nature, but in 2016, the Constitutional Court firmly committed their full implementation. The high court found a violation of due process where the lower court's ruling was unreasonable for failure to fully appreciate the significance of the new ecocentric constitutional paradigm. The change, the Court said, consisted in a "paradigm shift on the basis of which, nature – as a natural being – is considered a subject of rights. In this sense", the Court continued, the Constitution "consecrates a double meaning (dimension) on nature, and the environment in general, conceiving of it not only on the basis of the traditional paradigm as the object of rights but also as an independent subject of its own specific rights"[114]. This is not a simple question of recognition of an additional right into a stable constitutional order; rather it demands a complete rethinking of the constitutional order: "In this way, the sumac kawsay (indigenous term for living well, in harmony with nature) constitutes a primordial purpose of the state, where this new conception plays

---

of nature from a provincial court in Ecuador", *Review of European Community & International Environmental Law*, Vol. 1, 2012, p. 21.

114 Sentencia N. 0 166-15-Sep-CC, Corte Constitucional del Ecuador, at 10 (Translation from Spanish by Erin Daly).

a transcendental role in the promotion of social and economic development in harmony with nature"[115].

In two 2017 decisions, the High Court at Uttarakhand in India recognized the rights of important water bodies and flows. First, the Court held that the Rivers Ganges and Yamuna along with their tributaries, are juristic persons[116]. It thus held that "the Rivers Ganga and Yamuna, all their tributaries, streams, every natural water flowing with flow continuously or intermittently of these rivers, are declared as juristic/legal persons/living entities having the status of a legal person with all corresponding rights, duties and liabilities of a living person in order to preserve and conserve river Ganga and Yamuna"[117]. Ten days later, the same Court declared that rivers, forests, lakes, water bodies, air, glaciers and springs have a right to exist, persist, maintain, sustain and regenerate their own vital ecology system and have the status of legal persons with all corresponding rights[118]. The Court focused on the importance of nature for the planet and for human development, citing a wide variety of literary, spiritual, ecological, as well as domestic and foreign legal sources, and held that the fundamental human rights on which human survival depends are Nature's rights.

In 2016, the Colombian Constitutional Court issued a landmark decision recognizing the Rio Atrato's legal ability to assert its rights in court[119]. Like the Ecuadorian court, the Colombian Court based its findings not only on a simple provision of the Constitution, but on the ecological nature of the Constitution which reflected a new way of thinking about nature, about rights, and about the role of the courts in protecting nature through the vindication of rights, ruling that "nature must be treated as a subject of rights"[120]. Thus, the Court decided to take a "step forward in its jurisprudence toward the constitutional protection of one the most important

---

115 *Ibid.*

116 *Mohd Salim v State of Uttarakhand & others*, WPPIL 126/2014 (High Court of Uttarakhand at Nainital 2017) at paras. 17, 19, http://lobis.nic.in/ddir/uhc/RS/orders/22-03-2017/RS20032017WPPIL1262014.pdf.

117 *Ibid.* at para. 19.

118 *Lalit Miglani v State of Uttarakhand & others*, WPPIL 140/2015 (High Court of Uttarakhand) 2017 64, http://lobis.nic.in/ddir/uhc/RS/judgement/31-03-2017/RS30032017WPPIL1402015.pdf. As of this writing, these cases are under review in the Supreme Court of India.

119 T-622 of 2016.

120 *Ibid.* at para. 9.28.

founts of biodiversity: the Rio Atrato"[121]. Collectively, these provisions allow the recognition of the transcendent importance of a healthy environment, its interdependent links with human beings, and the State.

In 2018, the Colombian Supreme Court of Justice then took another giant leap by recognizing the Colombian Amazon as a subject of rights. The Court therefore found that

> in reality, there exists a causal nexus between climate change generated by the progressive reduction of forest cover, caused by the expansion of agriculture, the cultivation of narcotics, mining and other illicit activities, which presumptively negatively affect the health of those who live in the Colombian territory, and [...] the uncontrolled degradation of the rainforest, which directly impairs the human rights to live in dignity, to water, and to food of the petitioners[122].

The constitutions of some Brazilian states specifically elevate the interests of nature. For example, Bahia's says that "[i]t is incumbent upon the State, beyond all powers that are not prohibited by the Federal Constitution, to [...] protect the environment and fight pollution in any of its forms, preserving the forests, fauna and flora". It remains to be seen whether provisions such as this create a "right" on behalf of nature. Regardless, this recognition of the rights of the rivers and the rainforest to claim legal personhood not only affirms the ecocentric paradigm shift of the Constitution but also places the courts squarely in the heart of the protection of those most essential ecosystems.

IV) Environmental Dignity Rights

Dignity rights[123] are playing an increasingly important role in environmental constitutionalism. The first, most important recognition of human dignity in a legal instrument is in the 1948 Universal Declaration of Human Rights, whose preamble begins with an acknowledgment of every person's dignity: "Whereas recognition

---

121 *Ibid.* at para. 9.31.

122 Corte Suprema de Justicia (Colombia), STC4360-2018, cited.

123 This section is largely adopted from Erin Daly, James R. May, "Environmental Dignity Rights", *in*: Sandrine Maljean-Dubois (ed.), *The Effectiveness of Environmental Law*, Intersentia, 2017; Erin Daly, James R. May, "Bridging Constitutional Dignity and Environmental Rights Jurisprudence", *Journal of Human Rights and the Environment*, Vol. 7, 2016, p. 218.

of the inherent dignity and of the equal and inalienable rights of all members of the human family is the foundation of freedom, justice and peace in the world". Human dignity has since dispersed into the next generation of international law in the common language of both International Covenants, which begin by recognizing that the rights enumerated therein "derive from the inherent dignity of the human person". It can be conceptualized simply, but profoundly, as the right to have rights – recognized as both a right in and of itself and the progenitor and justification for all other rights. These various ways of thinking about dignity rights are reflected in current global constitutionalism: approximately 160 of the world's constitutions have incorporated dignity in some fashion and by now, hardly a new Constitution is adopted without reference to the right to dignity.

Human dignity and environmental outcomes are inextricably intertwined. International law is beginning to recognize the interdependence and indivisibility of human dignity and environmental rights. In 2015, more than 190 nations of the U.N. General Assembly issued the 2030 Agenda for Sustainable Development, which identifies mitigating environmental harm and advancing human dignity as core Sustainable Development Goals.

As constitutional courts around the globe are turning their attention to environmental human rights, they also are becoming increasingly aware of the impact of environmental degradation on human dignity. One of the earliest cases to see this connection is from Nigeria. In *Gbemre*, noted above, the lower court held that gas flaring violated the petitioners' constitutional "right to respect for their lives and dignity of their persons and to enjoy the best attainable state of physical and mental health as well as the right to a general satisfactory environment favourable to their development" and that the gas flaring activities "a violation of their said fundamental rights to life and dignity of human person and to a healthy life in a healthy environment". Although a declaratory judgment without remedy or continuing judicial oversight, the case signals a growing appreciation of the connection between dignity and environmental conditions.

Since 2014, the cases have become more numerous and more emphatic. In that year, for instance, Kenya's Environmental and Land Court in Nairobi acknowledged that environmental rights must be read in light of the constitutional commitment to human dignity:

> The Preamble to the Constitution […] proclaims that the people of Kenya, when making the Constitution were committed to nurturing and protecting the well-being of the individual, the family, communities and the nation. Likewise, the national values and principles that bind this Court … include human dignity, equity, social justice, human rights, non-discrimination, protection of the marginalized and sustainable development.

The following year would see cases from both Nepal and Pakistan. The Nepalese Supreme Court said:

> Article 12(1) of the Interim Constitution has also incorporated the right to live with dignity under the right to life. It shall be erroneous and incomplete to have a narrow thinking that the right to life is only a matter of sustaining life. Rather it should be understood that all rights necessary for living a dignified life as a human being are included in it. Not only that, it cannot be imagined to live with dignity in a polluted environment rather it may create an adverse situation even exposing human life to dangers[124].

The High Court of Lahore in Pakistan also recognized the connection between life, dignity, and environmental and climate justice in 2015, in Ashgar Leghari, as noted above, and again when it revisited the same case in 2018:

> Fundamental rights, like the right to life (article 9) which includes the right to a healthy and clean environment and right to human dignity (article 14) read with constitutional principles of democracy, equality, social, economic and political justice include within their ambit and commitment, the international environmental principles of sustainable development, precautionary principle, environmental impact assessment, inter and intra-generational equity and public trust doctrine[125].

And in 2017, as noted above, the High Court of Ireland held that the Irish Constitution recognized that a "right to an environment that is consistent with the human dignity and well-being of citizens at large is an essential condition for the fulfilment of all human rights. It is an indispensable existential right that is enjoyed universally, yet which is vested personally as a right that presents and can be seen always to have presented, and to enjoy protection, under […] the Constitution"[126].

---

124 *Pro Public v Godavari Marble Industries Pvt. Ltd. and Others* (Supreme Court of Nepal 2015).

125 *Ashgar Leghari*, Lahore High Court, 2018.

126 *Merryman v. Fingal County Council*, High Court of Ireland, Judgment of Mr. Justice Max Barrett (2017).

Dignity can be a useful concept in environmental litigation for several reasons. First, it provides a vocabulary for foregrounding the damage *to people* from environmental and climate harms. Second, it draws attention to how environmental harms affect all of the essential aspects of a person's life: where food security, access to clean water, and breathable air are threatened, a person's ability to design her own life plan is weakened and her ability to live in material comfort is impossible.

V) Sustainability Constitutionalism

The next trend in global environmental constitutionalism concerns sustainability[127]. Sustainability's advent as a legal construct recently entered its fifth decade. In 1972, the Stockholm Declaration on the Human Environment became the first international instrument officially to recognize a principle of sustainability. In 1987, the World Commission on Environment and Development released its pioneering study, *Our Common Future*, defining 'sustainable development' as "development [...] that [...] meets the needs of the present without compromising the ability of future generations to meet their own needs"[128].

The above-mentioned 2030 Agenda for Sustainable Development describes sustainability's role as one to "Promote peaceful and inclusive societies for sustainable development, provide access to justice for all and build effective, accountable and inclusive institutions at all levels"[129]. The 2030 Agenda incorporates the UN's 17 Sustainable Development Goals, designed to advance human dignity, adapt to

---

127 This section is largely adopted from James R. May, "Sustainability Constitutionalism", *University of Missouri-Kansas City Law Review*, Vol. 86, 2018, p. 1–13, available at: https://ssrn.com/abstract=3149930; James R. May, Erin Daly, *Global Environmental Constitutionalism*, cited, App. E and associated text (denoting role of sustainability in the development of international and national law, and analyzing constitutional provisions that embed sustainability from around the world); James R. May, "The North American Symposium on the Judiciary and Environmental Law: Constituting Fundamental Environmental Rights Worldwide", *Pace Environmental Law Review*, Vol. 23, 2006, p. 113, App. B (listing countries that have constitutionally entrenched environmental policies as a governing principles, some including sustainability).

128 UN A/42/427, Secretary-General, 4 August 1987, para. 27, available at: http://www.un-documents.net/our-common-future.pdf.

129 G.A. Res. 70/1, Transforming our World: the 2030 Agenda for Sustainable Development, at 14 (Sept. 25, 2015).

climate change, ensure clean water, air and soil, reduce poverty, promote gender equity, and respect sovereignty, among other ambitious objectives, by 2030.

Sustainability is also an emerging constitutional feature. Yet trends in what we call "sustainability constitutionalism" are dichotomous. While the constitutions of nations now regularly incorporate sustainability, jurists and advocates have been slow to promote it as a proper legal outcome instead of merely a silent guiding principle.

More than three-dozen countries have incorporated sustainability in their constitutions by advancing 'sustainable development', 'future generations', or some combination of these themes. Nearly 20 countries expressly recognize a constitutional goal of 'sustainability' or 'sustainable development' though most of these are in sections of the constitutions or written in language that suggests non-enforceability. For example, Belgium's bespeaks a commitment to "pursue the objectives of sustainable development in its social, economic and environmental aspects," and Colombia's requires policy makers to "plan the handling and use of natural resources in order to guarantee their sustainable development [...]" The constitutions of Greece, Mozambique, Poland, Serbia, and Thailand also expressly require that environmental policy be developed in accordance with 'sustainable development.'

The constitutions of a dozen countries specifically recognize responsibilities owed to future generations. For example, Brazil's Constitution specifies that: "The Government and the community have a duty to defend and to preserve the environment for present and future generations." The constitutions of both Niger and Vanuatu provide for protection of the environment in the "interests of future generations". And Germany's Constitution expresses "its responsibility toward future generations".

The strongest embodiment of environmental sustainability promotes sustainable development *for the purpose of* protecting the interests of future generations. The constitutions from nearly twenty countries contain this sort of hybrid pronouncement. For example, France's Constitution proclaims that: "Care must be taken to safeguard the environment along with other fundamental interests of the Nation [...]. In order to ensure sustainable development, choices designed to meet the needs of the present generation should not jeopardise the ability of future generations and other peoples to meet their own needs [...]".

The constitutions of some countries require that specific resources be developed with future generations in mind. For example, the Dominican

Republic provides that "nonrenewable natural resources, can only be explored and exploited by individuals, under sustainable environmental criteria [...]" and provides for the protection of the environment "for the benefit of the present and future generations". The Dominican Republic is the only country on the planet with a Constitution to address sustainability, future generations, and climate change.

While sustainability has gained a foothold in many national constitutions, it has yet to capture the imagination of jurists and advocates in particular. And until it does, sustainability constitutionalism is likely to remain under-valued and under-evaluated, and warranting additional study.

VI) Subnational Environmental Constitutionalism

Subnational governments around the globe have constitutionalized substantive and procedural environmental rights, environmental duties, and sustainable development for present and future generations, often more elaborately than provided in national constitutions[130].

Most examples of environmental standards in subnational constitutionalism are narrative. Spurred initially by the Rio Declaration in 1992 (and buttressed by the Rio+20 Conference in 2012), the most ardent examples of subnational environmental constitutionalism occur at the state level in Brazil[131]. The constitutions for all of Brazil's 26 states – and the Federal District – promote environmental protection, often in intricate ways. State constitutions delineate extensive governmental functions in the service of substantive environmental rights, including promoting biodiversity and sustainability, protecting species and water quality, advancing conservation and environmental education, and enforcing environmental requirements.

Notably, the constitutions of most Brazilian states and the Federal District embed a substantive right to a quality environment in some form, most commonly to a "balanced" environment. For example, the

---

130 This section is adopted from James R. May, "Subnational Environmental Constitutionalism and the Prospects for Reform in New York State", *Widener Law Review*, Vol. 38, 2017, p. 121; and, James R. May, Erin Daly, *Global Environmental Constitutionalism*, cited, Chapter7, App. H.

131 Paulo Affonso Leme Machado, *Direito Ambiental Brasileiro*, Malheiros Editores, 2018.

Constitution of Mato Grosso's provides that: "All have the right to an ecologically balanced environment". A couple of states vary slightly from the "balanced" formula, including Mato Grosso Sol, which provides that "All have the right to enjoy an environment free of physical and social factors harmful to health".

States in the United States have a long tradition of constitutionalizing environmental protection. The State of New York's Constitution was perhaps the first in the world to embody environmental constitutionalism – and the first to develop a corresponding 'standard' of no degradation – in what is known as its "Forever Wild" mandate from 1894. Presently, there are at least 207 natural resource or environment-related provisions in 46 state constitutions, addressing 19 different categories of natural resources or the environment, including water, timber and minerals.

Currently, five states instantiate a substantive right to a quality environment: Hawai'i, Illinois, Massachusetts, Montana, Rhode Island, and Pennsylvania. These provisions are independent of state laws that allow citizens to enforce pollution control statutes. While most of these five provide a "right" to the "environment," the adjectival objective – "clean" or "healthful" or "quality" – differs from state to state. Thus, subnational environmental constitutionalism can contribute to the normalization of environmental constitutionalism in a country and can goad activity at the national level.

Yet, amid the varied manifestations of constitutionally-embedded environmental provisions at the subnational level, one commonality stands out: they are seldom subject to substantive application. This dearth in linked jurisprudence is likely due to judicial concerns about recognizing and enforcing emerging constitutional features, restraining economic development and property rights, entering what are often seen as political thickets, or providing causes of action that may displace other legislative prerogatives granted to affected persons, such as state citizen suits to enforce state pollution control requirements.

There are profound examples, however, of judicial engagement of environmental constitutionalism at the subnational level, again led by the State of Pennsylvania in the United States. In 2017, a majority of the Supreme Court in *Pennsylvania Environmental Defense Foundation v Commonwealth of Pennsylvania (PEDF)*, decided that the state constitution's environmental rights amendment is self-executing and that it imposes on the state a constitutional obligation to manage state lands as a trustee, including in granting licenses for oil and gas development[132] and that it must "dispose of any proceeds generated from the sale of its public natural resources"[133] consistently with the environmental mandate.

VII) Procedural Environmental Rights

The last trend[134] in global environmental constitutionalism is constitutional incorporation of process rights access to information, participation and justice in environmental matters. Procedural rights raise awareness, provide opportunities to participate, foster public empowerment, strengthen local communities, facilitate government accountability, increase public acceptance of decisions, and contribute to the legitimacy of governmental action.

About three-dozen countries specifically provide for procedural rights in environmental matters. For example, Article 50 of Ukraine's Constitution declares: "Everyone is guaranteed the right of free access to information about the environmental situation [...] and also the right to disseminate such information". Other examples include Brazil, Colombia, Ecuador, Eritrea, Ethiopia, Finland, France, Kosovo, Poland and Zambia. Some constitutions expressly provide for expansive or open standing to the judicial process to pursue environmental rights. A leading example is Brazil, whose Constitution declares that "[a]ny citizen has standing to bring a popular action to annul an act injurious to the public patrimony or the patrimony of an entity in which the State participates [...] to the environment [...]". In addition, many countries' judicial systems include environmental tribunals, chambers, or courts that have special procedures designed to facilitate the bringing of actions to promote vindication of environmental rights.

---

132 161 A.3d 911, 916 (Pa. 2017). For commentary, *see, e.g.*, John C. Dernbach, Kenneth Kristl, James May, "Pennsylvania Environmental Defense Foundation v. Commonwealth of Pennsylvania: Recognition of Environmental Rights for Pennsylvania Citizens", *Ruthers University Law Review* (March 9, 2018), *Rutgers Law Review*, Forthcoming: Widener Law Commonwealth Research Paper No. 18–02, available at: https://ssrn.com/abstract=3137074.

133 *Ibid.*

134 This section is largely adopted from James R. May, Erin Daly, *Global Environmental Constitutionalism*, cited, Chapter 9, App. I; and, James R. May, "Constitutional Directions in Procedural Environmental Rights", *Journal of Environmental Law and Litigation*, Vol. 28, 2013, p. 101.

There is also a growing body of judicial decisions concerning constitutional rights to participate in environmental matters[135]. For example, the Constitutional Court of Colombia found that its Constitution requires that certain indigenous populations be "formally and substantially consulted" about a plan to engage in oil exploration in culturally important lands[136]. In *Federacion Independiente del Pueblo Shuar del Ecuador c. Arco Oriente s/Amparo*, the Ecuador Constitutional Tribunal found that a government license to permit hydrocarbon exploration violated citizens' constitutional right to be "consulted and [...] participate in the design, implementation and evaluation of national and regional development plans and programs potentially affecting them directly"[137]. In *Mineral Development v. Save the Vaal Environment*, the Supreme Court of Appeal of South Africa held that a decision to allow mining operations had violated constitutional rights of notification and participation, and "since environmental rights are fundamental, this requires that environmental considerations be accorded recognition and respect in the administrative process of the country"[138]. This suggests that notwithstanding the Aarhus Convention's and domestic constitutional identification of three independent pillars, some courts tend to implement the rights holistically: information is necessary for participation and access to justice may be necessary to vindicate informational and participatory rights.

VIII) Conclusion

Global environmental constitutionalism is a relatively recent phenomenon that integrates constitutional law, international law, human rights, and environmental law. Already most national and many sub-national constitutions include provisions aimed at protecting the environment, many by creating explicit and enforceable substantive

---

[135] See generally, James R. May, Erin Daly, "The Future we Want and Constitutionally Enshrined Procedural Rights", *in*: Robert V. Percival, Jolene Lin, William Piermattei, *Global Environmental Law at a Crossroads*, Edward Elgar 2014, p. 42–43.

[136] Sentence T-766 (Constitutional Court of Colombia 2015), available at: http://www.corteconstitucional.gov.co/relatoria/2015/t-766-15.htm.

[137] *Federación Independiente del Puebo Shuar del Ecuador (FIPSE) c. Arco Oriente s/ Amparo* [ENG] (Tribunal Constitucional de Ecuador, Sala Primara April 2000).

[138] *Mineral Development v. Save the Vaal Environment*, Case No. 133 (Supreme Ct. of Appeal of South Africa, 12 Mar. 1999).

and procedural environmental rights. The spread of environmental constitutional provisions has given rise to a growing jurisprudence of linked cases that vindicate these rights.

This chapter has recounted some notable trends in global environmental constitutionalism to show how the field has grown in recent years and where it is likely to go next. We have described innovations concerning climate change, rights of nature, dignity, sustainability, subnational incorporation, and procedural rights in environmental matters. Each of these trends underscores the growing importance of environmental constitutionalism worldwide.

Chapitre 3

La Charte de l'environnement comme modèle du constitutionnalisme environnemental ?

I) Introduction

II) La Charte, un texte modèle ?

A) Un standard intéressant : un texte constitutionnel assez complet et directement applicable

B) Un paradigme non exemplaire : un texte imparfait et incomplet

III) La Charte, un modèle diversement applicable et appliqué

A) Une source d'inspiration pour d'autres pays ?

B) Un modèle timidement appliqué en France

IV) Conclusion

Chapter 3

The French Charter on the Environment: A Model for Environmental Constitutionalism?

I) Introduction

II) The French Charter, a Legal Instrument with Model Character?

A) A Valuable Benchmark: Comprehensive and Directly Enforceable Constitutional Provisions

B) A not Convincing Paradigm: Flawed and Incomplete Provisions

III) The Charter, a Legal Model Diversely Applicable and Applied

A) A Source of Inspiration for Other Countries?

B) A Model Timidly Implemented in France

IV) Conclusion

Marie-Anne COHENDET

Professeur de droit public
École de droit de la Sorbonne
(Co)directrice de l'axe environnement de l'Institut des sciences juridique et philosophique de la Sorbonne,
Université Paris 1 Panthéon-Sorbonne, France

Résumé : Cette contribution examine la portée de la Charte de l'environnement. S'agit-il d'un instrument constitutionnel qui pourrait servir de modèle au-delà du contexte français ? Est-elle correctement appliquée par le Conseil constitutionnel ? Il est démontré que la Charte a effectivement un caractère paradigmatique en droit constitutionnel comparé de l'environnement avec son dispositif assez complet et directement applicable. À ce titre elle constitue une source d'inspiration pour d'autres pays. Toutefois, cela ne signifie pas que la Charte convainc complètement par son exemplarité. En effet, elle se présente comme un texte imparfait et incomplet. Par ailleurs, il incombe aux autorités françaises, et plus particulièrement aux juges, d'achever l'œuvre du constituant en appliquant correctement la Charte.

Abstract: This contribution examines the scope of the French Charter on environment. Is it a legal instrument with worldwide model character? Is it applied correctly within France, by the *Conseil constitutionnel*? The author shows that the Charter represents indeed a global benchmark for comparative environmental constitutional law with its comprehensive and directly enforceable provisions. As a result, the Charter is capable of providing inspiration for other countries. However, the Charter cannot be said to be entirely successful since it is also flawed and incomplete. Furthermore, French authorities and particularly judges still have homework to do in order to fully implement the Charter.

I) Introduction

C'était un grand plaisir pour l'auteur de ces lignes de participer à ce beau colloque sur le constitutionnalisme environnemental, pratiquement le premier en France, en dehors du colloque sur les dix ans de la Charte de l'environnement[139], et quelques mois avant le colloque de Paris 1 sur

---

[139] Carolina Cerda-Guzman, Florian Savonito (dir.), *Les 10 ans de la Charte de l'environnement. 2005–2015*, Éditions de l'Institut universitaire Varenne, coll. Colloques et essais, 1re éd., 2016 (2e éd. à paraître).

le droit constitutionnel de l'environnement[140]. Jochen Sohnle, qui est également intervenu dans ce colloque international et dont les travaux sont très appréciés par votre serviteur(e) depuis des années, en est ici chaleureusement remercié.

Arrogance ou bienveillance, nombrilisme ou générosité, idéalisme ou réalisme… la France ou pour le moins les Français aiment à se présenter comme modèles. Dès 1789, nous avons l'ambition d'éclairer la terre entière de nos lumières et de proclamer des droits reconnus à tous les hommes, quels qu'ils soient (mais pas encore les femmes). Aujourd'hui, face à un président des États-Unis déterminé à dénoncer l'accord de Paris, le Président français se présente comme le fer de lance d'un vaste mouvement mondial pour « make the planet green again »[141]. Dans la même veine, le Président du Conseil constitutionnel, avec une conception peu orthodoxe de ses fonctions, contribue à faire rédiger par des acteurs privés dont il n'est pas établi qu'ils soient dépourvus de tout lien avec les milieux industriels, un projet de troisième pacte mondial pour l'environnement, qui s'ajouterait aux deux grands pactes de l'ONU de 1966. Cette idée, qui avait été émise depuis des décennies par des auteurs de droit de l'environnement et plus récemment au niveau de l'ONU[142], trouve ainsi un début de concrétisation. Un autre projet de pacte mondial pour l'environnement est parallèlement proposé par une ONG internationale animée par des universitaires des quatre coins de la planète, le Centre International pour le droit comparé de l'environnement, sous la direction de Michel Prieur[143].

Quelques mois plus tard, dans le cadre du projet de révision de la Constitution du 4 octobre 1958 adopté en Conseil des ministres le 9 mai 2018, il est seulement envisagé par le Gouvernement d'ajouter l'action contre les changements climatiques aux matières dont les principes ne peuvent être définis que par le législateur, à l'article 34 de la Constitution. Certes, il serait facile de faire respecter cette norme, mais elle n'impliquerait pratiquement aucun progrès pour le constitutionnalisme environnemental.

---

140 Marie-Anne Cohendet (dir.), *Droit constitutionnel de l'environnement, regards croisés*, Paris, École de droit de la Sorbonne, Université Paris 1 Panthéon-Sorbonne, 6 et 7 mars 2018, actes à paraître, Mare et Martin, 2019.

141 L'un des slogans de M. Trump était « Make America great again ».

142 Assemblée générale des Nations unies, résolution A/RES/72/277 du 10 mai 2018, « Vers un pacte mondial pour l'environnement ».

143 Site du centre : <www.cidce.org>.

La normativité de cette réforme ne serait donc guère contestable, mais elle serait à peu près inutile. Cette formulation pourrait conduire à penser que les gouvernants entendent jeter de la poudre aux yeux des Français en inscrivant l'action contre les changements climatiques dans la Constitution alors que cela n'aurait pratiquement aucun effet, puisque le législateur est déjà compétent pour définir les principes en matière d'environnement et qu'il ne serait toujours pas possible de l'obliger à agir en ce sens.

Cependant d'autres voix se font entendre dans la doctrine[144], dans les milieux associatifs et au Parlement – jusqu'au Sénat[145] – pour inscrire non pas à l'article 34, mais à l'article 1 de notre Constitution, non pas seulement une règle de compétences restrictive, mais de grands principes environnementaux et de véritables obligations d'action qui s'imposeraient à tous. Ainsi, tout comme elle garantit la laïcité, l'indivisibilité de la République et le principe d'égalité, la République devrait assurer l'action contre les changements climatiques. Elle devrait en outre assurer le respect de la biodiversité, voire le principe de non-régression et/ou les limites planétaires. Certains objectent que la Charte de l'environnement devrait suffire à garantir l'action contre les changements climatiques. Mais le fait est que le Conseil constitutionnel a donné une interprétation très contestable de la Charte sur certains points, et notamment sur l'article 6 relatif au développement durable[146]. Moins de quinze ans après son adoption, il serait donc nécessaire de modifier la Constitution pour compléter la Charte de l'environnement et la rendre plus effective. Si la France veut être un modèle sur la scène internationale, il serait en effet judicieux qu'elle commence par être un modèle sur le plan interne

---

144 V. notes précédentes. V. aussi : Dominique Bourg (dir.), avec Julien Bétaille, Marie-Anne Cohendet, Jean-Michel Fourniau, Bastien François, Philippe Marzolf, Yves Sintomer, *Pour une 6e République écologique*, Odile Jacob, 2011, p. 162 ; Dominique Bourg (dir.), avec Floran Augagneur, Loïc Blondiaux, Marie-Anne Cohendet, Jean-Michel Fourniau, Bastien François, Michel Prieur, *Inventer la démocratie du XXIe siècle. L'Assemblée citoyenne du futur*, Les liens qui libèrent, 2017.

145 Matthieu Orphelin avait annoncé cette intention du Président du Sénat, Gérard Larcher, en mai 2018, sur Twitter (https://twitter.com/m_orphelin/status/994258342532009986?s=21). V. aussi les interventions de diverses associations de protection de l'environnement en ce sens.

146 Nous verrons en effet plus bas que le Conseil constitutionnel a fait le choix – très contestable et contesté – de considérer que l'article 6 de la Charte, relatif au développement durable, n'était pas invocable en question prioritaire de constitutionnalité (QPC) et donc ne pouvait pas permettre de vérifier la conformité des lois anciennes aux dispositions de la Charte.

dans l'application de la Charte. Cet effet boule de neige entre les normes environnementales internationales et internes est d'ailleurs très typique de l'évolution du droit constitutionnel de l'environnement[147]. Plus, même, par le développement du droit de l'environnement à différents niveaux, droit européen de la Cour européenne des droits de l'homme (CEDH), droit de l'UE, droit international, et du dialogue plus ou moins pacifique des juges, on constate une large convergence générale des normes constitutionnelles environnementales et ainsi l'émergence d'un droit constitutionnel global de l'environnement, mis en lumière par James May et Erin Daly[148].

Le modèle est le patron en relief d'une statue ou d'un autre ouvrage d'art d'après lequel on travaille pour ensuite exécuter ce qu'on s'est proposé. « Se dit aussi figurément, tant des ouvrages d'esprit que des actions morales et signifie exemplaire qu'il faut suivre[149]. » Le modèle c'est l'archétype, le canon, l'étalon, l'exemple, le paradigme, la référence, la règle, le standard, le prototype, mais c'est aussi celui qui est bon, édifiant, exemplaire, comme l'élève modèle. Pour qu'un texte juridique soit un modèle, doit-il donc être le premier, le pionnier ? Être exemplaire, comme un enfant modèle ? Être tellement parfait qu'il conviendrait de l'imiter toujours, partout, en tout, et par tous ? Les règles de droit ne sont-elles pas, par définition, des modèles de conduite établis pour être suivis par tous ? Ce modèle a vocation à être suivi et mis en œuvre fidèlement, un peu comme le patron est le modèle du couturier qui l'applique sur le tissu pour fabriquer un vêtement. Certains auteurs ont contesté ou nuancé cette image, pour considérer que la règle de droit ne se réduit pas à un tel modèle, comme Antoine Jeammaud[150]. Néanmoins, bon nombre des règles de droit, et en particulier les règles constitutionnelles, doivent être regardées comme des modèles de conduite qui s'imposent à tous, pouvoirs publics, particuliers ou juges. En droit, l'être (le *sein*) doit en principe se conformer au devoir être (le *sollen*).

---

[147] Même si cette dynamique n'est pas spécifique au droit constitutionnel de l'environnement mais concerne beaucoup de domaines du droit, spécialement en matière de droits de l'homme (ou de droits humains).

[148] James R. May, Erin Daly, *Global Environmental Constitutionalism*, Cambridge University Press, 2015.

[149] *Dictionnaire de l'Académie française*, Duplain, Lyon, 1777, v° modèle.

[150] Antoine Jeammaud, « La règle de droit comme modèle », *Recueil Dalloz* 1990, Chroniques p. 199–210.

À la fin des années 1960, aucune Constitution au monde n'évoquait explicitement la protection de l'environnement, même si certaines normes constitutionnelles classiques pouvaient déjà et peuvent encore être utilisées pour protéger l'environnement. Progressivement, depuis les années 1970, la plupart des pays du monde ont inscrit dans leur Constitution des normes environnementales. Tandis que la France n'a constitutionnalisé ces droits qu'en 2005, dans le texte intégré à la Constitution qu'est la Charte de l'environnement, il semble incongru de la présenter comme un modèle. Pourtant, certains arguments peuvent plaider en ce sens. Il conviendra donc de nous demander si, pourquoi, comment et dans quelle mesure la Charte de l'environnement peut être regardée comme un modèle pour d'autres pays, pour tous les pays dans tous les temps, voire pour le droit européen et international. Parallèlement, en France, la Constitution est conçue comme un modèle qui doit s'imposer à tous, du fait de sa primauté dans l'ordre juridique, même si, là encore, la concurrence ou l'émulation avec les droits européens et international est très sensible. Si l'on se réfère au seul texte de la Charte, on peut constater qu'il s'agit d'un modèle intéressant, même s'il n'est pas exemplaire et qu'il peut être amélioré (II). Si l'on s'intéresse à l'application de ce modèle, on observera que cette application par d'autres pays peut être conçue avec des adaptations mais que la mise en œuvre de ce modèle en France est encore bien loin d'être exemplaire (III).

II) La Charte, un texte modèle ?

La Charte de l'environnement comporte de réelles qualités (A), même si elle reste imparfaite et qu'elle mériterait d'être complétée (B).

A) Un standard intéressant : un texte constitutionnel assez complet et directement applicable

Il s'en faut de beaucoup que la France soit pionnière dans la constitutionnalisation de normes environnementales. David Boyd a démontré que l'émergence des premières dispositions constitutionnelles relatives à l'environnement est très liée à la progression du droit international[151] : la déclaration de Stockholm, qui affirme notamment

[151] David R. Boyd, *The Environmental Rights Revolution: A Global Study of Constitutions, Human Rights, and the Environment*, University of British Columbia Press, 2012, p. 47.

le droit de l'homme à un environnement sain en 1972, est suivie de la constitutionnalisation de droits environnementaux dans plusieurs pays, en particulier ceux qui accèdent à la démocratie après une dictature. Ensuite, c'est la déclaration de Rio, en 1992, où le droit de l'homme à un environnement sain est réaffirmé, qui favorise la multiplication de normes constitutionnelles environnementales, notamment dans les pays issus de l'ex-bloc soviétique. La Cour européenne des droits de l'homme (CEDH) interprète alors la Convention européenne des droits de l'homme, évidemment muette sur le sujet puisqu'elle date de 1950, comme pouvant fonder un droit de l'homme à un environnement sain, par le biais de l'article 8 relatif au droit à une vie familiale normale, dans l'arrêt *Lopez Ostra contre Espagne* en 1994, et aussi ensuite en 2004 par le biais de l'article 2 affirmant le droit à la vie dans l'arrêt *Öneryildiz contre Turquie*. Craignant alors d'être condamnés par la CEDH s'ils ne respectent pas ce droit, plusieurs pays révisent leur Constitution pour y introduire des normes environnementales. Il en va de même après la Convention d'Aarhus, en 1998. Or il faut attendre 2005 pour que la Charte de l'environnement, adoptée en 2004, soit intégrée à la Constitution en France.

Mais même si la Charte n'est pas le premier texte constitutionnel environnemental, elle est intéressante sur plusieurs points.

Ce texte a *pleine valeur constitutionnelle*. En effet, il est placé dans la Constitution aux côtés de la Déclaration des droits de l'homme et du citoyen de 1789 et du préambule de la Constitution de 1946. Ainsi, quand « (l)e peuple français proclame solennellement son attachement »[152] à ces textes et notamment aux droits et devoirs définis dans la Charte de l'environnement, c'est bien lui qui donne pleine valeur constitutionnelle à ces textes et non pas le juge constitutionnel, comme l'écrivent parfois les étudiants, car le juge constate cette valeur constitutionnelle, il n'aurait le droit de la créer que si nous étions dans une aristocratie de robe et non pas en démocratie. Le Conseil constitutionnel, tout comme le Conseil d'État, ont d'ailleurs rapidement constaté la pleine valeur constitutionnelle de la Charte, spécialement en 2008. Tous les considérants et tous les articles de la Charte ont la même valeur constitutionnelle. Comme toute norme constitutionnelle et à l'opposé des directives de l'Union européenne ou de certaines conventions internationales, la Charte est évidemment *directement applicable et invocable devant tous les juges*. Peu

[152] Constitution de 1958, préambule.

importe l'imprécision ou la généralité de ces normes, elles s'imposent à tous, exactement comme les principes de liberté ou d'égalité, qui sont eux aussi très généraux. Enfin, lorsque certains articles prévoient l'intervention d'une loi, cela ne signifie aucunement qu'ils ne seraient pas applicables en l'absence de loi, mais seulement que le législateur est seul compétent pour préciser leur application. Il en va de même pour le droit de grève. Il « s'exerce dans le cadre des lois qui le réglementent » (7e alinéa du préambule de la Constitution de 1946), et en l'absence de loi, il doit être respecté, il ne disparaît pas. Il en va de même pour le 10e alinéa de la Déclaration des droits de l'homme et du citoyen, relatif à la liberté d'expression. Tous ces caractères-là ne sont pas très innovants non plus, on les retrouve dans bon nombre de dispositions constitutionnelles d'autres pays[153].

Ce qui est relativement plus novateur dans la Charte, en revanche, c'est le fait qu'il s'agit d'un texte assez substantiel, important, structuré et complet.

Bien d'autres constitutions contiennent des normes environnementales, mais elles sont généralement plus brèves, incomplètes et parfois, même si elles sont assez substantielles, elles sont souvent un peu dispersées dans le texte constitutionnel, comme dans la Constitution de Saint-Domingue.

Quand on regarde de quelle manière a été composée la Commission Coppens, qui a rédigé la Charte, la qualité de ce texte relève presque du miracle. Dominique Bourg rappelle en effet que la plupart des membres de cette commission soit ne connaissaient presque rien à l'environnement soit n'étaient guère favorables à sa protection. Il a fallu la détermination du Président Chirac et de quelques autres personnes pour que ce texte aboutisse et ne soit pas totalement creux[154].

Aux termes de la Charte, « (l)e peuple français » énonce sept considérants puis proclame dix articles. Les sept considérants semblent *a priori* d'une normativité relativement faible, puisqu'ils constatent surtout des situations de fait. Ainsi, « les ressources et les équilibres naturels ont conditionné l'émergence de l'humanité » (cons. 1) et « l'avenir et l'existence même de l'humanité sont indissociables de son

---

153 David R. Boyd, cité; James R. May, Erin Daly, cité.

154 V. Dominique Bourg, « La rédaction de la Charte de l'Environnement », *in* : Marie-Anne Cohendet (dir.), *Droit constitutionnel de l'environnement, regards croisés*, Mare et Martin, à paraître.

milieu naturel » (cons. 2). De même, le constat selon lequel « l'homme exerce une influence croissante sur les conditions de la vie et sur sa propre évolution » (cons. 4) et « la diversité biologique, l'épanouissement de la personne et le progrès des sociétés humaines sont affectés par certains modes de consommation ou de production et par l'exploitation excessive des ressources naturelles » (cons. 5). D'autres impliquent cependant plus clairement l'existence d'une norme, en ce qu'ils affirment par exemple un statut juridique et/ou en ce qu'ils dictent l'orientation des lois ou de tous les autres actes juridiques. Il en va ainsi de l'affirmation « l'environnement est le patrimoine commun des êtres humains » (cons. 3), ou « la préservation de l'environnement doit être recherchée au même titre que les autres intérêts fondamentaux de la nation » (cons. 6), ou encore « qu'afin d'assurer un développement durable, les choix destinés à répondre aux besoins du présent ne doivent pas compromettre la capacité des générations futures et des autres peuples à satisfaire leurs propres besoins » (cons. 7). Tous ces considérants ont pleine valeur constitutionnelle et doivent pour le moins servir à interpréter la Charte de l'environnement et les autres dispositions de la Constitution. Même ceux de ces considérants qui semblent les moins impératifs contiennent des orientations pour l'ensemble des conduites humaines. Par exemple une loi relative aux aides fiscales à tel type de carburant doit prendre en compte les données scientifiques rappelées par ces considérants et ne peut donc pas s'y opposer clairement[155].

La Charte contient ensuite *dix articles*. Ils peuvent être considérés essentiellement comme des dispositions visant à assurer l'effectivité du premier, qui affirme le « droit » de « chacun » « à vivre dans un environnement équilibré et respectueux de la santé ». Ce droit est immédiatement suivi de plusieurs devoirs : prendre part à la préservation et à l'amélioration de l'environnement (art. 2), prévenir ou limiter les atteintes que l'on peut porter à l'environnement (art. 3) et contribuer à la réparation des dommages qu'on lui cause (art. 4). Ensuite, l'article 5 affirme le principe de précaution, en des termes relativement restrictifs[156]

---

155 Sur les relations entre les carburants et l'environnement, v. Marie-Anne Cohendet, « Sciences et droits de l'homme, quelles implications réciproques? », *in* : Rafael Encinas De Munagorri, Alexandra Bensamoun, Estelle Brosset, Marie-Anne Cohendet (dir.), *Sciences et droits de l'homme*, Mare et Martin, 2017, p. 11–23.

156 Art. 5 : « Lorsque la réalisation d'un dommage, bien qu'incertaine en l'état des connaissances scientifiques, pourrait affecter de manière grave *et* irréversible

et l'article 6 énonce le principe du développement durable : « les politiques publiques doivent promouvoir le développement durable. À cet effet, elles concilient la protection et la mise en valeur de l'environnement, le développement économique et le progrès social ». Puis l'article 7 reprend pour l'essentiel des droits procéduraux affirmés dans la Convention d'Aarhus, comme le droit à l'information et à la participation[157], mais pas le droit d'accès à la justice, peut-être parce que les rédacteurs estimaient qu'il était déjà acquis, ce qui peut se discuter[158]. Les articles 8 et 9 disposent que l'éducation, la formation et la recherche doivent contribuer à l'exercice des droits et devoirs contenus dans cette charte et à la protection de l'environnement. Enfin, selon l'article 10, « la présente Charte inspire l'action européenne et internationale de la France », ce qui signifie que la France ne saurait agir dans ces cadres de manière contraire à la Charte.

Si ce texte n'a pas l'ampleur de la Déclaration de 1789, il a du moins une certaine allure. Pour autant il comporte des faiblesses.

B) *Un paradigme non exemplaire : un texte imparfait et incomplet*

Parmi les principales critiques formulées à l'encontre de la Charte, certaines semblent peu pertinentes, d'autres paraissent plus fondées rationnellement.

Les adversaires de la protection de l'environnement ont vertement critiqué certaines de ses règles. Certains lui reprochent de ne pas consacrer le principe d'innovation, alors même que l'article 9 dispose que « la recherche et l'innovation » doivent apporter leur concours à la préservation et à la mise en valeur de l'environnement. L'innovation est donc protégée, si elle conduit à la protection et non pas à la destruction de l'environnement, ce qui semble

---

l'environnement, les autorités publiques veillent, par application du principe de précaution et dans leurs domaines d'attributions, à la mise en œuvre de procédures d'évaluation des risques et à l'adoption de mesures provisoires et proportionnées afin de parer à la réalisation du dommage » (souligné par nous).

157 Art. 7 : « Toute personne a le droit, dans les conditions et les limites définies par la loi, d'accéder aux informations relatives à l'environnement détenues par les autorités publiques et de participer à l'élaboration des décisions publiques ayant une incidence sur l'environnement. »

158 Sur cette notion en général et sur l'application de la Convention d'Aarhus, v. Julien Bétaille (dir.), *Le droit d'accès à la justice en matière d'environnement*, LGDJ-Lextenso, Presses universitaires de Toulouse, 2015.

assez raisonnable à l'époque actuelle. Le principe de précaution est souvent leur cible favorite, alors qu'il ne s'agit guère que d'une application moderne du principe de prudence du bon père de famille qui existait déjà en droit romain. Ce principe est, aujourd'hui encore, très souvent et injustement décrié et parfois même accusé de paralyser toute l'économie française[159] alors que les faits ont prouvé le contraire. Or, non seulement le principe de précaution est indispensable à une époque de destruction massive de l'environnement et de mise en danger de très nombreuses vies par notre incurie, mais encore il est rédigé dans la Charte de manière très faible : il n'est applicable qu'en cas de risque de dommages graves *et* irréversibles sur l'environnement et non pas dès qu'il y a des risques d'effets graves *ou* irréversibles, comme c'est le cas dans d'autres textes, ce qui est donc très restrictif. Au point que l'on a pu se demander si certains ne souhaitaient pas l'adoption de la Charte afin d'opposer un écran constitutionnel à des normes européennes ou internationales plus exigeantes[160].

Tout comme le principe de précaution, d'autres dispositions de la Charte ont également une formulation relativement molle, au regard des lois ou de conventions internationales existantes. Le principe pollueur-payeur n'est pas explicitement rappelé et il est même plutôt affaibli. En effet, chacun doit seulement « contribuer » à la réparation des dommages causés à l'environnent, ce qui est bien faible au regard des dispositions de ce qui était encore alors l'article 1382 du Code civil[161]. Un autre point a été très contesté : le fait que dans l'article 6 de la Charte relatif au développement durable, l'économie soit placée au même niveau que l'environnement,

---

[159] V. notamment les propos de Bernard Accoyer devant la Commission Bartolone-Winock sur l'avenir des institutions : Claude Bartolone, Michel Winock, *Refaire la démocratie*, Rapport n° 3100, Assemblée nationale, XIVe législature, en ligne : http://www2.assemblee-nationale.fr/static/14/institutions/Rapport_groupe_travail_avenir_institutions_T1.pdf.

[160] Marie-Anne Cohendet, *Revue juridique de l'environnement (RJE)*, numéro spécial, 2003, « La Charte constitutionnelle en débat », p. 51–68. Et, avant : Nicolas Huten, « Chronique sur la Charte de l'environnement », *RJE*, notamment en 2005, 2007, 2010 et 2018. Pour une analyse de la Charte et des principes qu'elle contient, v. Michel Prieur, Julien Bétaille, Marie-Anne Cohendet, Hubert Delzangles, Jessica Makowiak, Pascale Steichen, *Droit de l'environnement*, Dalloz, 2016 (prochaine édition à paraître en 2019).

[161] La loi n° 2016-1087 du 8 août 2016 complète le Code civil avec notamment l'article 1246 : « Toute personne responsable d'un préjudice écologique est tenue de le réparer. »

alors que la survie de l'économie est conditionnée par la préservation d'un environnement équilibré. Quant au droit à l'information, il est restreint aux informations détenues par les personnes publiques, ce qui est très discutable.

Si le modèle qu'est la Charte n'est pas exemplaire, cela tient aussi à son incomplétude. Certains principes pourraient y être intégrés. Le principe de *non-régression*, qui a obtenu une valeur simplement législative dans la loi sur la biodiversité[162], pourrait très utilement être constitutionnalisé, comme l'a préconisé Michel Prieur[163]. L'action contre les *changements climatiques* doit être imposée plus clairement à tous, à une époque où les scientifiques annoncent des températures de l'ordre de 55 degrés à Paris dans quelques années et où les scientifiques du GIEC constatent que ce sont actuellement les scénarios les plus pessimistes qui se réalisent dans l'aggravation accélérée des dérèglements climatiques[164]. Sans doute, la Charte contient-elle déjà des éléments importants pour lutter contre ces phénomènes, mais ils ont été interprétés de manière très contestable par le Conseil constitutionnel et il conviendrait donc d'affirmer clairement l'obligation d'agir en ce sens, à condition qu'elle soit assortie d'une obligation de protéger la biodiversité et plus globalement de respecter les limites planétaires[165]. Le principe de respect des limites planétaires ou de prise en compte de la finitude des ressources planétaires « vise à interdire toute forme de pari insensé sur l'avenir, à obliger les autorités

---

[162] Code de l'environnement, art. L 110-1, modifié par la loi n° 2016-1087 du 8 août 2016.

[163] Michel Prieur, « Le principe de non-régression face à la logique du marché », *in* : Jochen Sohnle, Marie-Pierre Camproux Duffrène (dir.), *Marché et environnement*, Bruylant, 2014, p. 478–488 ; Michel Prieur, « Une vraie fausse création juridique : le principe de non-régression », *in* : *RJE*, numéro spécial, 2016, *La doctrine en droit de l'environnement*, p. 319–326.

[164] Dominique Bourg, *Une nouvelle terre. Pour une autre relation au monde*, Desclée de Brouwer, 2018, et les travaux de Jean Jouzel, ancien vice-président du groupe scientifique du GIEC (groupes d'experts intergouvernemental sur l'évolution du climat) et prix Nobel de la paix en 2007, notamment Jean Jouzel, Pierre Larrouturou, *Pour éviter le chaos climatique et financier*, Odile Jacob, 2018.

[165] Dominique Bourg, Marie-Anne Cohendet, Jean Jouzel, Bastien François, Valérie Masson-Delmotte, Marie-Antoinette Mélières, « Inscrire la protection du climat dans la Constitution ne suffit pas : il faut agir contre l'ensemble des atteintes aux limites planétaires, comme les pertes de biodiversité, l'acidification des océans, les aérosols atmosphériques, la pollution chimique, etc. », *Le Monde*, 07.03.2018, https://www.lemonde.fr/idees/article/2018/03/07/inscrire-la-protection-du-climat-dans-la-constitution-ne-suffit-pas_5267222_3232.html#k7D3gRpr6oAZu059.99.

publiques à considérer les limites des systèmes naturels et celles de nos capacités d'action et d'adaptation à leur égard, mais également à fournir un principe d'évaluation (voire de jugement) de la conformité de l'action publique aux exigences du long terme »[166]. Ainsi, l'obligation de respecter les *limites planétaires*, qui s'impose actuellement très fortement sur le plan scientifique dans tous les pays, devrait être également constitutionnalisée pour que les citoyens, les pouvoirs publics et les juges puissent plus aisément assurer non seulement la survie des générations futures mais aussi notre propre survie dans quelques décennies.

Le plus logique semblerait être de compléter directement la Charte elle-même. Cependant, dans des travaux de la doctrine dès 2011[167] puis dans des amendements proposés à la révision constitutionnelle envisagée en 2018–2019, c'est directement dans la Constitution à l'article 1 qu'il a été suggéré d'inscrire ces principes[168]. D'abord parce qu'ils figureraient ainsi parmi les grands principes de la République, et donc les principales obligations qui s'imposeraient à tous comme la garantie de l'égalité, de la laïcité, de l'indivisibilité de la République. Ensuite, parce qu'il paraît contestable de retoucher un texte placé aux côtés des textes fondateurs de la démocratie, spécialement alors que les contestations de certains principes comme le principe de précaution restent fortes dans certains milieux très influents. La normativité de ces principes dépendrait non seulement de leur place dans la constitution, mais aussi de la formulation, plus ou moins contraignante, qui serait adoptée pour les affirmer. Comme nous l'avons vu, une simple évocation à l'article 34 serait un miroir aux alouettes et si le peuple et ses représentants veulent effectivement « make the planet green again », il conviendrait pour le moins que la République assure (ce qui signifie : doit assurer, a l'obligation d'assurer) le respect de ces principes, comme elle doit assurer l'égalité ou la laïcité.

---

166 Dominique Bourg (dir.), *Pour une 6e République écologique*, Odile Jacob, 2011, p. 163.

167 Dominique Bourg (dir.), *Pour une 6e République écologique*, cité, p. 162 : La formulation suivante de l'article 1 de la Constitution avait alors été proposée (les éléments nouveaux proposés sont en italiques) : « La France est une république indivisible, laïque, démocratique et sociale. Elle assure l'égalité devant la loi de tous les citoyens sans distinction d'origine, de race ou de religion. Elle respecte toutes les croyances. Son organisation est décentralisée. La République veille à un usage économe et équitable des ressources, respectueux des limites de la biosphère. Elle organise le financement des investissements nécessaires à l'adaptation publique aux grands changements naturels en cours et à venir [...]. »

168 *Ibid.*

D'autres propositions, assez nombreuses, ont été formulées pour modifier et/ou compléter la Charte de l'environnement, mais qui ne font peut-être pas l'objet d'un consensus suffisant pour être constitutionnalisées et/ou qui peuvent être, déjà ou plus tard, défendues par certaines dispositions existantes de la Charte et/ou par d'autres niveaux normatifs, par exemple la notion de droits de l'humanité, les droits des animaux, le statut de la nature[169], la notion de biens communs, le crime d'écocide, ou la création d'un procureur général de l'environnement. Le droit constitutionnel comparé de l'environnement est cependant un instrument très précieux et en plein essor pour étudier les révisions constitutionnelles envisageables sur ces points.

III) La Charte, un modèle diversement applicable et appliqué

L'application du modèle de la Charte pourrait donner lieu à certaines adaptations dans divers pays (A) et elle pourrait surtout être nettement renforcée en France, où elle reste très limitée, même si elle n'est pas inexistante (B)

A) Une source d'inspiration pour d'autres pays ?

Plus qu'un véritable archétype à suivre en tous points, la Charte pourrait plutôt être considérée comme une source d'inspiration pour d'autres pays ou groupes de pays.

Le modèle de la Charte de l'environnement pourrait inspirer les pays ou groupes de pays qui n'ont pas du tout de texte imposant des dispositions constitutionnelles environnementales. Les cartes du monde de ces dispositions dressées par David Boyd puis par James May et Erin Daly montrent que de grands pays – qui sont aussi souvent les

---

[169] Entretien avec Michel Serres, « Le droit peut sauver la nature », *Pouvoirs*, n° 127, Droit et environnement, 2008, p. 5 ; Christopher Stone, *Les arbres doivent-ils pouvoir plaider ?*, préface Catherine Larrère, Le Passager clandestin, 2017 ; Marie-Pierre Camproux-Dufrène, Jochen Sohnle (dir.), *La représentation de la nature devant le juge : approches comparative et prospective*, Les Éditions en environnement VertigO, 2015, aussi en ligne : http://vertigo.revues.org/16159 ; Marie-Angèle Hermitte, *Les natures en questions – Quels rapports entre artificialisation de la nature et droit(s) du vivant ?*, à paraître ; Pierre Brunet, « Des innovations jurisprudentielles en Inde : l'attribution de la personnalité juridique à des fleuves », *in* : Marie-Anne Cohendet (dir.), *Droit constitutionnel de l'environnement, regards croisés*, à paraître.

plus gros émetteurs de gaz à effets de serre – comme les États-Unis, le Canada ou l'Australie n'ont pas de dispositions relatives à la protection de l'environnement dans leur Constitution nationale. Il convient cependant de nuancer cette observation très négative par le constat du fait que quand ce sont des États fédéraux, les États membres ont parfois des constitutions qui évoquent la protection de l'environnement. La situation est ainsi très contrastée entre les différents États membres des États-Unis, dont certains ont été pionniers en adoptant des normes constitutionnelles environnementales dès le début des années soixante-dix, tandis que d'autres sont toujours muettes sur ce point.

Le modèle de la charte peut aussi intéresser des groupements d'États dénués de normes environnementales, comme la Convention européenne des droits de l'homme, dont le texte pourrait être modernisé avec l'adoption d'un protocole additionnel relatif à l'environnement, ou le droit de l'Union européenne. Notons cependant que dans certains États ou groupes d'États, il n'y a pas de normes constitutionnelles environnementales écrites, mais les juges ont adapté l'interprétation du texte à l'évolution de l'environnement, comme en Italie par exemple ou comme on l'a vu dans le droit appliqué par la Cour européenne des droits de l'homme.

Comme la plupart des pays sont déjà dotés de dispositions constitutionnelles environnementales (plus de 167 en 2018[170]), le modèle de la Charte peut aussi inspirer des États (ou des groupes d'États pour des conventions bilatérales, régionales ou globales) qui ont déjà des dispositions de ce type, mais qui souhaitent les renforcer. La possibilité et la volonté de s'inspirer de la Charte dépendra, dans chaque pays, de nombreux facteurs qui tiennent d'une part aux règles constitutionnelles, comme le fédéralisme et d'autre part au système de variables déterminantes[171], qui comprend à la fois des éléments juridiques, comme la tradition juridique, et des éléments extrajuridiques, comme la stratégie politique d'un Premier ministre ou comme la conception de la nature dans les mentalités traditionnelles.

D'une manière générale, le *mimétisme constitutionnel* peut s'expliquer par plusieurs facteurs. Il est assez classique de la part des anciennes colonies.

---

[170] James R May, Erin Daly, « Les droits, devoirs et principes environnementaux reconnus pas les constitutions dans le monde », *in* : Marie-Anne Cohendet (dir.), *Droit constitutionnel de l'environnement, regards croisés*, à paraître.

[171] On entend par là l'ensemble des éléments, juridiques ou extra-juridiques qui, seuls ou combinés, contribuent à déterminer l'interprétation d'une norme. V. Marie-Anne Cohendet, *Droit constitutionnel*, coll. Cours, LGDJ-Lextenso, 4e éd. 2019.

Ainsi, les anciennes colonies de la Grande-Bretagne sont souvent dépourvues de dispositions constitutionnelles environnementales. Au contraire, la Tunisie, par exemple, s'est inspirée de la Charte de l'environnement dans sa nouvelle constitution, tout en allant plus loin qu'elle sur certains points. Plus récemment, ce mimétisme peut au contraire être le fait de démocraties anciennes qui s'inspirent de la modernité des jeunes constitutions des pays qui ont accédé plus récemment à la démocratie. En effet, ces pays ayant des constitutions postérieures aux années 1970 ou aux années 1990, elles contiennent presque toutes ces dispositions de droit constitutionnel de l'environnement et sont imitées par les anciennes démocraties. Ainsi, la France s'est-elle inspirée de jeunes constitutions pour l'élaboration de la Charte de l'environnement, avant de devenir à son tour un modèle.

Par ailleurs, en dehors du passé colonial et de la *date des constitutions*, plusieurs facteurs vont déterminer l'importance du droit constitutionnel environnemental. Et donc l'aptitude ou la volonté de s'inspirer de la Charte de l'environnement.

D'abord le *caractère démocratique* des pays. Globalement, plus un pays est démocratique, plus il a de chances d'avoir établi des normes constitutionnelles environnementales. Le niveau de pollution de l'ex-URSS et des pays de ce bloc était élevé, tout comme il l'est aujourd'hui en Chine. Aujourd'hui, nos collègues chinois restent un peu pantois lorsque nous leur parlons de droit de l'homme à un environnement sain. Il est clair que l'avènement de la démocratie se traduit pratiquement toujours par l'instauration de normes constitutionnelles environnementales depuis les années 1970. Cependant, quand un pays connaît une régression démocratique, comme les États-Unis, ou la Pologne ou la Turquie, cela se manifestera soit par la tentative de supprimer des normes environnementales, soit par la conservation de ces normes mais sans qu'elles soient effectives, comme en Turquie. Rappelons que les pays qui se revendiquent d'une oxymorique « démocratie illibérale » ne sont tout simplement pas des démocraties, si l'on admet avec Kelsen que c'est précisément la synthèse de la liberté et de l'égalité qui est la caractéristique de la démocratie[172]. Cette corrélation entre démocratie et constitutionnalisme environnemental est cependant nuancée par le fait que bon nombre de démocraties ont des constitutions anciennes, souvent difficiles à réviser, d'autant plus que ce sont souvent des États fédéraux

172 Hans Kelsen, *La démocratie, sa nature, sa valeur*, Economica, 1988, p. 17, dont le premier chapitre est justement consacré à la liberté, v. aussi la préface de Michel Troper (p. 9). V. aussi : Marie-Anne Cohendet, *Droit constitutionnel*, cité, n° 88 et s.

(comme les États-Unis et le Canada). On constate aussi que les pays qui sont de très gros émetteurs de gaz à effet de serre (GES), comme les États-Unis, le Canada, l'Australie ou le Japon, n'ont pas de telles normes, pour des raisons diverses. On peut aussi observer que les pays de tradition romano-germanique, comme la France, accordent plus d'importance au texte et donc à l'inscription de telles dispositions dans la Constitution, tandis que les pays de tradition anglo-saxonne se soucient moins de grands principes, croient davantage en l'efficacité des dispositions procédurales et font surtout confiance aux juges pour adapter les règles de droit à l'évolution de la société. Ils sont donc moins enclins à adopter des normes constitutionnelles environnementales et quand ils le font, ce sont surtout des normes de procédure. Ces influences combinées se traduisent dans les textes internationaux, comme la Convention européenne des droits de l'homme ou la Convention d'Aarhus. La Charte de l'environnement pourrait par exemple être un modèle pour un protocole additionnel à la Convention européenne des droits de l'homme, ou au droit de l'Union européenne, mais il est clair qu'il y aurait alors une adaptation au moins partielle de ce modèle aux traditions juridiques anglo-saxonnes.

L'existence et surtout le contenu des normes environnementales ainsi que l'aptitude ou la volonté de certains pays de s'inspirer du modèle de la Charte peuvent aussi dépendre d'*autres traditions*, des mœurs au sens large où les entendait Montesquieu dans l'esprit des lois, comme la conception de la nature. Par exemple, dans un certain nombre de pays notamment en Amérique latine les habitants présents avant la colonisation ont assez souvent une *conception de la nature* très différente de la nôtre, elle a une place centrale dans la société et un très grand respect lui est dû. Ils pourront donc se montrer plus exigeants que nous ne le sommes pour sa protection. Parfois, certains éléments de la nature, comme un fleuve, se sont récemment vu reconnaître une personnalité juridique, notamment en Nouvelle-Zélande[173] et en Inde[174], ce qui reste assez difficile à concevoir en France[175].

---

173 Catherine J. Iorns Magallanes, « Nature as an Ancestor : Two Examples of Legal Personality for Nature in New Zealand », *in* : Marie-Pierre Camproux-Dufrène, Jochen Sohnle (dir.), *La représentation de la nature devant le juge : approches comparative et prospective*, cité, p. 81–103.

174 Pierre Brunet, « Des innovations jurisprudentielles en Inde : l'attribution de la personnalité juridique à des fleuves », *in* : Marie-Anne Cohendet (dir.), *Droit constitutionnel de l'environnement, regards croisés*, à paraître.

175 Sauf pour certains territoires d'outre-mer, v. Province des îles Loyautés de la Nouvelle Calédonie avec sa Charte de l'environnement de 2012 et son Code de l'environnement de 2016.

La situation politique et l'influence des groupes de pression favorables ou hostiles à la protection de l'environnement peuvent aussi exercer une influence sur le fait que tel pays sera enclin ou non à s'inspirer du modèle de la Charte. Parfois des hommes politiques plutôt proches des groupes industriels et peu enclins à se soucier de l'environnement *a priori* peuvent annoncer qu'ils souhaitent adopter de telles normes, soit parce que leur leader est en réalité très au fait des questions environnementales et très soucieux de protéger l'environnement, comme ce fut le cas pour Jacques Chirac[176], soit parce qu'ils espèrent ainsi attirer la ferveur populaire sur une réforme globale dans laquelle ils incluraient des dispositions moins populaires, comme il semble que cela ait été le cas au Japon dans les discours du Premier ministre en 2018.

S'il est un point sur lequel la Charte de l'environnement n'est pas exemplaire, c'est bien sur son application par les pouvoirs publics et par les juges, car elle reste très étriquée.

B) Un modèle timidement appliqué en France

L'ineffectivité ou pour le moins l'effectivité[177] relativement faible de la Charte de l'environnement en France s'explique par plusieurs facteurs.

Déjà, lors de l'élaboration de la Charte, avant même son adoption, on assista à une charge massive d'une partie de la doctrine et de certains avocats pour annoncer qu'elle n'aurait pas ou peu de valeur normative, ou pour le moins qu'il y aurait une gradation très élaborée pour ne pas dire byzantine entre la normativité de ses différents articles[178]. Des échanges doctrinaux

---

176 V. Dominique Bourg, « De nouvelles formes de démocratie pour l'élaboration de la Charte de l'Environnement », *in* : Marie-Anne Cohendet (dir.), *Droit constitutionnel de l'environnement, regards croisés*, à paraître.

177 Sur la notion d'effectivité : Julien Bétaille, *Les conditions juridiques de l'effectivité de la norme en droit public interne : illustrations en droit de l'urbanisme et en droit de l'environnement*, thèse, Limoges, 2012 (sous la direction de Michel Prieur) ; Marie-Anne Cohendet, « Légitimité, effectivité et validité », *in* : Collectif, *La République – Mélanges Pierre Avril*, LGDJ, 2001, p. 201–234.

178 Nicolas Huten, *La protection de l'environnement dans la Constitution française : contribution à l'étude de l'effectivité différenciée des droits et principes constitutionnels*, thèse, Paris I, 2011 (sous la direction de Laurent Fombaustier) ; Marie-Anne Cohendet, « Science et conscience, de la neutralité à l'objectivité », *in* : *Pour un droit commun de l'environnement – Mélanges en l'honneur de Michel Prieur*, Dalloz, 2007, p. 75–89 ; Marie-Anne Cohendet, « La doctrine et la charte

assez vifs eurent lieu sur ce sujet[179]. Certains constitutionnalistes firent une interprétation très contestable de la volonté populaire exprimée par les représentants du peuple français en affirmant que certaines dispositions de la Charte ne seraient pas des normes constitutionnelles, directement applicables, mais simplement des objectifs de valeur constitutionnelle, qui s'imposeraient seulement au législateur.

Certains auteurs doutèrent de l'invocabilité de la Charte devant les juges, par exemple au motif de la généralité de ses termes ou du fait du renvoi au législateur effectué dans certains de ses articles, mais on a vu que ces arguments ne tiennent pas. David Boyd a d'ailleurs observé que ces mêmes arguments sont systématiquement brandis dans les pays où l'on instaure des normes environnementales constitutionnelles pour tenter de les rendre ineffectives[180]. Ce type d'arguments a d'ailleurs été invoqué aussi en France précédemment par des auteurs qui s'opposaient aux droits sociaux, pour des motifs qui pouvaient être plus politiques que juridiques. Tous les droits reconnus dans les textes auxquels renvoie le préambule sont invocables devant tous les juges, puisque c'est leur fondement juridique qui détermine leur valeur juridique[181]. Ensuite, il sera plus ou moins facile pour les juges de leur donner une portée concrète importante. Mais c'est une autre question.

Cette charge massive d'une partie de la doctrine exerça une influence sur le reste de la doctrine, sur les avocats et sur les juges. Aujourd'hui encore, la très grande majorité des manuels de droit constitutionnel et de libertés fondamentales brillent par leur indigence sur le droit de l'homme à un environnement sain et plus largement sur les droits constitutionnels environnementaux. Guy Carcassonne alla jusqu'à commenter le devoir de protéger l'environnement énoncé à l'article 2 de la Charte par cette seule formule : « Je suis parti débroussailler et ramasser des papiers gras, mais je reviens de suite[182]. » Ce laconisme qui se voulait élégant est en réalité très

---

de l'environnement, nos choix et leurs conséquences, *in* : « La doctrine en droit de l'environnement », *RJE*, numéro spécial, 2016, p. 296–318.

179 V. notamment les échanges entre Bertrand Mathieu et Marie-Anne Cohendet, « La Charte et le Conseil constitutionnel : point de vue », *RJE*, numéro spécial, 2005, p. 107–136.

180 David Boyd, cited, p. 245–248.

181 Sur l'invocabilité des droits v. Cédric Roulhac, *L'opposabilité des droits et libertés*, thèse, Paris 10 (Nanterre), 2016 (sous la direction de Véronique Champeil-Desplats).

182 Guy Carcassonne, Marc Guillaume, *La Constitution, introduite et commentée*, 12e éd. 2014, n° 583, voir aussi sa charge contre la Charte n° 4 et l'ensemble du commentaire n° 579 et s.

éloquent sur l'ignorance – pour ne pas dire l'incurie voire l'hostilité – d'une grande partie de la doctrine, notamment constitutionnelle, sur les questions environnementales. La plupart des manuels sont quasiment silencieux sur la Charte. Dès lors, les étudiants demeurent ignorants sur ce sujet quand ils deviennent avocats ou magistrats. Sans doute, on sait que le climato-scepticisme concerne pour les deux tiers des personnes âgées de plus de 60 ans, tandis que les jeunes générations sont mieux informées, mais il demeure que les pouvoirs publics auraient dû déduire de l'article 8 de la Charte que l'enseignement du droit de l'environnement est obligatoire pour tous les juristes, dans les premiers cycles d'études puis dans les écoles d'avocats et de magistrats ainsi qu'à Sciences Po et à l'ENA. Ceux qui dirigeront majoritairement les politiques publiques et ceux qui plaideront ou trancheront les litiges doivent en effet être en mesure de comprendre les obligations qui s'imposent à eux comme à chacun. Il serait utile que les juges leur rappellent cette obligation, mais cela supposerait qu'ils soient eux-mêmes conscients de leurs obligations.

Le Conseil constitutionnel et le Conseil d'État affirmèrent bientôt la pleine valeur normative de la Charte et de ses considérants, dans deux décisions retentissantes de 2008[183]. Le Conseil constitutionnel a clairement souligné que les dispositions de l'article 5 de la Charte, relatives au principe de précaution,

> comme l'ensemble des droits et devoirs définis dans la Charte de l'environnement, ont valeur constitutionnelle ; qu'elles s'imposent aux pouvoirs publics et aux autorités administratives dans leur domaine de compétences respectif ; que, dès lors, il incombe au Conseil constitutionnel, saisi en application de l'article 61 de la Constitution, de s'assurer que le législateur n'a pas méconnu le principe de précaution et a pris les mesures propres à garantir son respect par les autres autorités publiques[184].

Il a aussi précisé dans le cadre d'une décision « question prioritaire de constitutionnalité » (QPC) que les sept considérants qui précèdent les articles de la Charte « ont valeur constitutionnelle »[185].

L'article 7 de la Charte est de très loin celui qui est le plus souvent et le plus efficacement invoqué. Peut-être parce qu'il est plus facile à interpréter et à appliquer pour le Conseil et peut-être aussi car le Conseil constitutionnel sait qu'en cas de violation des droits à l'information et à la participation, le

---

183 Cons. Const., 2008-564 DC, 19 juin 2008, *OGM* ; CE, Ass., 3 octobre 2008, n° 297931.

184 Cons. Const., 2008-564 DC, 19 juin 2008, *OGM*, cons. 18.

185 Cons. Const., 2014-394 QPC, 7 mai 2014, *Société Casuca*.

comité qui veille au respect de la Convention d'Aarhus pourrait clouer la France au pilori, ce qui n'est guère glorieux.

Le Conseil constitutionnel a cependant une jurisprudence qui reste très étriquée sur la Charte. Il admet fort heureusement l'invocabilité devant lui de tous les considérants et de tous les articles de la Charte dans le contentieux *a priori* de l'article 61. En revanche, dans le cadre de l'article 61-1, c'est-à-dire pour le contentieux *a posteriori* de la QPC, il a bien admis l'invocabilité des quatre premiers articles de la Charte, ainsi que l'article 7 sur les droits à l'information et à la participation, en reconnaissant qu'ils sont bien « des droits et libertés que la Constitution garantit », mais il a refusé ce label aux considérants de la Charte et à l'article 6 relatif au développement durable. La rationalité de cette exclusion reste très contestée[186], en effet, lorsque la Constitution impose des obligations aux pouvoirs publics, cela signifie que chacun a droit à ce que les pouvoirs publics prennent ces mesures[187]. En outre, il est assez curieux de voir le Conseil constitutionnel refuser l'invocabilité des considérants de la Charte en QPC alors qu'il a lui-même déduit le principe de dignité du préambule de la Constitution de 1946 et qu'il a admis que ce principe fait partie des droits et libertés constitutionnellement garantis et donc invocables en QPC[188]. Sur l'article 5 relatif au principe de précaution, il a éludé la question, constatant à juste titre dans l'affaire qui lui était soumise qu'en l'espèce ce n'était pas le principe de précaution qui s'appliquait mais le principe de prévention, car il n'y avait aucun doute sur le caractère polluant de l'activité concernée[189]. Enfin, il n'a pas eu à se prononcer sur ce point en ce qui concerne les autres articles de la Charte.

La question prioritaire de constitutionnalité aurait dû permettre le développement d'un contentieux abondant pour assurer l'effectivité de la Charte. En principe, il n'est pas possible de saisir le juge constitutionnel par voie de QPC (donc par le filtre des autres juridictions) quand les dispositions contestées de cette loi avaient déjà été contrôlées par le Conseil

---

186 Véronique Champeil-Desplats, « Charte de l'environnement : la QPC bute sur l'incipit. À propos de la décision n° 2014- 394 QPC du 7 mai 2014 », *La Revue des droits de l'homme*, Lettre Actualités Droits-libertés, mai 2014.

187 V. notamment Julien Bétaille, « Le principe de précaution, un "droit" garanti par la Constitution ? », *Revue française de droit constitutionnel*, 2016, p. e29-e60.

188 Cons. Const., 2010-25 QPC, 16 septembre 2010, cons. 11.

189 En l'espèce la fracturation hydraulique pour l'exploitation des gaz de schiste, Cons. Const., 2013-346 QPC, 11 octobre 2013, *Société Schuepbach Energy LLC*. L'article 5 est en l'espèce inopérant et non pas non invocable en QPC.

constitutionnel, sauf en cas de changement de circonstances de droit ou de fait. Or, justement, l'avènement de la Charte de l'environnement est un changement de circonstances de droit, ce qui permet de saisir le Conseil constitutionnel *a posteriori* même quand la loi contestée a déjà été contrôlée par lui. De même, l'évolution de l'état de l'environnement et/ou des connaissances sur l'environnement constitue un changement de circonstances de fait qui autorise la contestation de dispositions législatives déjà contrôlées par le Conseil constitutionnel. Et pourtant, dix ans après son entrée en vigueur, la Charte n'a fait l'objet que d'une trentaine de décisions du Conseil constitutionnel, dont les deux tiers ont été rendues dans le cadre du contentieux de la QPC[190].

Les associations de protection de l'environnement ne se donnent bien souvent même plus la peine d'invoquer la Charte de l'environnement devant le Conseil constitutionnel tant sa jurisprudence est peu protectrice pour l'environnement. Pour autant, le Conseil constitutionnel ne s'est pas totalement opposé à la Charte. Il a reconnu sa pleine valeur normative. Il a déduit de la combinaison des articles 1 et 2 l'existence d'une obligation de vigilance environnementale, qui n'est pas sans évoquer l'obligation de *due diligence* reconnue en droit international de l'environnement[191]. Il a également pu considérer que l'exploitation des gaz de schiste par fracturation hydraulique pouvait à bon droit limiter la liberté d'entreprendre puisque la Charte de l'environnement énonçait des droits environnementaux de valeur constitutionnelle[192]. C'est également grâce à la Charte que le législateur a

---

190 Pour une analyse précise de ce contentieux : Michel Prieur, Julien Bétaille, Marie-Anne Cohendet, Hubert Delzangles, Jessica Makowiak, Pascale Steichen, *Droit de l'environnement*, Dalloz, 2019, n° 29 et s. ; Marie-Anne Cohendet, « Chronique sur la Charte de l'environnement », avec Nicolas Huten entre 2007 et 2010 et avec Marine Fleury à partir de 2018, *RJE* ; aussi les chroniques d'autres revues et l'ensemble des manuels de droit de l'environnement, notamment ceux d'Agathe Van Lang, *Droit de l'environnement*, PUF, Thémis, 2016 et d'Éric Naim-Gesbert, *Droit général de l'environnement*, LexisNexis, 2014 ; Patricia Rrapi, « La Charte de l'environnement devant le Conseil constitutionnel », *in* : Marie-Anne Cohendet (dir.), *Droit constitutionnel de l'environnement, regards croisés*, à paraître. V. aussi Jochen Sohnle, « Judicial Implementation of Environmental Constitutionalism in France : A Fertile Ground from the Charter of the Environment », *in* : Erin Daly, James R. May (dir.), *Implementing Environmental Constitutionalism – Current Global Challenges*, Cambridge University Press, 2018, p. 159–179.

191 Cons. Const., 2011-116 QPC, 8 avril 2011, *Michel Z. et autre*. V. aussi : Brice Crottet, « Le Conseil constitutionnel et l'obligation de vigilance environnementale », *Revue française de droit constitutionnel*, n° 90, 2012/2, p. 239–267.

192 Cons. Const., 2013-346 QPC, 11 octobre 2013, *Société Schuepbach Energy LLC*.

dû créer ou perfectionner selon les cas les modalités d'information et de participation du public pour les décisions publiques ayant une incidence sur l'environnement. Il demeure que la Charte recèle un potentiel important en matière de QPC, qui est très loin d'avoir encore été exploité[193].

Le Conseil constitutionnel est en mesure de concilier les droits et obligations reconnus par la Charte de l'environnement avec l'ensemble des autres droits et libertés de valeur constitutionnelle. Notamment avec la liberté. Il convient de rappeler que la liberté étant le droit de faire « tout ce qui ne nuit pas à autrui », aux termes de l'article 4 de la Déclaration des droits de l'homme et du citoyen, nul n'a jamais eu la liberté de polluer ou de détruire l'environnement. Rappelons aussi que d'autres normes antérieures à la Charte peuvent être invoquées pour renforcer son effectivité, comme l'alinéa 10 du préambule de la Constitution de 1946, aux termes duquel « la Nation assure à l'individu et à la famille les conditions nécessaires à leur développement ». Il en va de même pour le 11e alinéa : « Elle garantit à tous [...] la protection de la santé, la sécurité matérielle, le repos et les loisirs. »

Les autres juges ont également appliqué la Charte à de très nombreuses reprises. Déjà, en 2014, on avait pu recenser plus de 250 décisions du Conseil d'État sur la Charte[194], et Simon Jolivet apportera un regard plus actualisé sur ce point ci-après. Il en va de même pour les juges judiciaires, qui sont bien évidemment en mesure d'appliquer directement la Charte de l'environnement[195]. Simplement, on constate ici aussi les conséquences d'une insuffisante formation des juristes en droit de l'environnement en général et sur la Charte en particulier, de sorte que ce contentieux est plus restreint qu'il devrait l'être.

---

193 V. notamment Marie-Anne Cohendet, « QPC et droit public de l'environnement », *in* : Mustapha Mekki, Éric Naim-Gesbert (dir.), *Droit public et droit privé de l'environnement : unité dans la diversité ?*, LGDJ, coll. Grands colloques, 2016, p. 147–169.

194 Christian Huglo, « La QPC, quelle utilisation en droit de l'environnement », *Nouveaux Cahiers du Conseil constitutionnel*, n° 43, 2014, p. 63.

195 Contribution orale non publiée d'Émilie Gaillard au colloque à l'origine de la présente publication ; Pascale Steichen, « La Charte devant les tribunaux judiciaires, un contentieux en voie de développement », *in* : Marie-Anne Cohendet (dir.), *Droit constitutionnel de l'environnement, regards croisés*, à paraître.

IV) Conclusion

Loin de générer les torrents de contentieux annoncés par ses adversaires, la Charte de l'environnement a été appliquée par tous les juges, avec une prudence et une lenteur assez inquiétantes pour ceux qui sont informés sur l'urgence climatique et sur la rapidité de la destruction de l'environnement de manière plus générale.

La Charte de l'environnement n'est donc pas un texte modèle qui devrait être immédiatement copiée par tous. Pourtant, ce texte de valeur constitutionnelle, invocable devant tous les tribunaux, est suffisamment cohérent et intéressant pour servir d'inspiration dans d'autres pays ou pour le droit européen, et on peut gager qu'il sera appliqué de plus en plus sérieusement par chacun, particuliers, pouvoirs publics et juges notamment. L'invocation de plus en plus fréquente des dispositions constitutionnelles environnementales dans les contentieux climatiques émergents aux quatre coins de la planète est assez porteuse d'espoirs pour beaucoup de requérants[196].

---

[196] V. les travaux de Christel Cournil et Marta Torre Schaub, spécialement Christel Cournil, « L'invocation croissante du droit constitutionnel environnemental dans le contentieux climatique », *in* : Marie-Anne Cohendet (dir.), *Droit constitutionnel de l'environnement, regards croisés*, à paraître.

Chapter 4

"Environmental Constitutional Law" in Germany: Legal Nature, Scope and Content of the Principle of Environmental Protection

I) Introduction

II) The Environmental Protection Principle of the *Grundgesetz*

A) Negotiating History

B) Legal Nature of the Environmental Protection Principle

C) Scope of the Environmental Protection Principle

D) Content of the Environmental Protection Principle

E) Addressees of the Environmental Protection Principle

III) The Environmental Protection Principle in the Constitutions of the Federal States

IV) Conclusion

Chapitre 4

« Le droit constitutionnel de l'environnement » en Allemagne : nature juridique, domaine d'application et contenu du principe de protection environnementale

I) Introduction

II) Le principe de protection de l'environnement de la loi fondamentale

A) Les travaux préparatoires

B) La nature juridique du principe de protection environnementale

Alexander PROELSS

Chair in the International Law of the Sea and International Environmental Law, Public International Law and Public Law Faculty of Law, University of Hamburg, Germany

Abstract: This contribution gives an introduction to the normative features of "environmental constitutional law" in Germany. Its main focus is on the development, legal nature, scope, content and addressees of the environmental protection principle codified in the German Constitution (*Grundgesetz*) as well as in the constitutions of selected Federal States. Notwithstanding its objective nature, this principle has been applied in legal practice as a basis for justifying environmental-oriented conduct of the State, even if that conduct may lead to conflicts with other constitutional principles. It constitutes a horizontal clause on the level of constitutional law, which as such is not limited to individual fields of environmental law, but rather has the potential to guide the interpretation and application of the entire sub-constitutional legal system. Viewed from this perspective, the environmental protection principle may be regarded as a keystone for building what has been referred to as the "environmental State".

Sommaire : Cette contribution propose une introduction à la dimension normative du droit constitutionnel de l'environnement en Allemagne. Elle vise essentiellement l'évolution, la nature juridique, le domaine d'application, le contenu et les destinataires du principe de protection environnementale codifié à la fois dans la Constitution fédérale (loi fondamentale) et les constitutions de quelques Länder sélectionnés. Malgré sa nature objective, ce principe a été mis en œuvre dans la pratique pour servir de fondement à un comportement environnemental de l'État et cela même s'il y a des conflits avec d'autres principes constitutionnels. Il se présente ainsi comme une clause horizontale au niveau constitutionnel dont l'application n'est pas limitée à des domaines spécifiques du droit de l'environnement, mais dont la fin est de guider l'interprétation et l'application de l'ensemble des normes infraconstitutionnelles. De ce point de vue, le principe de protection environnementale se présente comme la clé de voûte de la construction de ce qui est appelé l'« État environnemental ».

I) Introduction

This article intends to give an introduction to the normative features of "environmental constitutional law" in Germany. Its main focus is on the environmental protection principle codified in the German Constitution (*Grundgesetz*)[197] as well as in the constitutions of the Federal States. It analyzes the development, legal nature, scope, content and addressees of this principle, and assesses whether and, in case of affirmation, to what extent it has been able to produce normative impacts in legal practice. It thereby aims at contributing to a mutual understanding of the basis of environmental constitutional law within the Member States of the European Union, which may ultimately result in the development of regional environmental constitutionalism.

While the first part of this paper examines in a more detailed manner the environmental protection principle of the *Grundgesetz* (II) the second part provides an overview of this principle in the Constitutions of the Federal States (III).

II) The Environmental Protection Principle of the *Grundgesetz*

Taking into account that the provisions of the *Grundgesetz* take precedence over the law of the Federal States, including their constitutions[198], attention will first be turned to the constitutional legal

---

[197] An authentic translation of the *Grundgesetz* in English is available at: https://www.gesetze-im-internet.de/englisch_gg/englisch_gg.html#p0026, a French version can be retrieved at: https://www.btg-bestellservice.de/pdf/80202000.pdf.

[198] See Article 31 *Grundgesetz*: "Federal law shall take precedence over *Land* law." The terms "Land" (singular) and "Länder" (plural) are the technical terms used by the *Grundgesetz* for the Federal States.

situation on the federal level. This part presents the development (A), the legal nature (B), the scope (C), the content (D) and the addressees (E) of the environmental protection principle.

A) Negotiating History

On the federal level, the environmental protection principle is codified in Article 20a *Grundgesetz*. The first part of this provision, which addresses the protection of the natural foundations of life, was included into the text of the Constitution in 1994. In 2002, the then already existing Article 20a *Grundgesetz* was complemented by inclusion of a reference to the duty of the State to protect animal welfare. As it stands today, Article 20a *Grundgesetz* reads:

"Mindful also of its responsibility toward future generations, the state shall protect the natural foundations of life and animals by legislation and, in accordance with law and justice, by executive and judicial action, all within the framework of the constitutional order".

Attempts to include a duty of the State to protect the environment into the Constitution had begun in the course of the 10th legislative period (1983–1987) of the Federal Parliament (*Bundestag*), but initially remained unsuccessful due to controversies concerning the scope of the pertinent obligation. Although not substantively related with the issue of reunification, the debate on including the duty to protect the environment into the text of the Constitution was resumed in the context of the general discussions concerning the need to amend the *Grundgesetz* following achievement of the German reunification in 1990. While the Members of the Joint Constitutional Commission of the *Bundestag* and the *Bundesrat* (representing the interests of the *Länder* on the federal constitutional level) generally agreed on a corresponding principle to be included in the text of the *Grundgesetz*[199], views were divided on whether the provision concerned should be based on an ecocentric or anthropocentric approach[200]. Moreover, the relationship between the future environmental protection principle and other constitutional objectives, as well as the scope of power of the legislator

[199] See Rupert Scholz, "Artikel 20a", *in*: Theodor Maunz, Günter Dürig, *Grundgesetz-Kommentar*, C.H. Beck, 2017, para. 19.

[200] Stefan Huster, Johannes Rux, "Artikel 20a", *in*: Volker Epping, Christian Hillgruber, *BeckOK Grundgesetz*, C.H. Beck, 2018, para. 3.

to further substantiate the environmental protection principle, were subject to debate[201]. Only after the chairman of the Joint Constitutional Commission, Rupert Scholz, announced that he would step back should no agreement on the environmental principle be achieved, did the members of the Commission agree on the compromise formula that was later on enacted as the new Article 20a *Grundgesetz*. While the advocates of an anthropocentric view did not insist anymore on that view being expressly mentioned in the wording of Article 20a *Grundgesetz*, those supporting the notion that the environmental protection principle should reflect an ecocentric perspective abandoned their position that the obligation contained in the provision should demand a "particular" level of protection (which would have arguably implied that the protection of the environment would outbalance other constitutional objectives in case of conflict)[202].

As far as animal welfare (which was held to be not, or at least not to the full extent, covered by the environmental protection principle) is concerned, the Joint Constitutional Commission in 1993 refrained from recommending to the constitutional legislator to also include the issue of animal protection into the text of that provision. It argued that this would bear the risk that the overall balance of the system of values enshrined in the *Grundgesetz*, which was held to exclusively refer to human beings, would be put into question[203]. Notwithstanding this, following several (and initially unsuccessful) legislative initiatives to change the wording of the newly adopted Article 20a *Grundgesetz*, the parliamentary groups of the *Bundestag* agreed in 2002 on amending the text of this provision by the words "and animals". As far as the reasons for this paradigm shift are concerned, the explanatory memorandum referred, *inter alia*, to the need of safeguarding an ethically responsible treatment of animals by man, as well as to the ability to suffer and the sensitivity of higher developed animal species[204]. It should also be taken into account that the general elections that took place in 1998 resulted for the first time in German history in the formation of a government coalition between

---

[201] Rupert Scholz, "Artikel 20a", *in*: Theodor Maunz, Günter Dürig, cited, para. 22.

[202] Stefan Huster, Johannes Rux, "Artikel 20a", *in*: Volker Epping, Christian Hillgruber, cited, para. 4.

[203] Rupert Scholz, "Artikel 20a", *in*: Theodor Maunz, Günter Dürig, cited, para. 59.

[204] *Official publication of the Bundestag (BT-Drucks)*, No. 14/8860 of 23 April 2002, p. 3, available (in German language) at: http://dip21.bundestag.de/dip21/btd/14/088/1408860.pdf.

the Social Democratic Party (*SPD*) and the Green Party (*Grüne*) – a fact that explains why environmental issues played a more dominating role in German politics at the beginning of the 21st century than in the past. Prior to the amendment of the *Grundgesetz* in 2002, the issue of animal welfare had been governed by sub-constitutional law, in particular by way of the Protection of Animals Act.

B) Legal Nature of the Environmental Protection Principle

Article 20a *Grundgesetz* is the constitutional legal basis for the protection of animals and the environment. It is generally accepted that it ought to be regarded as a State objective (*Staatszielbestimmung*) and, as such, a binding principle of constitutional law (and not merely a soft law recommendation)[205]. Its main legal relevance becomes evident in the context of substantiating vague legal concepts included in sub-constitutional law. Article 20a *Grundgesetz* also serves as guideline for the interpretation of lower-ranking law and can, in light of its nature as principle of constitutional law, be relied upon in order justify interferences with basic rights[206]. Viewed from this perspective, it can be characterized as an inherent constitutional limitation to the basic rights and freedoms codified in Articles 2 to 19 *Grundgesetz*.

The normative power of the environmental protection principle is limited from the outset, though, as the legislator enjoys a broad scope of discretion in deciding upon the implementation of animal and environmental protection issues within sub-constitutional law[207]. In particular, as has been confirmed by the Federal Constitutional Court (*Bundesverfassungsgericht*), Article 20a *Grundgesetz* does not provide a subjective right of individuals vis-à-vis the public authorities, and it

205 For references see Michael Kloepfer, *Umweltrecht*, C.H. Beck, 4th ed., 2016, p. 121 *et seq.*; Reiner Schmidt, Wolfgang Kahl, Klaus Ferdinand Gärditz, *Umweltrecht*, C.H. Beck, 9th ed., 2014, p. 68 *et seq.*

206 A note on terminology: The *Grundgesetz* speaks of "human rights" when referring to individual rights contained in international treaties (see Article 1 para. 2). The crucially important individual constitutional rights that are codified in the *Grundgesetz* itself are called "basic rights" (see Article 1 para. 3).

207 BVerfGE 118, p. 79, at 110; BVerfG, *Neue Zeitschrift für Verwaltungsrecht*, 2010, p. 114–120, at 116 *et seq.*; in relation to the protection of animals BVerfGE 127, p. 293, at 328; see also Michael Kloepfer, *Umweltrecht*, cited, p. 128 with further references.

may thus not be relied upon individually in order to file a constitutional complaint[208]. That said, it has yet to be decided whether and to what extent the environmental principle can be used in order to "charge" the basic rights in terms of Articles 2 to 19 *Grundgesetz*, whose violation can be asserted, following exhaustion of ordinary remedies, by recourse to the constitutional complaint under Article 93 para. 1 No. 4a *Grundgesetz* before the Federal Constitutional Court, with environmental content[209].

C) Scope of the Environmental Protection Principle

Article 20a *Grundgesetz* refers to the "natural foundations of life". This term is generally held to be synonymous with the broad concept of the natural environment. As such it covers humans, animals, plants, microorganisms, soil, water, air, climate, atmosphere, landscape, biological diversity and the interrelationship between these goods[210]. In contrast, the issue of animal welfare was and is not considered as being part of the concept of the "natural foundations of life"[211], a fact that prompted the constitutional legislator to include the words "and animals" in Article 20a *Grundgesetz* in 2002. Since that time, it is beyond doubt that the legislator is obliged by virtue of Article 20a *Grundgesetz* to take measures to protect individual animals from suffering harm[212].

Commentators disagree on whether the reference being made in Article 20a *Grundgesetz* to the responsibility of the State "toward future generations", in conjunction with the terminology used ("natural foundations") as well as the crucial constitutional legal importance of the basic rights of life and physical integrity codified in Articles 1 and 2 *Grundgesetz*, necessarily imply that the environmental protection

---

208 BVerfG, *Neue Zeitschrift für Verwaltungsrecht*, 2001, p. 1148–1150, at 1149.

209 In the affirmative Reiner Schmidt, Wolfgang Kahl, Klaus Ferdinand Gärditz, *Umweltrecht*, cited, p. 69 *et seq*.

210 BVerfGE 128, p. 1, at 65; see also Reiner Schmidt, Wolfgang Kahl, Klaus Ferdinand Gärditz, *Umweltrecht*, cited, p. 70; Klaus Ferdinand Gärditz, "Artikel 20a Grundgesetz", *in*: Martin Beckmann, Wolfgang Durner, Thomas Mann, Marc Röckinghausen, *Landmann/Rohmer – Umweltrecht*, Vol. I, C.H. Beck, 2017, para. 9 with further references.

211 But see Christian Calliess, *Rechtsstaat und Umweltstaat*, Mohr Siebeck, 2001, p. 109.

212 For details see Michael Kloepfer, "Artikel 20a", *in*: Rudolf Dolzer, Klaus Vogel, Karin Graßhof, *Bonner Kommentar zum Grundgesetz*, C.F. Müller, Vol. 5, 2017, para. 66 *et seq*.

principle is first and foremost based on an anthropogenic viewpoint[213]. While the wording of the provision is the outcome of a historical compromise (see A above) and thus cannot be held to reflect either of the two positions, it seems safe to conclude that Article 20a *Grundgesetz* is sufficiently flexible in order to support the enactment of measures that reflect a holistic approach to environmental protection, also taking into account the broad scope of discretion allocated to the legislator in the development of the environmental protection principle. That said, in case of conflict between the protection of the environment for its own sake on the one hand and legitimate human interests on the other, the principle of human dignity codified in Article 1 para. 1 *Grundgesetz*, which constitutes the fundament of the entire constitutional system, will often result in precedence being allocated to the latter[214].

Article 20a *Grundgesetz* only addresses the protection of the "natural" foundations of life. While most commentators agree that purely artificial objects are thus not covered by the environmental protection principle, anthropogenic impacts on parts of the natural environment do not result in the inapplicability of Article 20a *Grundgesetz*, provided that the modified environment is still exercising parts of its ecological functions[215]. Therefore, artificial habitats and reintroduced animal species are part of the natural environment, and it is difficult to see why genetically modified organisms should automatically be treated differently[216].

The reference in Article 20a *Grundgesetz* to the "responsibility toward future generations" subjects the constitutional legal obligation to take measures of environmental and animal protection to a long-term understanding. Thus, it reflects an extract (i.e., the ecological dimension) of the broader the principle of sustainability[217]. As the environmental

---

[213] For analysis see Christian Calliess, *Rechtsstaat und Umweltstaat*, cited, p. 111 *et seq.*; Klaus Ferdinand Gärditz, "Artikel 20a Grundgesetz", *in*: Martin Beckmann, Wolfgang Durner, Thomas Mann, Marc Röckinghausen, *Landmann/Rohmer, Umweltrecht*, cited, para. 10; Michael Kloepfer, *Umweltrecht*, cited, p. 125 (arguing in favor of an anthropogenic approach).

[214] Christian Calliess, *Rechtsstaat und Umweltstaat*, cited, p. 113 *et seq.*

[215] Klaus Ferdinand Gärditz, "Artikel 20a Grundgesetz", *in*: Martin Beckmann, Wolfgang Durner, Thomas Mann, Marc Röckinghausen, cited, para. 11; Christian Calliess, *Rechtsstaat und Umweltstaat*, cited, p. 108 *et seq.*

[216] But see Astrid Epiney, "Artikel 20a", *in*: Hans v. Mangoldt, Friedrich Klein, C. Starck, *Kommentar zum Grundgesetz*, Vol. II, C.H. Beck, 6th ed., 2010, para. 18.

[217] Cf. BVerfGE 118, p. 79, at 110 (holding that the principle of sustainability would require the legislator to take measures in order to further reduce greenhouse gas

protection principle is also valid for present generations, however, the specific legal consequences of the intergenerational shape of Article 20a *Grundgesetz* are far from clear. Commentators have argued that the environmental protection principle would prohibit measures that may result in a deterioration of the overall state of the environment. This would imply a constitutional legal duty to manage natural resources in a careful and precautionary manner, as future generations would otherwise be deprived of their right to have equal access to these resources[218]. If this view is correct, Article 20a *Grundgesetz* can be considered as the constitutional legal basis for the precautionary principle[219].

D) Content of the Environmental Protection Principle

The environmental protection principle first and foremost obliges the State authorities, in terms of a mandate to act, to take measures of environmental and animal welfare protection, and to take into account these values in decision-making processes. Notwithstanding the broad scope of discretion allocated to the legislator, Article 20a *Grundgesetz* is thus not limited to the prevention or removal of environmental damage, but requires that the State actively counters the emergence of such damage, e.g. by implementing risk management and environmental impact assessment procedures[220]. The constitutional threshold that must in any event be observed by the legislator can best be described in terms of a general principle[221] of ecological non-regression[222]. While in exceptional cases, the environmental protection principle may give rise to an unequivocal duty of the State authorities to intervene vis-à-vis private

---

emissions); see Klaus Ferdinand Gärditz, "Artikel 20a Grundgesetz", *in*: Martin Beckmann, Wolfgang Durner, Thomas Mann, Marc Röckinghausen, cited, para. 11; Christian Calliess, *Rechtsstaat und Umweltstaat*, cited, p. 121.

218 Christian Calliess, *Rechtsstaat und Umweltstaat*, cited, p. 124. See also Reiner Schmidt, Wolfgang Kahl, Klaus Ferdinand Gärditz, *Umweltrecht*, cited, p. 71.

219 See Michael Kloepfer, "Artikel 20a", *in*: Rudolf Dolzer, Klaus Vogel, Karin Graßhof, *Bonner Kommentar zum Grundgesetz*, C.F. Müller, Vol. 5, 2017, paras. 48, 72.

220 *Ibid.*, para. 72; Reiner Schmidt, Wolfgang Kahl, Klaus Ferdinand Gärditz, *Umweltrecht*, cited, p. 72.

221 "General" implies that the non-regression principle does not refer to individual cases, but to the overall situation.

222 Michael Kloepfer, *Umweltrecht*, cited, p. 129; Reiner Schmidt, Wolfgang Kahl, Klaus Ferdinand Gärditz, *Umweltrecht*, cited, p. 72. – Note that the Federal Constitutional Court has so far never determined a violation of this threshold.

conduct if that conduct jeopardizes, or is likely to jeopardize respectively, the needs of environmental protection and/or animal welfare[223], the principle codified in Article 20a *Grundgesetz* on the one hand and other constitutional legal values on the other generally possess equal status – a fact that in cases of conflict gives rise to a duty of the State authorities of balancing the colliding interests involved.

The case-law of the Federal Constitutional Court demonstrates that the environmental protection principle, while only having achieved limited relevance so far, cannot be regarded as lacking sufficient legal power. Concerning the protection of animal welfare, the Federal Constitutional Court confirmed that Article 20a *Grundgesetz* demands the protection of the individual animal[224], and that the animal protection principle ought to be fairly balanced with other constitutional principles and objectives as well as basic rights[225], without automatically enjoying priority in case of conflict[226]. In its decision on the constitutionality of caging of laying hens, it held that if the federal legislator has enacted laws that establish protection-oriented conditions for the enactment of governmental regulations in relation to the treatment of animals, a violation of these requirements by a governmental agency would at the same time violate the constitutional principle of environmental protection[227]. The Federal Constitutional Court also ruled that by deciding to accelerate the nuclear power phase-out following the Fukushima accident, the German legislator pursued a legitimate regulatory objective by which it accommodated the environmental protection principle codified in Art. 20a *Grundgesetz*[228].

The most sophisticated statement that has been made by the Federal Constitutional Court concerning the relevance of Art. 20a *Grundgesetz* so far can be found in its judgment on the constitutionality of the Act on Genetic Engineering. The Court held that the task of the legislator arising from that provision could require the taking of both preventive and risk management measures, taking into account that the scope of the environmental principle

223 Michael Kloepfer, “Artikel 20a”, *in*: Rudolf Dolzer, Klaus Vogel, Karin Graßhof, *Bonner Kommentar zum Grundgesetz*, cited, para. 73.

224 BVerfGE 127, p. 293, at 328.

225 BVerfGE 117, p. 126, at 138; BVerfGE 127, p. 293, at 328; BVerfGE 128, p. 1, at 41 *et seq*.

226 BVerfGE 110, p. 141, at 166; BVerfGE 127, p. 293, at 328.

227 BVerfGE 127, p. 293, at 329.

228 BVerfGE 143, p. 246, at para. 283.

would also cover the conservation of biodiversity and the protection of appropriate living conditions for endangered animal and plant species[229]. The legislator's responsibility enshrined in the environmental protection principle would be circumvented, would it not be considered to be under the duty to submit descendants of genetically modified organisms to a control scheme[230]. Against the background of persisting scientific uncertainty concerning the long-term consequences of deploying genetic engineering, the State would thus be bound to observe, by virtue of Art. 20a *Grundgesetz*, a due diligence obligation to protect the protection of the natural foundations of life also in favor of future generations[231]. Therefore, the Court implicitly acknowledged that the content of the environmental protection principle indeed extends to the precautionary principle.

E) Addressees of the Environmental Protection Principle

While all State authorities in terms of Article 20 para. 2 *Grundgesetz*, and all State organs, no matter what level of governance they are allocated to, and irrespective of whether they act in the form of public or private law, are bound to observe the principle codified in Article 20a *Grundgesetz*, the environmental protection principle cannot be relied upon by private individuals, or in the context of legal relationships between private individuals respectively[232]. The legislator, which has a broad scope of discretion in implementing and further developing it (see C above), is the primary addressee of the environmental protection principle. Taking into account that Article 20a *Grundgesetz* embodies a substantive principle in terms of a constitutional State objective, it leaves untouched the allocation of competences between the Federation and the Federal States in relation to law-making powers laid down in Articles 70 to 74 *Grundgesetz*. Thus, the mere fact that Article 20a *Grundgesetz* is a provision of the Constitution of the Federation does not result in the law-making powers automatically being allocated to the Federation[233].

With regard to the executive authority on the one hand and the judiciary on the other, the relevance of the principle of environmental protection

---

229 BVerfGE 128, p. 1, at 37.

230 *Ibid.*, at 39 *et seq.*

231 *Ibid.*, at 37.

232 Reiner Schmidt, Wolfgang Kahl, Klaus Ferdinand Gärditz, *Umweltrecht*, cited, p. 72.

233 *Ibid.*, p. 72.

becomes manifest in the context of interpreting sub-constitutional law in line with Article 20a *Grundgesetz*, in connection with the taking – and controlling respectively – of discretionary decisions as well as with planning deliberations[234], and in relation to the need to justify interferences with individual basic rights or other constitutional legal values[235].

III) The Environmental Protection Principle in the Constitutions of the Federal States

Parallel to the legal situation on the federal level, the environmental protection principle is meanwhile included in all constitutions of the Federal States[236], even though with varying legal structure and content. For example, the Constitution of Brandenburg in Article 39 contains a very detailed provision addressing the protection of the natural foundations of life, which in its paragraph 2 acknowledges the existence of an individual right to be protected from injuries and unacceptable threats resulting from interferences with the environment. Furthermore, Article 39 para. 8 of the Constitution of Brandenburg recognizes the existence and admissibility of group actions in relation to the protection of the environment. The Bavarian Constitution contains in its Article 141 para. 3 a basic right of everyone to have free access to the scenic attractions of the State and to recreate in the open air. Most *Länder* constitutions follow the structure of Article 20a *Grundgesetz*, however[237]. This will be demonstrated in the following by taking a closer look at the relevant provisions of the Constitution of Rhineland-Palatinate.

---

234 Michael Kloepfer, *Umweltrecht*, cited, p. 130; Michael Kloepfer, "Artikel 20a", *in*: Rudolf Dolzer, Klaus Vogel, Karin Graßhof, *Bonner Kommentar zum Grundgesetz*, cited, paras. 53–58 and paras. 59–61.

235 For details see Christian Calliess, *Rechtsstaat und Umweltstaat*, cited, p. 128–132; Michael Kloepfer, *Umweltrecht*, cited, p. 131.

236 As a matter of constitutional law, the *Länder* are quasi-sovereign entities characterized by the existence of all State authorities. While they even have, under the strict conditions set out in Article 32 (3) *Grundgesetz*, the competence to conclude international treaties, the external dimension of sovereignty is predominantly allocated to the Federation (*Bund*). Also, from an internal perspective, the scope of competences of the *Länder*, in particular as far as the field of legislation is concerned, has significantly decreased over the decades to the advantage of the *Bund*.

237 Or rather *vice versa*: Several of the constitutions of the *Länder* already contained codifications of the environmental protection principle before this provision was

In this respect, the environmental protection principle is codified in Article 69 of the Constitution. Similar to Article 20a *Grundgesetz*, it has been framed in terms of a constitutional State objective, i.e., a legally binding principle of constitutional law. Concerning its scope, Article 69 Constitution of Rhineland-Palatinate refers to the "protection of nature and the environment", but it has convincingly been demonstrated that no difference exists between these terms on the one hand and the concept of "natural foundations of life" under Article 20a *Grundgesetz* on the other[238]. The issue of animal welfare has been subjected to a separate provision (Article 70), which requires that animals must be respected as fellow creatures, and that they ought to be protected within the framework of sub-constitutional law from pain and injuries.

Article 69 para. 1 Constitution of Rhineland-Palatinate contains a reference to nature and the environment being the foundations of "present and future" life, and para. 2 prescribes that the use of soil, air and water (which must be specifically protected according to the first sentence of this paragraph) is devoted to "the general public and future generations". It thus becomes obvious that the amended wording of this provision, which abandons the anthropogenic approach which its predecessor provision of 1985 was held to reflect, echoes the focus on the environmental dimension of the principle of sustainability included in Article 20a *Grundgesetz*[239]. That Article 69 para. 2 Constitution of Rhineland-Palatinate demands "special protection" of soil, air and water, and that para. 3 requires the careful management of natural resources, does not result in these environmental goods being allocated higher rank in comparison to nature and the environment in general under the Constitution. The legal relevance of these special provisions is limited, inasmuch as their effects do arguably not go beyond mere political appeals.

The content of the environmental protection and animal welfare principles on the level of Rhineland-Palatinate corresponds to that of Article 20a *Grundgesetz*. Thus, also Articles 69 and 70 Constitution

---

included in the *Grundgesetz*. For an analysis see Daniel Hahn, *Staatszielbestimmungen im integrierten Bundesstaat*, Duncker & Humblot, 2010, p. 118–181.

238 Cf. Jürgen Held, "Artikel 69", *in*: Lars Brocker, Michael Droege, Siegfried Jutzi, *Verfassung für Rheinland-Pfalz*, Nomos, 2014, para. 10.

239 Article 69 Constitution of Rhineland-Palatinate was amended in 2000, i.e., after the inclusion of Article 20a in the *Grundgesetz*.

of Rhineland-Palatinate oblige the authorities of the *Land* to take corresponding measures, and to take into account these values in decision-making processes. As in the case of Article 20a *Grundgesetz*, the *Land* legislator enjoys a broad scope of discretion in relation to the development of these principles, which is delimited by the minimum threshold to generally prevent deterioration of the state of the environment[240]. At the same time, it is generally recognized that Articles 69 and 70 Constitution of Rhineland-Palatinate are not limited to prevention, but also include precautionary measures and the duty to remove or compensate environmental damage[241]. The legal consequences arising from the environmental protection and animal welfare principles on the level of Rhineland-Palatinate are essentially the same as those on the federal level[242]. In respect of the task of the legislator to implement and develop them further, it should be noted, though, that the legislative powers of the Federal States are limited in light of the fact that the pertinent competences of the Federation have been significantly extended over time[243].

In all that, it is not possible to rely on Articles 69 and 70 Constitution of Rhineland-Palatinate in order to justify interferences with basic rights and other constitutional values guaranteed under the *Grundgesetz* due to the higher rank of the latter vis-à-vis the *Länder* constitutions. Similarly, ordinary (i.e., sub-constitutional) law enacted by the federal legislator cannot be interpreted in conformity with the environmental protection and animal welfare principles codified in the Constitution of Rhineland-Palatinate, taking into account that the precedence of federal law under Article 31 *Grundgesetz* also extends to the constitutions of the *Länder*[244].

As far as the addressees of the environmental protection and animal welfare principles are concerned, reference can be made to the corresponding submissions made in relation to Article 20a *Grundgesetz*. All State authorities, including the organs of the municipalities, are therefore bound to observe the constitutional principles codified in Articles 69 and 70 Constitution of Rhineland-Palatinate. Article 69 para. 1 Constitution

---

[240] Jürgen Held, "Artikel 69", *in*: Lars Brocker, Michael Droege, Siegfried Jutzi, *Verfassung für Rheinland-Pfalz*, cited, para. 17 *et seq*.

[241] *Ibid*., para. 17.

[242] *Ibid*., paras. 19–21 and 24–34. For details see sections II, D and E above.

[243] *Ibid*., paras. 26–27.

[244] *Ibid*., para. 2.

of Rhineland-Palatinate contains a special clause, though, inasmuch as it prescribes that the protection of nature and the environment is also an obligation of "all humans"[245]. The meaning and consequences of this clause are not completely clear. One commentator has suggested that the obligation concerned would emphasize the principle of cooperation, according to which the protection of the environment would be a task of both State and society[246]. Be that as it may, in light of the objective nature of the environmental protection principle it seems difficult to conclude that Article 69 para. 1 Constitution of Rhineland-Palatinate establishes a duty of individuals which could directly be enforced by the State administration. Also taking into account that the environmental protection principle is in need of development by the legislator, the correct view arguably is that the pertinent obligation established by the wording of Article 69 para. 1 Constitution of Rhineland-Palatinate is only a moral one[247].

IV) Conclusion

At first glance, it may seem to appear that the environmental protection principle has not lived up to the high expectations that were expressed by some[248] following the amendment of the *Grundgesetz*. It is true that the legal impacts of this principle, in particular with regard to the further development of sub-constitutional law, have so far remained comparatively narrow. On closer examination, however, this is only natural, taking into account that the Joint Constitutional Commission refrained from taking into account to frame the environmental protection principle in terms of a subjective right. It should also not be forgotten that the State authorities were already entitled to take measures for the protection of the environment prior to

245 A similar rule is contained in Article 143 para. 3 of the Bavarian Constitution which includes individuals in the general duty to treat nature and landscape with care.

246 Jürgen Held, "Artikel 69", *in*: Lars Brocker, Michael Droege, Siegfried Jutzi, *Verfassung für Rheinland-Pfalz*, cited, para. 16. For details on the principle of cooperation see Michael Kloepfer, *Umweltrecht*, cited, p. 200–205.

247 Consenting Jürgen Held, "Artikel 69", *in*: Lars Brocker, Michael Droege, Siegfried Jutzi, *Verfassung für Rheinland-Pfalz*, cited, para. 16.

248 See, e.g., Heinz-Joachim Peters, "Art. 20a – Die neue Staatszielbestimmung des Grundgesetzes", *Neue Zeitschrift für Verwaltungsrecht*, 1995, p. 555–557, at 556.

the codification of the respective principle on the constitutional level[249]. The case law of the Federal Constitutional Court demonstrates that Article 20a *Grundgesetz*, notwithstanding its objective nature, has been applied in legal practice as a basis for justifying environmental-oriented conduct of the State, even if that conduct may lead to interferences with other constitutional principles. In this respect, one commentator has convincingly argued that the mere existence of the environmental protection principle has gained and will continue to gain political momentum[250]. From a legal perspective, particular relevance can be allocated to the fact that this principle constitutes a horizontal clause on the level of constitutional law, which as such is not limited to individual fields of environmental law, but rather has the potential to guide the interpretation and application of the entire sub-constitutional legal system[251]. Viewed from this perspective, Article 20a *Grundgesetz* may one day turn out to be a keystone for the construction of what has been referred to as the "environmental State"[252].

249 Michael Kloepfer, "Artikel 20a", *in*: Rudolf Dolzer, Klaus Vogel, Karin Graßhof, *Bonner Kommentar zum Grundgesetz*, C.F. Müller, Vol. 5, 2017, para. 93.

250 *Ibid.*, paras. 95, 97 *et seq.*

251 See *ibid.*, para. 96.

252 Michael Kloepfer, "Auf dem Weg zum Umweltstaat?", *in*: Michael Kloepfer (ed.), *Umweltstaat*, Springer, 1998, p. 39–78, at 43.

Chapitre 5

La protection environnementale en droit constitutionnel suisse

Chapter 5

Environmental Protection in Swiss Constitutional Law

Anne-Christine FAVRE

Professeure ordinaire en droit public à l'Université de Lausanne, Suisse Faculté de droit, des sciences criminelles et d'administration publique

Résumé : Le droit constitutionnel suisse en matière environnementale repose essentiellement sur un catalogue de tâches confiées à la Confédération et aux cantons. Les dispositions en la matière n'attribuent aucun droit subjectif aux particuliers. Cependant, depuis la révision de la Constitution fédérale, en 1999, certains principes en matière de protection de l'environnement ont acquis le rang de principes constitutionnels ; ils peuvent, dans une certaine mesure, être invoqués par les particuliers ou les organisations non gouvernementales dans un litige. Cette situation a permis le développement d'une jurisprudence montrant la prévalence des intérêts environnementaux dans nombre de situations, et laisse augurer de potentielles évolutions.

Abstract: Given that in environmental matters the Swiss Constitution contains no provisions creating subjective rights of private individuals, Swiss environmental constitutionalism essentially relies on a catalogue of duties assigned to the Confederation and the cantons. However, since the revision of the federal Constitution of 1999, some environmental principles have been imbued with constitutional rank. These principles may be invoked by private individuals and NGOs in disputes before the courts. Therefore, it has become possible to uphold environmental interests in an increasing number of cases. This bodes well for environmental constitutionalism and constitutional case law in the future.

I) Introduction

La constitutionnalisation de la protection de l'environnement se voit renforcée depuis la révision de la Constitution en 1999, par l'inscription des principes de durabilité, de prévention des atteintes et du pollueur-payeur[253]. Ceux-ci acquièrent le rang de principes constitutionnels[254] de portée générale qui orientent l'action sur l'ensemble du droit de l'environnement[255]. Nous nous pencherons dans un premier temps sur la portée de ces principes (II).

La Constitution suisse[256] invite par ailleurs la Confédération à légiférer sur la protection de l'homme, des êtres vivants et de leur environnement naturel[257]. Cette tâche est placée au même rang que les autres missions à caractère social ou économique découlant de la Constitution, rang auquel s'inscrivent également les droits fondamentaux classiques[258];

---

253 Art. 73 et 74 de la Constitution fédérale du 18 avril 1999 (Cst.).

254 Les principes de prévention et du pollueur-payeur étaient déjà évoqués aux art. 1 et 2 de la Loi fédérale sur la protection de l'environnement du 7 octobre 1983 (LPE ; RS 814.01).

255 Fabia Jungo, *Le principe de précaution en droit de l'environnement suisse, avec des perspectives de droit international et européen*, Schulthess, 2012, p. 163–173 ; Ursula Marti, *Das Vorsorgeprinzip im Umweltrecht, Am Beispiel der internationalen, europäischen und schweizerischen Rechtsordnung*, Schulthess, 2011, p. 149 s.

256 Constitution fédérale du 18 avril 1999 (Cst. ; RS 101). Nous n'évoquerons pas dans ce texte les obligations découlant des constitutions cantonales.

257 Art. 73 à 79 Cst.

258 Message du Conseil fédéral relatif à une nouvelle Constitution fédérale (Message Cst.), Feuille fédérale (FF) 1997 I, p. 129 et 247. V. aussi : Reto Morell, Klaus A. Vallender, « Art. 74, N. 5 », *in* : Bernhard Ehrenzeller, Benjamin Schindler, Rainer J. Schweizer, Klaus A. Vallender (dir.), *Die schweizerische Bundesverfassung, St. Galler Kommentar*, Dike/Schulthess, 2014 ; Anne-Christine Favre, « Entre nature et culture », *in* : Anne-Christine Favre, Alexandre Flückiger (dir.), *Droit et culture*, Recueil de textes à l'occasion des 75 ans de Pierre Moor, Éditions de la Faculté de droit, des sciences criminelles et d'administration publique, 2015, p. 26.

l'ensemble de ces obligations et droits constituent autant d'intérêts[259] à gérer par la collectivité publique. Nous examinerons, dans un second temps, comment le législateur, puis les autorités d'exécution – au stade de la mise en œuvre –, tranchent la question des conflits d'intérêts en concours (III).

À défaut de consacrer expressément un « droit subjectif » en matière d'environnement, la Constitution suisse n'exclut pas que l'on puisse déduire une certaine justiciabilité des principes précités, au moins dans leur portée interprétative. À ce titre seront évoquées dans un dernier temps les possibilités de faire reconnaître un droit fondamental à un environnement sain en droit constitutionnel suisse (IV).

II) Les principes environnementaux consacrés par la Constitution

La Constitution fédérale suisse mentionne les principes de durabilité (A), de prévention et de précaution (B) et du pollueur-payeur (C). Au-delà de ces principes explicitement consacrés, on peut s'interroger sur la pertinence de principes constitutionnels non écrits en matière environnementale (D).

A) Le principe de durabilité

La Constitution de 1999 se veut toute empreinte d'un principe de « pérennité »[260], qui a pris place dans le texte sous des désignations diverses (responsabilité envers la Création et devoir d'assumer des responsabilités envers les générations futures[261], développement durable et conservation durable des ressources naturelles[262], équilibre durable entre la nature, en particulier sa capacité de renouvellement, et son utilisation par l'être humain[263]). Cette mise en perspective d'une relation forte entre la société civile et le milieu naturel, en tant que base de la vie, constitue le

---

259 Sur cette notion, v. *infra*, note 287.

260 V. Message Cst., FF 1997 I p. 85, 126, 247–259, 271, 298, 302, 370.

261 Préambule de la Constitution.

262 Art. 2 al. 2 et 4 Cst. et art. 104 al. 1 lit. b Cst.

263 Art. 73 Cst.

ciment d'une approche précautionneuse des ressources qui doivent être préservées pour les générations futures[264].

Plus encore, au stade des débats parlementaires, il a été décidé de renforcer le volet écologique du développement durable par l'introduction d'un article 73 Cst. : cette disposition invite la Confédération et les cantons à œuvrer « à l'établissement d'un équilibre durable entre la nature, en particulier sa capacité de renouvellement, et son utilisation par l'être humain ». Figurant en tête du chapitre relatif à la protection de l'environnement et à l'aménagement du territoire, l'article 73 Cst. est assurément appelé à évoquer le caractère général et transversal du principe de durabilité. Le développement durable y tient un rôle de « super-principe » ou de principe fondamental[265] qui oriente l'ensemble des tâches de l'État, celle du législateur comme celles des autorités d'exécution et des tribunaux[266]. Bien que cette norme ait parfois été qualifiée de purement programmatoire[267], les contours de sa portée interprétative tendent à se dessiner peu à peu, au gré d'une jurisprudence certes hésitante à mentionner expressément le principe en tant que tel, mais qui permet de dégager les tendances suivantes :

- le principe de durabilité a rapidement été associé au principe de précaution[268] et à une gestion parcimonieuse des ressources[269] ;

---

264 Message Cst., FF 1997 I p. 125.

265 Anne-Christine Favre, *Entre nature et culture*, cité, p. 27.

266 Raphaël Mahaim, *Le principe de durabilité et l'aménagement du territoire, Le mitage du territoire à l'épreuve du droit : utilisation mesurée du sol, urbanisation et dimensionnement des zones à bâtir*, Schulthess, Thèse Fribourg, 2014 ; Alexandre Flückiger, « Le développement durable en droit constitutionnel suisse », *Droit de l'environnement dans la pratique (DEP)*, 2006, p. 471–526 ; Anne Petitpierre-Sauvain, « Fondements écologiques de l'ordre constitutionnel suisse », *in* : Daniel Thürer *et al.* (dir.), *Droit constitutionnel suisse*, Schulthess, 2001, p. 579–590.

267 Arrêts du Tribunal Fédéral Suisse, *Recueil officiel* (ATF) 132/2006 II 305, c. 4 (arrêt de la vache folle) et la doctrine citée.

268 ATF 132/2006 II 305, c. 4.3 : « Sous sa dimension écologique, une politique de développement durable implique notamment de faire une place importante au principe de précaution, qui, selon la définition la plus couramment utilisée et la plus largement admise, postule qu'en cas de risque de dommages graves ou irréversibles, l'absence de certitude scientifique absolue ne doit pas servir de prétexte pour remettre à plus tard l'adoption de mesures effectives visant à prévenir la dégradation de l'environnement ».

269 ATF 114/1988 Ib 224, c. 10 dd (relatif à la gestion de forêts).

- en présence de ressources non renouvelables, il convient d'examiner toutes les alternatives, y compris les perspectives de matériaux de substitution[270] et de procéder à une analyse judicieuse du degré d'épuisement de la ressource ; cela peut impliquer que la gestion de la ressource soit décidée ou planifiée à un échelon national plutôt que local[271] ;
- un cours d'eau encore intact, et présentant des caractéristiques esthétiques devenant rares, peut justifier que l'on renonce à y exploiter une installation hydraulique, même si les besoins économiques font *a priori* apparaître cet usage comme indispensable[272].

La question qui fait le plus débat est sans doute celle de la justiciabilité de ce principe. En droit suisse, on distingue la portée interprétative d'un principe – qui oriente le juge sur le sens à donner à une norme dans une situation donnée –, de son invocabilité directe par un justiciable devant les tribunaux. Au final, dans l'argumentaire d'une sentence judiciaire, cette distinction peut être ténue, dans la mesure où, dans l'un ou l'autre cas, le contrôle du juge s'attachera à examiner la portée d'un principe dans une situation concrète, le plus souvent en appui à l'interprétation à donner au texte d'une loi[273]. Une partie de la doctrine considère néanmoins que le principe de durabilité déduit de l'article 73 Cst. est justiciable, de manière autonome[274]. Une telle disposition fait incontestablement partie du droit fédéral invocable en justice[275] ; seul son caractère indéterminé fait barrage à une pleine justiciabilité, mais cet

---

270 Arrêt non publié du Tribunal fédéral du 23 février 2004 (1A.115/2003, *Köniz*) : balance des intérêts nécessaire pour la prolongation de l'exploitation d'une gravière durant les 50 prochaines années, au regard des matériaux de substitution envisageables.

271 V. notamment l'arrêt non publié du Tribunal fédéral du 13 mars 2007 (1A.25/2006, *Arvel*), où un projet d'extension d'une carrière (de compétence cantonale) a été bloqué, tant qu'une planification de l'exploitation des roches dures n'était établie au niveau national.

272 ATF 140/2014 II 262, c. 8, *Obergoms*.

273 Pour des exemples dans ce sens, Raphaël Mahaim, *Le principe de durabilité et l'aménagement du territoire*, cité, p. 100.

274 *Ibid.*, p. 100 ; Klaus A. Vallender, « ad Art. 73, N. 29-41 », *in* : *Die schweizerische Bundesverfassung*, cité.

275 Au sens de l'art. 95 de la Loi sur le Tribunal fédéral du 17 juin 2005 (LTF ; RS 173.110).

aspect est évolutif, et profitera de la jurisprudence appelée à se développer à chaque fois que le principe est concrétisé dans la loi.

B) Les principes de prévention et de précaution

L'article 74 alinéa 2 Cst. consacre les principes de prévention et de précaution, concrétisés également dans le texte de plusieurs lois. Si ces principes invitent le législateur à leur donner un contenu précis selon les situations visées, ils exercent également une incidence directe importante sur les mesures d'exécution, par leur portée interprétative, voire leur applicabilité directe, en l'absence de norme de concrétisation, de telle sorte que l'on peut leur rattacher des obligations s'adressant aux autorités (et non aux particuliers directement)[276]. L'ancrage constitutionnel de ces principes permet d'augurer le développement du droit prétorien, notamment dans le contexte des obligations positives à charge des autorités.

Tels que concrétisés dans la loi, ces principes d'anticipation des atteintes invitent à prendre toutes les mesures économiquement supportables, à la source[277], et selon un processus d'évaluation continu, spécialement s'agissant de risques sécuritaires[278]. Les mesures doivent être prises assez tôt[279], même en l'absence de preuves scientifiques claires de la potentialité d'une atteinte ou d'un risque ; dans cette dernière situation, qui fait appel au principe de précaution, la jurisprudence commande le respect d'une « marge de sécurité »[280] permettant de rester en deçà de la limite de la zone de risque ou d'atteintes. Le Tribunal fédéral a par ailleurs précisé que les atteintes et les risques dépassant les normes d'acceptabilité doivent être catégoriquement évités lorsqu'aucune mesure n'est envisageable ; il n'est toutefois pas possible de viser le risque zéro, de telle sorte que la perspective selon

---

[276] Alain Griffel, Heribert Rausch, *Kommentar zum Umweltschutzgesetz, Ergänzungsband zur 2. Auflage*, Schulthess, 2011, « Art. 1, N. 21 » ; ces auteurs évoquent des situations où l'applicabilité directe du principe de prévention s'est manifestée (essentiellement au niveau procédural, en invitant l'autorité à apprécier les impacts le plus en amont possible).

[277] V. notamment les art. 1 al. 2 et 11 al. 2 LPE.

[278] ATF 139/2013 II 185, c. 10, *Centrale nucléaire de Mühleberg*.

[279] Art. 1 al. 2 LPE et 2 al. 1 de la Loi fédérale sur l'application du génie génétique au domaine non humain, du 21 mars 2003 (RS 814.91).

[280] Fabia Jungo, *Le principe de précaution en droit de l'environnement suisse*, cité, p. 121.

laquelle des mesures pourraient être encore possibles ultérieurement permet d'accepter certains risques[281].

C) Le principe du pollueur-payeur

Le principe du pollueur-payeur figure à l'article 74 alinéa 2 Cst. en tant que principe général de « responsabilité environnementale ». Il signifie que toute personne qui cause des atteintes à l'environnement doit s'attendre à devoir en payer le coût par des mesures de prévention ou de réparation, ou par un régime de taxes[282]. Ce principe invite incontestablement à une concrétisation par le législateur. Néanmoins, la portée interprétative du principe a pu conduire le Tribunal fédéral à développer une jurisprudence intéressante en relation avec des situations où la question de savoir qui devait prendre en charge les coûts de certaines mesures n'était pas claire[283].

L'internalisation des coûts des atteintes à l'environnement par un régime de taxes reste largement défaillante en Suisse. La justiciabilité du principe est pratiquement impossible dans ce contexte, puisqu'elle inviterait à remettre en cause des carences dans l'activité législative de la Confédération ; le Tribunal fédéral est en effet tenu d'appliquer les lois fédérales telles qu'elles se présentent (art. 190 Cst.). Cette situation réduit d'autant la portée du principe du pollueur-payeur au niveau constitutionnel.

D) Des principes constitutionnels non écrits en matière environnementale ?

Les principes constitutionnels non écrits peuvent naître d'un travail interprétatif à partir non seulement du texte de la Constitution[284], mais aussi du droit international[285]. On a vu que la portée normative des principes constitutionnels qui animent le droit de l'environnement est

---

281 ATF 139/2013 II 185.

282 V. art. 2 LPE. Reto Morell, Klaus A. Vallender, « Art. 74, N. 28 s. », *in* : *Die schweizerische Bundesverfassung*, cité.

283 ATF 132/2006 II 371, *Sissach*.

284 Des principes tels que celui de la légalité, de l'intérêt public et de la proportionnalité relèvent du droit prétorien et étaient qualifiés de principes constitutionnels non écrits avant la nouvelle Constitution de 1999.

285 Message Cst., FF 1997 I p. 44.

en phase de développement ; à notre sens, plusieurs règles prescriptives peuvent être déduites de ceux-ci, au titre de sous-principes. On mentionnera l'obligation de trouver des solutions de substitution avant d'épuiser une ressource rare – tirée du principe de durabilité inscrit à l'article 73 Cst. – ou le principe de non-régression – jamais formellement évoqué à notre connaissance – mais que l'on peut déduire des principes de prévention et précaution (art. 74 Cst.), et qui s'est manifesté récemment lorsque le législateur a renoncé à assouplir les seuils d'émissions en matière de rayonnement non ionisant, en considérant que le doute quant aux atteintes générées devait profiter aux personnes exposées et non aux fournisseurs des nouvelles technologies[286].

III) Les tâches et intérêts environnementaux consacrés par la Constitution fédérale

Dans un État fédéraliste comme la Suisse, la répartition des tâches (législatives et d'exécution) entre la Confédération et les cantons est essentielle. Chacune de ces tâches est sous-tendue par des valeurs qui se traduisent par des intérêts publics ou privés[287], dont il convient de tenir compte tant au stade de l'élaboration de la législation que lors de la mise en œuvre.

Nous examinerons dans un premier temps les tâches confiées à la Confédération (A), puis la place des intérêts environnementaux dans celles-ci (B).

A) Les tâches fédérales en matière d'environnement

Le rôle de la Constitution fédérale est avant tout celui de fixer les attributions de la Confédération par rapport à la souveraineté reconnue

[286] À deux reprises, le Conseil des États a refusé de donner suite à une motion demandant d'élever les seuils applicables au rayonnement non ionisant, d'une part parce que cette compétence relève de la responsabilité du Conseil fédéral et d'autre part parce qu'il existe trop de doutes quant aux effets de l'électrosmog sur la population (*Bulletin officiel de l'Assemblée fédérale*, Conseil des États, 2016, p. 1082 et séance du Conseil des États du 5 mars 2018, en réponse à la motion 18.3006).

[287] En matière de protection de l'environnement, il existe ainsi un intérêt public à mettre en place une législation fixant les valeurs limites à respecter en matière d'atteintes nuisibles ou incommodantes, pour protéger la population et l'environnement, comme à exiger le respect de ces valeurs, au stade de la mise en œuvre ; cet intérêt public peut être doublé d'un intérêt privé à exiger que les seuils soient respectés.

aux cantons[288]. Or, en matière de protection de l'environnement, la Confédération s'est vu confier au fil des années de plus en plus de responsabilités législatives, dans un but d'unification de la matière[289] ; cela ne signifie pas nécessairement la suppression des compétences des cantons, qui restent concurrentes, voire exclusives, selon les domaines. Toutefois, la Confédération reçoit désormais une compétence générale en matière de protection contre les atteintes nuisibles ou incommodantes (art. 74 Cst.), en matière de protection des eaux (art. 76 Cst.), en matière forestière (art. 77 Cst.), ou en matière de chasse et de pêche (art. 79 Cst.) ; par ailleurs, elle dispose de compétences étendues en matière de protection de la nature et du patrimoine (art. 78 Cst.) et d'aménagement du territoire (art. 75 Cst.).

Le plus souvent, il incombe aux cantons de mettre en œuvre ces législations.

B) Vers une prééminence des intérêts environnementaux ?

Dans des situations plutôt exceptionnelles, la Constitution fédérale fait primer l'intérêt environnemental de telle sorte que l'autorité d'exécution ne peut plus procéder à une pesée des intérêts en présence[290]. Il s'agit ici de l'effet d'une singularité du droit suisse, par le jeu des initiatives populaires, qui permettent l'ancrage dans la Constitution de textes réputés parfois directement applicables[291], dont le contenu matériel aurait pu trouver place dans une loi. On évoquera spécialement :

- l'article 78 alinéa 5 Cst., relatif à la protection des marais et des sites marécageux d'une beauté particulière qui présentent un intérêt national ; selon cette disposition, il est interdit d'y aménager des installations ou d'en modifier le terrain[292] ;

---

288 Selon l'art. 3 Cst., « Les cantons sont souverains en tant que leur souveraineté n'est pas limitée par la Constitution fédérale et exercent tous les droits qui ne sont pas délégués à la Confédération ».

289 Art. 73 à 79 Cst.

290 ATF 138/2012 II 281 c. 6.2 et 6.5; 127/2001 II 184 c. 5b. Pour la marge de manœuvre subsistante, v. TF 1C_79/2016, du 5 avril 2017, surélévation du barrage du *Grimsel*.

291 Pour l'art. 78 al. 5 Cst., v. ATF 139/2013 II 243 c. 10.7 ; 127/2001 II 184 c. 5b/aa ; 123/1997 II 248 c. 3a/aa. Pour l'art. 75*b* Cst., v. ATF 139/2013 II 243.

292 Font exception les installations qui servent à la protection de ces espaces ou à la poursuite de leur exploitation à des fins agricoles.

- l'article 75*b* Cst., qui fixe le quota maximum de résidences secondaires à 20 % du parc des logements et de la surface brute au sol habitable de chaque commune. Cette disposition a pour objectif de préserver le sol et le paysage.

Dans les autres cas, les intérêts qui orientent les tâches en matière d'environnement entrent en concours avec les autres intérêts protégés par la Constitution ou la loi[293] : la politique énergétique peut ainsi s'opposer à la protection du paysage ; les intérêts environnementaux pourront entrer en conflit avec les droits fondamentaux classiques, comme la garantie de la propriété ou la liberté du commerce et de l'industrie.

En réalité, ainsi que l'a parfaitement démontré un auteur[294], la prise en compte des intérêts environnementaux – plus récente que celle des autres intérêts liés aux usages du sol et de l'espace (le droit de propriété, l'aménagement du territoire) –, façonne une nouvelle approche des enjeux territoriaux, dans laquelle la préservation des ressources, mais aussi de l'environnement contre les atteintes anthropiques, tend à l'emporter par rapport à d'autres valeurs. Ce constat se manifeste non seulement à l'appui de la formulation – souvent plus absolue – des textes de la loi[295], mais également dans l'argumentation du juge, lors d'une pesée des intérêts en présence. De plus en plus souvent, en effet, il est fait référence, explicitement ou non, aux principes de durabilité et de prévention des atteintes, pour restreindre les droits d'usages des particuliers[296].

---

293 On notera que le législateur peut, quant à lui, établir des priorités : v. dans ce sens l'art. 6 al. 2 de la Loi fédérale sur la protection de la nature et du paysage du 1er juillet 1966 (LPN ; RS 451) et l'art. 12 al. 2 et 3 de la Loi fédérale sur l'énergie du 30 septembre 2016 (LEne ; RS 730).

294 Jacques Dubey, *Espace – Temps – Propriété, Définition et restriction de la propriété privée du sol à l'heure du développement durable et de l'aménagement du territoire*, Schulthess, 2012, p. 91 s.

295 Notamment par les valeurs seuils fixées par la législation environnementale en matière d'atteintes ou de risques.

296 Deux affaires sont significatives à cet égard : v. ATF 139/2013 II 28, relatif à l'affaire *Misoxer Kraftwerke* où, sur la base des principes de proportionnalité et de prévention des atteintes, le Tribunal fédéral a établi une échelle standardisée des coûts économiquement supportables, pouvant être imputés aux exploitations hydrauliques anciennes, pour permettre de rétablir des débits résiduels conformes à la législation sur la protection des eaux (Thierry Largey, « L'assainissement des cours d'eau dans l'application de l'art. 80 LEaux – Les enseignements de l'arrêt Misoxer Kraftwerke », *DEP*, 2013, p. 92-112). V. également ATF 140/2014 II 262, *Kraftwerke Obergoms AG*, où le Tribunal fédéral a refusé d'autoriser un captage sur un torrent encore intact et participant à la beauté paysagère des lieux,

IV) Un droit fondamental à un environnement sain ?

Même s'il n'existe pas, au niveau fédéral[297], de consécration constitutionnelle d'un droit fondamental à un environnement sain (A), on peut s'interroger sur la question de savoir si un tel droit existe de manière non écrite (B). Une affaire concrète, à savoir l'action de l'Association des Aînées pour la protection du climat (*Verein KlimaSeniorinnen*), tend à faire évoluer la jurisprudence dans ce sens (C).

A) L'absence de consécration constitutionnelle

L'un des buts de la nouvelle Constitution de 1999 – non des moindres –, consistait à consacrer ou mieux formaliser le contenu des droits fondamentaux, cela tant au regard des textes de rang supérieur, comme la Convention européenne des droits de l'homme, qu'au vu du développement spectaculaire de la jurisprudence de ladite Cour en la matière[298].

La question d'un droit de l'homme à un environnement sain a été évoquée à plusieurs reprises, entre les années 1970[299] et le premier projet de révision totale de la Constitution de 1874[300]. Mais les réflexions n'ont pas conduit à le consacrer expressément, essentiellement par crainte de ne pouvoir donner un contenu suffisamment précis aux obligations positives de l'État qui en découleraient, ou de devoir reconnaître des effets horizontaux à un tel droit, dans un système où la portée des droits fondamentaux est essentiellement verticale[301].

---

cela en raison de sa rareté, quand bien-même l'exploitant évoquait une nécessité économique d'étendre les prélèvements à ce cours d'eau ; face à une telle situation, l'argumentation de la Cour a été d'exiger une adaptation des besoins en fonction des intérêts de la nature à préserver, ce d'autant que l'installation était subventionnée et devait se montrer exemplaire.

[297] Le Canton de Genève vient d'introduire un tel droit dans sa Constitution du 14 octobre 2012 (art. 19).

[298] Message Cst., FF 1997 I p. 13.

[299] Message relatif à l'art. 24^{septies} Cst., FF 1970 I p. 773 et 790.

[300] Francesca Magistro, *Le droit à un environnement sain revisité. Étude de droit suisse, international et comparé*, Schulthess, Thèse 2017, p. 204–206.

[301] En droit suisse, les effets horizontaux ne sont reconnus que de manière indirecte, sous réserve d'exceptions explicites ou implicites, qui tendent aujourd'hui à se multiplier (telles que l'égalité salariale entre hommes et femmes, l'interdiction de la discrimination). Aux termes de l'art. 35 al. 3 Cst., l'État doit veiller à ce que les droits fondamentaux – dans la mesure où ils s'y prêtent –, soient aussi réalisés dans les relations qui lient les particuliers entre eux ; ce mandat s'adresse au législateur,

Cependant le développement des obligations positives à charge de l'État, notamment sous les auspices de la Cour européenne des droits de l'homme (CEDH), change la donne, dans la mesure où un grand nombre d'entre elles visent les relations entre les particuliers[302] ; tel est précisément le cas du droit de l'environnement, dont les acteurs des atteintes et des risques sont le plus souvent des personnes privées. Cette circonstance amène incontestablement à de nouvelles réflexions. La doctrine prêche en tous les cas dans ce sens. Nous nous attarderons surtout sur les possibilités d'une reconnaissance d'un tel droit fondamental par le droit prétorien.

B) Un droit constitutionnel non écrit ?

L'une des particularités de la Constitution helvétique se caractérise par une grande souplesse, celle-là même qui a permis d'admettre, depuis le texte de 1874, de très nombreuses révisions partielles, mais aussi le développement d'un droit constitutionnel « non écrit »[303]. Ainsi, plusieurs libertés non écrites ont été reconnues par le Tribunal fédéral, telles que la garantie de la propriété ou la liberté personnelle[304]. Il ne s'agit pas à proprement parler du comblement d'une lacune, mais plutôt des possibilités laissées au juge, dans son travail d'interprétation – le cas échéant dynamique – des droits fondamentaux[305].

L'admissibilité d'un droit constitutionnel non écrit à vivre dans un environnement sain, de manière autonome ou indirecte, a été évoquée

qui doit assurer que les droits fondamentaux des particuliers ne subissent des atteintes de la part de tiers en leur permettant, par exemple, de se plaindre des nuisances produites par une installation polluante (Rainer J. Schweizer, « Art. 35, N. 48-61 », *in* : *Die schweizerische Bundesverfassung*, cité).

302 Vincent Martenet, « La réalisation des droits fondamentaux dans l'ordre juridique suisse », *Revue de droit suisse*, 130 (2011) I/3, p. 243–285, sp. 267 et 271.

303 Comme le relève le Conseil fédéral, dans son message (FF 1997 I p. 16), la Constitution suisse s'inscrit davantage dans la tradition de la souveraineté populaire selon Jean-Jacques Rousseau que dans celle des constitutions plus rigides selon l'orientation théorique de Benjamin Constant, qui a en particulier influencé fortement la tradition constitutionnelle française.

304 Peter Saladin, *Grundrechte im Wandel, Die Rechtsprechung des Schweizerischen Bundesgericht zu den Grundrechten in einer sich ändernden Umwelt*, Stämpfli, 1982, p. 114 ss.

305 Vincent Martenet, *La réalisation des droits fondamentaux dans l'ordre juridique suisse*, cité, p. 273.

à plusieurs reprises en doctrine[306]. En principe, un droit fondamental non écrit n'est reconnu qu'à des conditions restrictives, dont celle de la justiciabilité[307]. Il faut par ailleurs que l'adoption d'une règle par le juge plutôt que par le législateur soit possible, voire requise, analyse qui est toujours délicate[308]. Admettrait-on une compétence du juge en la matière qu'il conviendrait préalablement de se poser la question de savoir si l'affirmation d'un tel droit fondamental viendrait combler une réelle lacune, de manière à imposer à l'État de nouvelles limites dans l'exercice de ses activités et surtout à étendre les obligations positives en matière environnementale, ou si une telle reconnaissance s'inscrirait plutôt dans l'interprétation des droits fondamentaux existants.

Quelle que soit l'approche, admettre l'existence d'un droit fondamental inviterait à définir un noyau intangible au-delà duquel les conditions d'existence de l'homme et des autres êtres vivants sont menacées. Comme la garantie de la propriété, le contenu normatif d'un tel droit est élastique et dépend essentiellement d'un corpus de lois qui ne prédéterminent pas toujours la solution à adopter dans une situation donnée. Plus que les autres droits fondamentaux, celui lié à un environnement sain comporte ses propres tensions éthico-juridiques : même dans une perception minimaliste de l'équilibre à respecter entre les milieux vivants se posera la question de savoir quand la protection des intérêts autres que ceux de l'homme doit l'emporter. Si une partie du travail interprétatif peut être fait par le juge et reposer sur les droits fondamentaux existants[309], à l'instar de l'évolution suivie par la jurisprudence de la CEDH, force est de constater qu'une telle approche reste anthropocentrée. Cependant, plus les dégradations de l'environnement se font lourdes, plus il devient

---

306 Alexandre Flückiger, « Droits de l'homme et environnement », *in* : Maya Hertig Randall, Michel Hottelier (dir.), *Introduction aux droits de l'homme*, Schulthess, 2014, p. 606–620 ; Francesca Magistro, *Le droit à un environnement sain revisité*, cité, p. 244 ; Gregor T. Chatton, Caroline Cavaleri Rudaz, « L'eau à la croisée des droits sociaux et du service public : étude en marge des débats citoyens en République et canton de Genève », *Pratique juridique actuelle*, 2007, p. 217–246.

307 Selon une jurisprudence du Tribunal fédéral inaugurée dans les années 1970, la reconnaissance d'un tel droit est soumise à trois conditions cumulatives : il faut que le nouveau droit fondamental soit une condition d'exercice d'un autre droit constitutionnel, il doit représenter un certain consensus et sa justiciabilité doit être admise (ATF 115/1989 Ia 234, c. 10a ; ATF 107/1981 Ia 277, c. 2).

308 Vincent Martenet, *La réalisation des droits fondamentaux dans l'ordre juridique suisse*, cité, p. 271.

309 Droit à la vie, selon l'art. 10 al. 1 Cst., garantie de la propriété, selon l'art. 26 Cst., ou les droits déduits des art. 2 et 8 Convention européenne des droits de l'homme.

cohérent d'admettre que la défense d'un droit à un environnement sain – en tant que droit indirectement lié à la vie ou à la santé –, inclut aussi celle du support de vie et de ses interrelations avec les autres êtres vivants[310]. Les principes de durabilité et de précaution (articles 73 et 74 Cst.) invitent déjà à ménager au maximum ce capital nature.

Cela étant, dans la mesure où l'on peut d'ores et déjà déduire un certain nombre d'obligations à partir des principes constitutionnels ou du droit positif infraconstitutionnel, il faut se demander ce qu'apporterait réellement la reconnaissance d'une atteinte à un droit fondamental en matière environnementale. À notre sens, la principale perspective que l'on pourrait attendre – dans un premier temps – de la figure d'un tel droit subjectif est celle consistant à fixer des limites à la marge de manœuvre du législateur ou des autorités d'exécution, ce qui inviterait non seulement à mieux respecter la loi[311], mais aussi à légiférer[312], là où celle-ci est carencée. Le constat quant à des carences dans la mise en œuvre en matière environnementale n'est d'ailleurs pas propre à la Suisse ; la majorité des affaires ayant conduit à une violation de l'article 8 de la Convention européenne des droits de l'homme et portées devant la CEDH révélait que le problème ne résultait pas tant de l'absence de législation que d'un déficit d'action des autorités à la faire respecter[313].

Laissons pour une étape ultérieure les difficiles questions relatives à la titularité de ce droit, lorsqu'il est élargi à la possibilité d'évoquer non seulement des atteintes à la sphère individuelle, mais aussi à la biosphère et à l'humanité tout entière[314]. Pour ces questions, une jurisprudence protectrice peut, en l'état, se construire autour des procédures conduites par les organisations de protection de l'environnement.

---

310 La disparition drastique des abeilles ou des oiseaux met en évidence les interrelations entre les différentes espèces du milieu vivant et mobilise les décideurs politiques.

311 Le droit de l'environnement souffre surtout d'un manque de résultats par rapport aux objectifs fixés dans la loi, qui ne laisse pas toujours le pouvoir d'appréciation que l'autorité pense pouvoir s'accorder : on pense aux valeurs seuils en matière de bruit ou de pollution, qui restent largement dépassées, ou à l'obligation de ménager la biodiversité et de préserver les biotopes dignes de protection, pour lesquels les obligations sont relativement claires, mais les résultats très pauvres.

312 Sur cette question, d'une manière générale, Vincent Martenet, *La réalisation des droits fondamentaux dans l'ordre juridique suisse*, cité, p. 244, 256 et 271.

313 Alexandre Flückiger, *Droits de l'homme et environnement*, cité, p. 5 et les références citées.

314 Sur l'ensemble de ces questions, v. Alexandre Flückiger, *Droits de l'homme et environnement*, cité, p. 613 et s.

C) L'action de l'Association des Aînées pour la protection du climat (Verein KlimaSeniorinnen)

En illustration de ce qui précède, l'action de la « Verein KlimaSeniorinnen »[315] tend à démontrer que les carences du législateur et des autorités d'exécution en matière climatique mettent en danger la population, spécialement des groupes cibles comme les femmes âgées, qui souffrent le plus des pics de chaleur, avec le réchauffement climatique.

L'action tend tout d'abord à établir que la Confédération suisse ne respecte pas les objectifs minimaux qui lui incombent en matière climatique, au regard des engagements qu'elle a pris sur le plan international. Elle tend aussi à faire constater que par leurs actes et omissions, les autorités législatives et exécutives fédérales mettent en danger la vie des personnes les plus vulnérables. Le but est de faire reconnaître un manquement dans les obligations positives de la Confédération qui découlent des articles 73 et 74 Cst., mais aussi des articles 2 et 8 de la Convention européenne des droits de l'homme. La difficulté de cette démarche réside dans le fait que les requérantes ne mettent pas en cause une décision de l'autorité, mais plutôt une série d'actes matériels le plus souvent causés par omission (manquements dans la préparation de textes législatifs à revoir, dans les devoirs d'information, dans les obligations de surveillance, dans les mesures de réduction des émissions, etc.). Lorsque de tels actes sont illicites, et qu'ils touchent à des droits ou des obligations, toute personne qui dispose d'un intérêt digne de protection est en droit de solliciter de l'autorité compétente qu'elle statue par la voie d'une décision, notamment en vue de mettre fin à de tels actes ou d'en éliminer les conséquences[316]. La Confédération n'est pas entrée en matière sur cette requête[317] ; la procédure se poursuit devant les instances judiciaires fédérales[318].

---

[315] Il s'agit de l'action d'une association constituée de dames âgées de plus de 75 ans. V. Verein KlimaSeniorinnen ou Association des Aînées pour la protection du climat. En ligne : https://ainees-climat.ch/ueber-uns/.

[316] V. l'art. 25*a* de la Loi fédérale sur la procédure administrative du 20 décembre 1968 (RS 172.021).

[317] Décision du Département fédéral de l'environnement, de l'énergie et de la communication (DETEC/UVEK) du 25 avril 2017.

[318] Un recours a été interjeté en date du 26 mai 2017 devant le Tribunal administratif fédéral.

V) Conclusion

La constitutionnalisation de la protection de l'environnement se manifeste essentiellement par un catalogue des tâches à charge des autorités. Si ces tâches sont *a priori* de rang égal, une analyse plus fine de la législation montre que les intérêts environnementaux prennent souvent le pas dans la gestion des usages du sol et de l'espace.

L'élévation des principes de durabilité, de prévention des atteintes et du pollueur-payeur[319] au rang de principes constitutionnels a sans aucun doute favorisé cette approche. Dans la mesure où la Constitution suisse n'exclut pas que l'on puisse déduire une certaine justiciabilité des principes précités – au moins dans leur portée interprétative –, ils donnent ainsi corps aux obligations positives de l'État en matière de protection de l'environnement, et participent pour une bonne part au contenu normatif qui pourrait être associé à un droit fondamental à un environnement sain. L'argumentaire de l'action de la *Verein Klimaseniorinnen* est en grande partie construit autour des obligations de prévention des atteintes qui découlent pour la collectivité publique des articles 73 et 74 Cst. Alors que la législation suisse en matière climatique est peu centrée sur la protection des droits individuels, le caractère général accordé à ces dispositions permet incontestablement d'en déduire des obligations visant tant le législateur que les autorités d'exécution, de manière à éviter des atteintes à des droits absolus tels que la santé ou la vie.

De notre point de vue, les conditions sont actuellement favorables pour que le droit prétorien reconnaisse un droit fondamental à un environnement sain, au moins dans les mêmes limites que celles qui ont été définies par la CEDH. Les effets matériels d'une telle reconnaissance ne conduiraient vraisemblablement pas à des effets plus marquants que ceux tirés du texte de la loi. En revanche, ils permettraient de mieux inviter la collectivité publique à respecter la loi et à légiférer lorsque cela est nécessaire.

---

[319] Art. 73 et 74 Cst.

Chapter 6

Environmental Constitutionalism in India: Judicial Recognition and Application

I) Introduction
II) Explicit Environmental Constitutionalism: Directive Principles of State Policy and Fundamental Duties
III) Derivative Environmental Constitutionalism: Fundamental Right to Life
IV) Justiciable Environmental Constitutionalism: Standing and Access to Justice
V) Conclusion

Chapitre 6

Le constitutionnalisme en Inde : reconnaissance et mise en œuvre judiciaire

I) Introduction
II) Le constitutionnalisme environnemental explicite : principes directeurs de la politique de l'État et devoirs fondamentaux
III) Le constitutionnalisme environnemental dérivé : le droit fondamental à la vie
IV) Le constitutionnalisme environnemental devant le juge : la capacité procédurale d'agir et l'accès à la justice
V) Conclusion

Gitanjali Nain GILL

Professor of Environmental Law, Northumbria University, Newcastle upon Tyne, UK

School of Business and Law

Abstract: The paper focuses on the manner and effectiveness of the Supreme Court of India in addressing the many environmental issues facing modern India. An account is presented of how the Indian senior judiciary adjudicates environmental constitutionalism through the 'environmental care' paradigm. It presents and analyses explicit and derivative environmental constitutionalism through judicial engagement with the directive principles of state policy, fundamental duty and right to a quality environment as a part of the fundamental right to life. The paper concludes by examining how the senior Indian judiciary has promoted environmental constitutionalism through the liberal use of Public Interest Litigation (PIL) and relaxed *locus standi* to access and achieve environmental justice and governance.

Sommaire : De quelle manière et avec quelle effectivité la Cour suprême de l'Inde envisage-t-elle les nombreux enjeux environnementaux auxquels est confronté ce pays ? La présente contribution expose le constitutionnalisme environnemental indien tel qu'il est mis en œuvre par ses hautes autorités judiciaires à travers de ce que l'on peut appeler le paradigme du respect de l'environnement. La contribution analyse et approfondit le constitutionnalisme environnemental appliqué de manière explicite et dérivé par les juges à partir du cadre posé par des principes directeurs de la politique de l'État ainsi que par le devoir et le droit fondamental à un environnement de qualité qui découle du droit fondamental à la vie. La contribution termine en insistant sur la promotion du constitutionnalisme environnemental par les juges suprêmes de l'Inde grâce à un maniement libéral de stratégies contentieuses comme l'action dans l'intérêt public (*Public Interest Litigation*) ou la mise en œuvre souple de la capacité procédurale d'agir (*locus standi*). Il en résulte un accès effectif à la justice environnementale et la réalisation d'une gouvernance environnementale.

I) Introduction

Paradigmatic environmental constitutionalism is experiencing global recognition. Of 196 national constitutions 148 reflect a degree of environmental constitutionalism[320]. The discourse on environmental constitutionalism remains an important conversation within the swirl of the constantly changing geo-political climate, environmental priorities

---

[320] Roderic O'Gorman, "Environmental Constitutionalism: A Comparative Study", *Transnational Environmental Law*, 2017, p. 435–462, at 436.

and ineffective environmental governance at both global and domestic levels. There is a growing recognition among scholars that environmental constitutionalism represents a new approach that focuses on both broader constitutional concepts and on the environmental governance movement[321]. For instance, Kotzé argues that "where environmental care is couched in constitutionalist language, it is termed environmental constitutionalism"[322]. Kotzé argues constitutionalising environmental care provides opportunities to reform environmental governance through constitutional features that include fundamental rights and duties and aspirational values of human dignity and equality. It improves participatory mechanisms that access environmental justice and remedies; dictating contents of law; establishes moral and ethical obligations with respect to the environment and requires proper performance of these obligations by state authorities[323]. May and Daly adopt a comparative approach and suggest that "environmental constitutionalism is a relatively recent phenomenon at the confluence of constitutional law, international law, human rights and environmental law. It embodies the recognition that the environment is a proper subject for protection in the constitutional texts and for vindication by constitutional courts worldwide"[324].

Environmental constitutionalism continues to gain a global foothold through textual recognition and judicial receptivity. Studies provide insights into substantive and procedural rights, directive policies and duties that illustrate environmental constitutionalism[325]. About ninety-two constitutions explicitly recognise the right to a quality or healthy environment. Some ninety-seven constitutions include reciprocal duties on the state and fifty-six constitutions recognize the responsibility of the citizens to protect the environment[326]. Another study illustrates

---

321 Brian J. Gareau, "Global Environmental Constitutionalism", *Boston College Environmental Affairs Law Review*, Vol. 40, 2013, p. 403–404; Douglas A Kysar, "Global Environmental Constitutionalism: Getting There from Here", *Transnational Environmental Law*, 2012, p. 83 94.

322 Louis J. Kotzé, "Arguing Global Environmental Constitutionalism", *Transnational Environmental Law*, 2012, p. 193–233, p. 208.

323 *Ibid.*

324 James R May, Erin Daly, *Judicial Handbook on Environmental Constitutionalism*, United Nations Environment Programme 2017, p. 1.

325 *Ibid.*

326 Klaus Bosselmann, "Global Environmental Constitutionalism: Mapping the Terrain", *Widener Law Review*, 2015, p. 171–185, at 173.

the categorisation of environmental constitutionalism based upon the historical inspection of the domestic situation at the time when environmental constitutionalism was first embraced[327]. It identifies three key categories – crisis change (moments of crisis, such as the creation of a newly independent state, are significant drivers of constitutional change); regime consolidation (promulgation of constitutions by non-democratic rulers to confer legitimacy on existing legal arrangements); non-crisis change (changes in the values that a nation holds, or in views on the effectiveness of institutional arrangements during non-crisis situation). These historical categories help in understanding the specific circumstances and factors that influence the chances of the successful adoption of environmental constitutionalism[328].

The active participation of a creative judiciary in environmental constitutionalism is critical. In most jurisdictions, the courts (general or specialised courts and tribunals) are achieving tangible environmental outcomes and providing enhanced environmental protection. May and Daly's exploratory work[329] analyses the extent of judicial receptivity to environmental constitutionalism. The national courts have increasingly been engaged in interpreting constitutional environmental rights as independent[330], dependent[331], derivative[332], or dormant[333] rights thereby developing, expanding and creating environmental obligations despite being formally absent in the constitution.

Contextualising within India, the constitutionalism narrative is based on notions of divided and checked powers, fundamental duties of the state to protect and enhance the interests and welfare of the people and the

---

327 Roderic O'Gorman, "Environmental Constitutionalism: A Comparative Study", cited, p. 441.

328 *Ibid*, p. 441–444.

329 James R. May, Erin Daly, *Judicial Handbook on Environmental Constitutionalism*, cited, p. 166–178.

330 Some courts recognize causes of action to enforce express constitutional rights to a quality environment and of nature (Central Europe and Latin America).

331 Some courts recognize a right to a quality environment as an adjunct of constitutional provisions that direct the government to protect the environment as a matter of duty or policy (Philippines).

332 Some courts recognize environmental rights as being implicitly incorporated into other substantive, enforceable constitutional rights, including a right to life (India, Pakistan).

333 Courts in some countries have yet to engage environmental rights provisions (Turkey).

promotion of egalitarian social order. The function of trans-formatting the Constitution rests primarily with the courts, particularly the Supreme Court of India[334]. The judicial role involves the expansive interpretation of the Constitution. The ineffectiveness of both political leadership and administrative authorities in discharging their constitutional role and statutory duties, coupled with widespread corruption within the public sector has cast the Indian judiciary, particularly within the Supreme Court, in the role of protector of the interests of the disadvantaged in matters of public interest[335].

India's environmental constitutionalism is a product of senior judicial decisions to interpret liberally key constitutional provisions and combine human rights and the environment to develop a new 'environmental care' jurisprudence. This judicial activity is a result of a collaborative process engaging innovative substantial and procedural approaches that depart from the traditional adversarial judicial process[336].

This chapter maps the way in which the Indian senior judiciary adjudicates environmental constitutionalism through the 'environmental care' paradigm[337]. It examines the role of the pro-active Supreme Court of India in creating strategies within a broader constitutional framework and environmental governance movement to uphold the rule of law, enforce fundamental rights of the citizens and constitutional propriety aimed at the protection and improvement of environment. Accordingly, the contribution is hereafter divided into three parts. Part 1 offers an account of explicit environmental constitutionalism in the form of

---

334 *Vikas Sankhala v Vikas Kumar* (2017) 1 SCC 350, p. 354.

335 South Asian Human Rights Documentation Centre, *Human Rights and Humanitarian Law: Developments in Indian and International Law*, OUP, 2008, p. 423.

336 Gitanjali N. Gill, *Environmental Justice in India: The National Green Tribunal*, Routledge UK, 2017, p. 44; Shyam Divan and Armin Rosencranz, *Environmental Law and Policy in India*, OUP, 2001, p. 133; Leelakrishnan, *Environmental Law in India*, Butterworths, 2005; Lavanya Rajamani, "Public interest litigation in India: exploring issues of access, participation, equity, effectiveness and sustainability", *Journal of Environmental Law*, 2007, p. 293; Geetonjoy Sahu, "Implications of Indian Supreme Courts' innovation for environmental jurisprudence", *Law, Environmental and Development Journal*, 2008, p. 377–387.

337 This contribution does not address the National Green Tribunal (NGT) of India. The NGT is a specialised statutory tribunal having expertise in adjudicating environmental issues and building upon the environmental jurisprudence of the Supreme Court of India.

directive principle of state policy and fundamental duty embracing environmental care and judicial interventions (II). Part 2 presents and analyses derivative environmental constitutionalism through judicial engagement with the right to a quality environment as a part of the fundamental right to life at the national level (III). Part 3 examines how the senior Indian judiciary has promoted environmental constitutionalism through the liberal use of Public Interest Litigation (PIL) to achieve environmental justice. The Court's self-created power and justiciable constitutional remedy is intended to make 'environmental care' both real and meaningful throughout India (IV).

II) Explicit Environmental Constitutionalism: Directive Principles of State Policy and Fundamental Duties

The Indian Constitution of 1950 is a lengthy, elaborate, detailed document. Following the Stockholm Declaration in 1972, the Constitution was amended by the 42nd amendment in 1976 to explicitly incorporate environmental protection provisions within the directive principles of state policy[338] and fundamental duties[339].

The directive principles of state policy though not enforceable in courts of law are accepted as fundamental moral principles and values in the governance of the country to secure social and economic freedoms. They constitute *fons-juris* in a welfare state and obligate the state to take positive action to promote the welfare of the people. They set forth the humanitarian socialist precepts that were the aims of the Indian social revolution[340].

Article 48 A, was added to the directive principles of state policy by the 42nd amendment to the Constitution. The article requires the state to "endeavour to protect and improve the environment and to safeguard the forests and wildlife of the country". Environmental constitutionalism recognises that 'environmental care' expressed through moral and ethical

---

338 Part IV of the Constitution of India.

339 Part IV-A of the Constitution of India.

340 *A.K. Thakur v Union of India* (2008) 6 SCC 1; *P. M.A. Shetty v State of Karnataka* 1989 Supp (1) SCC 696; *Shrilekha Vidyarthi v State of U.P* (1991) 1 SCC 212; *Kesvananda Bharati v State of Kerala* (1973) 4 SCC 225.

principles because of established cultural, social, and legal experiences and practices can help achieve such environmental protection necessary for human welfare[341]. Readings from ancient Indian law serve as a window on the varying interests and increasing demand on natural resources and the subsequent state policy responses[342]. For example, Kautilyan jurisprudence states that it is the *dharma* (duty) of the king not only to protect forests but also establish new forests. The dharma of protecting the environment was to sustain and ensure progress and welfare of all and balance the eco-system[343].

Today the responsibility for environmental protection rests with the Supreme Court of India. In *Ivory Traders and Manufactures Association v Union of India*[344], the court acknowledged that Article 48 A is based on moral values and ethics. It draws heavily from religious Hindu scriptures to show compassion towards nature, animals and birds as all are considered to have come from the same source. To quote:

> Lord Krishna in the Bhagavad Gita declared that '*sarve yonisu aham bija pradahpitah*' which means I am the father of all. The followers of the Gita are steeped in the belief that even the leaves of the trees, the petals and the flowers have life and God pervades in them. The state has a solemn duty to give effect to the Article 48 A [...] ensure that the survival of man co-exists with nature [...] to sub-serve the common good[345].

The ethical and moral prescription has assumed the legal status of imposing an obligation not only on government but also on courts to protect the environment. Thus, Article 48 A is not symbolic but rather creates a primary obligation directing environmental governance.

Article 51 A of the Constitution[346] lays down fundamental duties for the citizen concerning the value and preservation of the rich heritage of Indian composite culture, including the environment. Article 51 A

---

341 Louis J. Kotzé, *Global Environmental Constitutionalism in the Anthropocene*, Hart Publishing, 2016, p. 153.

342 V.K. Gupta, *Kautilyan Jurisprudence*, B.D Gupta and Company Delhi, 1987, p. 155.

343 *Ibid*, p. 155.

344 (1997) 67 DLT 145 (FB).

345 *Ibid*, p. 165.

346 Article 51 A enlists ten duties that are in line with Article 29 (1) of the Universal Declaration of Human Rights.

(g), added by the 42nd amendment, mandates "every citizen of India to protect and improve the natural environment including forests, lakes, rivers and wildlife, and to have compassion for living creatures".

The judiciary has energised the environmental constitutionalism discourse by interpreting Article 51 A (g) to include 'environmental care' as a foundational norm in Indian society and in its law and governance system. This is reflected in two ways. Firstly, 'environmental care' is prioritized as a moral and ethical obligation of the citizen to act affirmatively to respect nature and protect the environment, as referred by Kotzé as "the duties to respect, protect, promote and fulfil"[347]. Ancient Indian thought involves *Om Sarvesham Shantir bhavatu* (peace unto all living beings and entire environment) or *Ahimsa paramo tapah* (non-violence is the greatest duty and the greatest penance). In *Association for Environment Protection and State of Kerala*[348] the Supreme Court observed:

> [...] our [Indian] sages and saints always preached and taught the people to worship earth, sky, rivers, sea, plants, trees and every form of life. Majority of people still consider it as their sacred duty to protect the plants, trees, rivers, wells, etc., because it is believed that they belong to all living creatures[349].

Secondly, Article 51 A (g) encourages and promotes people's participation in environmental protection and human welfare. Though couched in the language of 'duty', Article 51 A (g) confers a corresponding right on the citizen to move to the court to ensure the state performs its duties in accordance with the law[350]. Thus, the moral and ethical obligation under Article 51 A (g) has broadened the scope of 'citizen' to permit public-spirited citizens, interested institutions and NGOs to approach the courts for environmental protection.

Together, Articles 48 A and 51 A (g) lay the foundation for a jurisprudence of 'environmental care' demonstrating shared moral and ethical obligations of a pluralistic society. Environmental constitutionalism thus creates a symbiotic relationship between the state and citizen by re-defining the boundaries to achieve better environmental care through accountability and participative governance.

---

347 Louis J. Kotzé, "Arguing Global Environmental Constitutionalism", cited, p. 206.

348 (2013) 7 SCC 226.

349 *Ibid*, p. 229.

350 *L.K. Koolwal v State* AIR 1988 Raj. 2.

To strengthen the above-mentioned non-enforceable constitutional commitments, the Supreme Court has interpreted them as complementary and supplementary to the enforceable fundamental rights, particularly Article 21 (as discussed below). In *Intellectuals Forum, Tirupathi v State of AP*[351], the Supreme Court observed:

> [...] the environmental protection and conservation of natural resources has been given a status of a fundamental right and brought under Article 21 of the Constitution of India. This apart, Articles 48 A and 51 A (g) are fundamental in the governance of the country and require the state to apply these principles in making laws and further these two articles are to be kept in mind in understanding the scope and purport of the fundamental rights guaranteed by the Constitution including Article 21[352].

Thus, the courts have been guided by the language of Articles 48 A and 51 A (g) thereby providing a testimony to the fact that these are not merely "moral and ethical obligations" but are being gainfully employed.

III) Derivative Environmental Constitutionalism: Fundamental Right to Life

In India, there is no direct articulation of the right to environment, neither in the Constitution of India nor in statute law. The Supreme Court has constructed environmental constitutionalism encapsulating 'environmental care' by adopting an expansionist approach to the substantive right to life under Article 21 of the Constitution of India. Article 21, a fundamental right[353], reflects the US Justice William Brennan's vision of a living Constitution helping to understand and provide an expansive formulation of human dignity[354]. The normative focus is "on the individual – in the dignity and worth of the human

---

[351] (2006) 3 SCC 549.

[352] *Ibid*, p. 576; also see *State of Uttaranchal v B.S. Chaufal* (2010) 3 SCC 402; *Virendra Gaur v State of Haryana* (1995) 2 SCC 571; *M.C. Mehta v Union of India* AIR 1988 SC 1037; Nagrik Chetna Manch v State of Maharashtra 2016 SCC OnLine Bom 30.

[353] Article 21 states that no person shall be deprived of his life or personal liberty except according to procedure established by law.

[354] W.J. Brennan, *The Constitution of United States: Contemporary Ratification*, Text and Teaching Symposium, Georgetown University, 12 October 1985.

person"[355]. In *Francis Coralie v Delhi*[356], Justice Bhagwati stated: "We think that the right to life includes the right to live with human dignity and all that goes along with it, namely, the bare necessities of life such as adequate nutrition, clothing and shelter over the head and facilities for reading, writing, and expressing oneself in diverse forms"[357].

However, the human dignity principle is illusionary in the absence of the right to environment. The court has used the "linkage argument"[358] to defend the right to life and quality environment thereby placing human rights within environmental discourse. In *Municipal Corporation of Greater Mumbai v Kohinoor 34 CTNL Infrastructure*[359] the court stated:

> [...] it must be noted that the right to a clean and healthy environment is within the ambit of Article 21, as has been noted in *Court on its Own Motion v Union of India* reported in 2012 (12) SCALE 307 in the following words: – The scheme under the Indian Constitution unambiguously enshrines in itself the right of a citizen to life under Article 21 of the Constitution. The right to life is a right to live with dignity, safety and in a clean environment[360].

Thus, in a catena of judicial decisions right to life, liberty, pollution free air and water is guaranteed by the Constitution under Articles 21, 48 A and 51 A (g)[361]. It is the duty of the state and citizen to take

---

355 Lavanya Rajamani, "Public interest litigation in India: exploring issues of access, participation, equity, effectiveness and sustainability", cited, p. 414.

356 AIR 1981 SC 746.

357 *Ibid*, p. 753.

358 H. Shue, *Basic Rights*, Princeton University Press, 1996, p. 24–25. Shue initiated the use of the 'linkage argument' to defend the right to subsistence: "no one can fully [...] enjoy any right that is supposedly protected by society if he or she lacks the essentials for a reasonably healthy and active life". Shue defined subsistence as meaning "unpolluted air, unpolluted water, adequate food, clothing, adequate shelter and minimal preventive care" (p. 80). See also, J.W. Nickel, *Making Sense of Human Rights*, Oxford Blackwell Publishing, 2007, p. 139 and Brian Orend, *Human Rights: Concept and Context*, Broadview Press, 2001.

359 (2014) 4 SCC 538.

360 *Ibid*, p. 556.

361 *Subhash Kumar v State of Bihar* AIR 1991 SC 420; *MC Mehta* v *Kamal Nath* (2000)6 SCC 213; *In re Noise Pollution* v AIR 2005 SC 3136; *Delhi Jal Board* v *National Campaign for Dignity and Rights of Sewerage and Allied Workers* 2011 8 SCC 574.

adequate measures to promote, protect and improve both the man made and the natural environment.

Principles underpinning international environmental law have been absorbed into Article 21 thereby expanding the 'environmental care' paradigm to refine and improve environmental governance. In the *Intellectual Forum, Tirupathi v State of AP*[362], the Supreme Court accepted that "all human beings have a fundamental right to a healthy environment commensurate with their well-being [...] ensuring that natural resources are conserved and preserved in such a way that present as well as the future generation are aware of them equally"[363]. This ruling strengthens the principle of inter-generational equity which is derivative from Article 21. Similarly, the precautionary and polluter pays principles are an essential part of the reach of Article 21[364].

The Supreme Court created a link between life and a quality environment through a liberal interpretation of Article 21 from an anthropocentric position. However, identifying the right to a quality environment is not without its problems. It is complicated both in terms of content and justiciability. Descriptors used by the judiciary including safe, decent, clean, healthy, unpolluted, wholesome, resource rich and preserved environment are unrealistic, vague and indeterminate. This terminological uncertainty raises the issue of the establishment of constitutional environmental standards. What are the appropriate levels of environmental standards? Should these levels be based upon relative experience or absolute targets? Should the figures reflect those of western, industrial societies or prevailing Indian situations? If the standards are based upon the relative experience of other countries can the pervasive use of "legal transplants"[365] in a globalized world help improve the content and design of national environmental standards of the receiving

---

362 AIR 2006 SC 1350.

363 *Ibid*, para 84.

364 *Vellore Citizen Welfare Forum v Union of India* AIR 1996 SC 2715; *AP Pollution Control Board v Prof M.V. Nayudu* AIR 1999 SC 812.

365 The academic discourse on legal transplantation reveals fundamental differences over transplant existence and its feasibility. See A. Watson, *Legal Transplant*, University of Georgia Press, 1993; Pierre Legrand, "The Impossibility of 'Legal Transplants' ", *Maastricht Journal of European and Comparative Law*, 1997, p. 111; Otto Kahn-Freund, "On Uses and Misuses of Comparative Law", *Modern Law Review*, 1974, p. 1.

nations? If so, can the courts ensure that legal transplants are not a 'copy-paste', 'cross-pollination' or a simple 'mimicry' exercise[366]?

Beyond the problem of quantification is the thorny issue of implementation. Effective state implementation of the right to a quality environment remains disappointingly low. For example, there is no such thing as 'clean and fresh air' in India's capital, Delhi[367]. In November 2017, doctors in Delhi declared a public health emergency as air quality plunged to levels likened to smoking at least 50 cigarettes in one day[368]. The Chief Minister of Delhi, Arvind Kejriwal described Delhi as 'gas chamber' prompting his government to close 4,000 schools for a week[369]. According to the World Health Organisation, ten of the world's 20 most polluted cities are in India and it has among the highest proportion of deaths related to air pollution[370]. The 2017 Global Burden of Disease estimated that early deaths related to PM2.5 in India are the second highest in the world and ozone-related deaths, though lower than PM2.5, are the highest in the world. Not only the tiny particulates but also the toxic gases that come from combustion sources pose a very serious health risk[371].

The ground level environmental reality reveals considerable shortcomings and continuing challenges. It is acknowledged that the inaction of the state or failures of state agencies to perform their statutory duties result in endangering or impairing people's quality of life as guaranteed by the constitution. A damning report commissioned by the

366 Louis Kotzé, Caiphas Soyapi, *Transnational environmental law: the birth of a contemporary analytical perspective*, *in*: D. Fisher, *Research Handbook on Fundamental Concepts of Environmental Law*, Edward Elgar, 2016, p. 94.

367 Another example of implementation failure is portable water. India has the highest number of people globally without safe water. Nearly 76 million people have no access to a safe water supply. Approximately 140,000 Indian children die annually from diarrhoea. Water-Aid, 'Water: at What Cost? The State of the World's Water' (2016), online: http://www.wateraid.org/news/news/water- at-what- cost-our-latest-report- reveals-the- state-of- the worlds- water.

368 online: https://www.theguardian.com/world/2017/nov/07/delhi-india-declares-pollution-emergency-as-smog-chokes-city.

369 online: https://www.nytimes.com/2017/11/08/world/asia/india-air-pollution.html.

370 online: https://mg.co.za/article/2017-12-25-delhi-should-follow-beijings-example-in-tackling-air-pollution/.

371 Environmental Pollution (Prevention and Control) Authority (EPCA), *Report 71*, 2017, p. 8.

Ministry of Environment, Forest and Climate Change[372] condemns its own regulatory agencies dealing with environmental matters by stating:

> [...] the Executive has not covered itself with glory – indeed it has invited the attention of the judicial branch through lack of basic care [...] The institutional failures include lack of enforcement, flawed regulatory regime, poor management of resources, inadequate use of technology; absence of a credible, effective enforcement machinery; governance constraints in management; policy gaps; disincentives to environmental conservation, and so on[373].

However, the Supreme Court through its recently established Social Justice Bench (SJB)[374] is advancing environmental constitutionalism and care by framing and mobilising responses to environmental protection, human rights and social justice issues. The SJB is adopting a novel, creative problem solving and accountability approach allowing adjudication within a social context. Social and environmental justice is at the heart of the Indian Constitution, which in turn, places a duty on the judiciary to protect the rights of every citizen so that they might live a life of dignity and well-being.

For example, an on-going issue before the SJB is ensuring that the right to a "clean and fresh air" is effectively implemented rather than remaining an "aspirational goal". The court (SJB) in 2017 directed all the concerned regulatory authorities to develop a time-bound Comprehensive Action Plan (CAP) to clear the toxic air of Delhi and neighbouring states because of vehicular and industrial sources[375]. The CAP lists a combination of short, medium and long-term actions for each source of pollution and indicates regulatory agencies responsible for its implementation. The Supreme Court was informed of the actions taken up to 2018 that included a network of extensive and robust monitoring air quality stations, the Graded Response Action Plan for emergency action and during high pollution periods and stringent fuel and exhaust emission standards[376].

---

[372] High Level Committee on Forest and Environment Related Laws Report (MoEF&CC) (2014), online: http://envfor.nic.in/sites/default/files/press- releases/ Final_Report_of_ HLC.pdf.

[373] *Ibid*, p. 8, 22.

[374] Gitanjali N. Gill, "The Social Justice Bench of the Supreme Court of India: A New Development", *Public Law*, 2016, p. 392–401.

[375] *M.C. Mehta v Union of India*, Order dated 6th February 2017.

[376] EPCA and CSE, *Air Pollution Report Card 2017–18*, (submitted to the SJB), p. 22–24.

Further, the implementation of international environmental principles has also met with limited success. For example, polluters abuse the court system by repeatedly filing applications to avoid compliance with the court's order or judgment. In the *Indian Council for Enviro-Legal Action v Union of India*[377], the litigation continued for 23 years before the court empowered the state government to recover the cost of remedial measures and compensation from "rogue industries" that caused serious harm to the land and ground water level. Delay became a prohibitive feature of the legal route for those seeking environmental and social justice. The words of Justice Frankfurter capture both the expectation and frustration "there is nothing judicially more unseemly nor more self-defeating than for the Court to make *in terrorem* pronouncements, to indulge in merely empty rhetoric, sounding a word of promise to the ear, sure to be disappointing to the hope"[378].

Despite the above-mentioned shortcomings, the proactive judiciary acting as '*amicus* environment' has innovatively created and expanded environmental obligations to recognise 'environmental care' as constitutional virtues and rights in environmental governance in a normative sense. The expansionist approach has brought new dimensions not only in the environmental constitutionalism but also in the discourse on human rights in India.

IV) Justiciable Environmental Constitutionalism: Standing and Access to Justice

The Indian judiciary promotes the justiciability of environmental rights and obligations thus bringing 'environmental care' under the constitutional aegis. Broad and diffused standing or *locus standi* opens constitutional remedies to 'environmental care' to enforce environmental rights and secure environmental justice. The use of Public Interest Litigation (PIL) since 1980s as a broad-based, people-oriented approach envisioned access to justice as a "wheel of transformation" through judge-fashioned processes and remedies in a wide variety of socio-economic cases[379]. PIL has emerged as a procedural tool "redressing public injury,

---

377 AIR 1996 SC 1446.

378 *Baker v Carr*, 369 U.S. 186 (dissenting opinion).

379 Gitanjali N. Gill, "Human Rights and the Environment in India: Access through Public Interest Litigation", *Environmental Law Review*, 2012, p. 201.

enforcing public duty, protecting social, collective, "diffused" rights and interests or vindicating public interest"[380].

Environmental PIL is a product of the higher judiciary's response to the inaction of the state or failures of state agencies to perform their statutory duties resulting in endangering or impairing people's quality of life as guaranteed by the constitution. This has prompted environmentalists, NGOs and affected citizens to approach the courts, particularly the higher judiciary, for remedial action[381]. In this context, environmental constitutionalism embodies PIL as a transformative approach to provide access to justice to victims of environmental degradation. The use of Article 32 as a 'constitutional remedy' for the enforcement of fundamental rights, in particular Article 21, in environmental PIL constitutionalises 'environmental care' to forge new remedies and fashion new strategies for environmental protection. "A right without a remedy is a legal conundrum of a most grotesque kind. Article 32 confers one of the highly- cherished rights"[382].

The Supreme Court has relaxed the traditional standing or *locus standi* rule in environmental PILs to provide access to environmental justice to people who otherwise would be denied it. Procedural technicalities take a back seat in environmental PILs when a matter of grave public importance is considered by the court. Strict rules of pleading may not apply to the PIL. Pleadings prepared by a layman are construed generously as he lacks the standards of accuracy and precision particularly when a wrong is committed to a determinate class[383]. Thus, the relaxation of the rule of *locus standi* has resulted in a major procedural innovation. Justice Krishna Iyer, one of the most socially aware and concerned judges in independent India, stated:

> [...] the truth is that a few profound issues of processional jurisprudence of great strategic significance to our legal system face us. We must zero in on

---

[380] S.P. Sathe, *Judicial Activism in India Transgressing Borders and Enforcing Limits*, OUP New Delhi, 2002, 217.

[381] Gitanjali N. Gill, *Environmental Justice in India: The National Green Tribunal*, cited, p. 42.

[382] Justice R. Pal and Justice S. Pal, *Indian Constitutional Law*, Butterworths, 2011, p. 1429.

[383] *State of M.P. v Narmada Bachao Andolan* (2011) 7 SCC 639; *Rural Litigation and Entitlement Kendra v State of U.P.* 1989 Supp (1) SCC 504; *D.N. Jeevaraj v State of Karnataka* (2016) 2 SCC 563. *In*: *Mumbai Kamgar Sabha v Abdulbhai Faizullabhai*

them as they involve problems of access to justice for the people beyond the blinkered rules of 'standing' of the British-India vintage. If the centre of gravity of justice is to shift, as the Preamble of the Constitution mandates, from the traditional individualism of *locus standi* to the community orientation of public interest litigation, these interests must be considered[384].

Traditional *locus standi* has been changed in two ways through representative standing and citizen standing. Representative standing means any member of the public acting *bona fide*, may advance claims against violations of the human and environmental rights of victims who, because of their poverty, disability or socially or economically disadvantaged position, cannot approach the court for judicial enforcement of their fundamental rights. NGOs and environmental activists working, for example, on behalf of poor and tribal people enter the courts through this procedure[385]. Citizen standing provides access to seek redress for a public grievance affecting society rather than an individual. Where public duties are to be enforced and social collective 'diffused' environmental rights need protection, the court allows public-spirited citizens and organizations to act for a general or group interests even though they may not be directly injured regarding their own rights[386].

Thus, the new and relaxed meaning of *locus standi* in environmental PIL has introduced a transformative environmental constitutionalism approach being polycentric, participatory and democratic. This ensures commitment and adherence to environmental rule of law that employs a rights-based approach to augment 'environmental care' intricately inter-linked with fundamental values including human dignity, equality, fairness and justice.

However, for several reasons environmental PIL is not without its critics. First, the question whether environmental PIL provides effective or merely symbolic justice remains undecided. For instance, Singh argues "a judge may talk of right to life as including right to food, education,

---

(1976) 3 SCC 832 at p. 837, the court, observed "procedural prescriptions are handmaidens, not mistresses, of justice and failure of fair play is the spirit in which courts must view (procession) deviances".

384 *Municipal Council Ratlam v Vardhichan* (1980) 4 SCC 162, p. 163.

385 *State of Uttaranchal v B.S. Chaufal* (2010) 3 SCC 402; *Narmada Bachao Andolan v Union of India* (2000) 10 SCC 664; *Centre for environment Law WWF-I v Union of India* 2013 SCC OnLine SC 345.

386 *Almrita Patel* v *Union of India* Writ Petition No. 888 of 1996; *M C Mehta* v *Union of India* AIR 1997 SC 734; *Judges' Transfer Case* AIR 1982 SC 149.

environment and a horde of social rights without exactly determining who has the duty and how such duty to provide positive social benefits could be enforced"[387]. Second, a climate of inconsistency and uncertainty exists regarding entertaining and rejecting environmental PILs. This has become a serious concern among public-spirited citizens who see the court as the last resort for protecting the environment and citizens' rights. Prashant Bhushan has rightly argued that:

> the right to environmental protection has thus been whimsically applied by individual judges according to their own subjective preferences usually without clear principles guiding them about the circumstances in which the court could issue a mandamus for environmental protection. It appears that when socio-economic rights of the poor come into conflict with environmental protection the court has often subordinated those rights to environmental protection. On the other hand, when environmental protection comes into conflict with what is perceived by the court to be 'development issues' or powerful commercial, vested interests, environmental protection is often sacrificed at the altar of 'development' or similar powerful interests[388].

Third, critics also accuse the Supreme Court through its environmental PIL hearings of being a hyper active law-making body. Judges on occasions have ignored the doctrine of separation of powers by trespassing upon areas traditionally within the domain of the executive and the legislature[389]. It has been suggested that the court is guilty of populism as well as adventurism, thereby in violation of the doctrine of

---

387 Mahendra Pal Singh, "Protecting the Rights of the Disadvantaged Groups through Public Interest Litigation", *in*: Mahendra Pal Singh, Helmut Goerlich, Michael von Hauff (eds.), *Human Rights and Basic Need*, Universal Law Publishing, 2008, p. 322.

388 Prashant Bhushan, "Misplaced priorities and class bias of the judiciary", *Economic and Political Weekly*, 2009, p. 32–37, p. 35. See also, Geetonjoy Sahu, "Why the underdogs came out ahead: an analysis of the Supreme Court's environmental judgments, 1980–2010", *Economic and Political Weekly*, 2014, p. 52–57, at p. 55; Gitanjali N. Gill, "Environmental protection and development interests: a case study of the River Yamuna and the Commonwealth Games", Delhi 2010, *International Journal of Law in the Built Environment*, Special Issue, 2014, p. 69–90; *T N Godavarman Thirumulpad v Union of India* and *In the matter of Vedanta Aluminium Limited (*2008) 2 SCC 222; *Orissa Mining Corporation v MoEF* (2013) 6 SCC 476; *DDA v Rajendra Singh* AIR 2010 SC 2516.

389 Upendra Baxi, "How not to judge the judges: notes towards evaluation of the judicial role", *Journal of the Indian Law Institute*, 1983, p. 211; Shubhankar Dam, "Law-making beyond lawmakers: understanding the little right and the great

separation of powers. The court, however, has denied any such usurpation. In its pronouncements, it has justified its actions either under a statutory provision or as an aspect of its inherent powers[390].

Despite these criticisms, environmental PIL has produced a major change to India's environmental constitutionalism landscape. Environmental PIL is transformative and promotes 'environment care' through "collaborative approach, procedural flexibility, judicially supervised interim orders and forward-looking relief"[391]. It is a "testament to Indian democracy"[392] to improve environmental governance through constitutional attributes including fundamental rights and duties, rule of law and separation of powers.

V) Conclusion

India a nation of 1.3 billion people continues to experience environmental challenges that are both significant and numerous. Within this context environmental constitutionalism helps augment environmental care through a transformative approach involving broader constitutional, environmental law and governance responses. The legitimacy of the environmental constitutionalism paradigm depends on the creativity of those working on the problem. In the Indian context, the role of the judiciary is critical as it shapes the normative interpretation of the constitutional and regulatory framework. The Indian Supreme Court, a bedrock institution, has earned public respect and increased credibility through innovative and creative judicial craftsmanship.

To promote environmental constitutionalism, the Supreme Court expanded the constitutional provisions and combined human rights and environment to achieve better 'environmental care' and environmental governance. The court's willingness to expand its jurisdictional boundaries by introducing substantive and procedural changes has strengthened the

---

wrong (analysing the legitimacy of the nature of judicial law-making in India's constitutional dynamic)", *Tulane Journal of International and Comparative Law*, 2005, p. 109.

390 Geetonjoy Sahu, "Implications of Indian Supreme Courts' innovation for environmental jurisprudence", cited, p. 389.

391 Lavanya Rajamani, "Public interest litigation in India: exploring issues of access, participation, equity, effectiveness and sustainability", cited, p. 1.

392 *Ibid*, p. 12.

constitutionalisation of environmental care. Substantive changes include the growth of fundamental rights, particularly the right to life (Article 21), the derivative application of principles of international environmental law and broadening the scope of unenforceable constitutional moral and ethical commitments (Articles 48 A and 51 A [g]). Associated procedural expansion has provided a platform for the implementation of these substantive rights through a broader understanding of *locus standi* under environmental Public Interest Litigation. The failure in India of the inherited Westminster model of democratic governance which allocates individual and separate functions to parliament, the executive and the judiciary has resulted in the judiciary being promoted to be *primus inter pares*. This primary role concerning the protection of the environment is supported through the adoption and application of environmental constitutionalism involving broad, plural and inclusive constructs for an effective environmental governance.

Chapitre 7

Le droit constitutionnel de l'environnement et la protection de l'animal : le Brésil en voie de régression

I) Introduction
II) La protection de l'animal comme acquis du constitutionnalisme environnemental brésilien
III) La décision du Tribunal suprême fédéral de 2016 favorable à la protection de l'animal
IV) La régression critiquable du constitutionnalisme environnemental brésilien suite à la décision du Tribunal suprême fédéral
V) Conclusion

Chapter 7

Constitutional Environmental Law and Animal Protection: Brazil in Regression

I) Introduction
II) The Protection of the Animal as an Achievement of Brazilian Environmental Constitutionalism
III) The Federal Supreme Court's Ruling of 2016 in Favor of Animal Protection
IV) The Regrettable Regression of Brazilian Environmental Constitutionalism as a Consequence of the Federal Supreme Court's Ruling
V) Conclusion

Letícia ALBUQUERQUE

Professeure à l'Université Fédérale de Santa Catarina, Brésil

Chercheuse à l'Université de Strasbourg au laboratoire Sociétés, Acteurs et Gouvernement en Europe (SAGE) dans le cadre d'une bourse de recherche postdoctorale de l'agence brésilienne Coordenação de Aperfeiçoamento de Pessoal de Nível Superior – CAPES, n° 88881.119039/2016-01 (septembre 2017-août 2018)

Sommaire : L'année 2018 marque les 30 ans de l'actuelle Constitution de la République Fédérative du Brésil, la première Constitution du pays à se référer expressément à la protection de l'environnement. Depuis ce moment, le droit à un environnement écologiquement équilibré est reconnu au Brésil comme un droit fondamental. La Constitution consacre aussi le devoir de protection de la faune, interdisant les cruautés envers les animaux. Malgré cela, le texte constitutionnel a été révisé à la suite d'une décision du Tribunal suprême fédéral de 2016. Désormais cette interdiction de cruauté est relativisée lorsqu'il s'agit de pratiques considérées comme appartenant au patrimoine culturel brésilien. Le but principal de cet article est d'alerter sur l'actuel moment de régression des droits fondamentaux acquis au Brésil depuis 1988.

Abstract: The year 2018 marks the 30th anniversary of the current Constitution of the Federative Republic of Brazil, which is the first Constitution of the country to explicitly refer to environmental protection. The right to an ecologically healthy and balanced environment is recognized in Brazil as a fundamental right. The Constitution also enshrines the duty to protect animals by prohibiting cruelty. Despite this, as a reaction to a Federal Supreme Court's decision of 2016, the constitutional text was modified to relativize this prohibition regarding practices that are considered part of the cultural heritage. The main purpose of this article is to warn about the current regression of acquired fundamental rights in Brazil.

I) Introduction

En 2018, l'actuelle Constitution de la République Fédérative du Brésil a célébré ses 30 ans[393]. Adoptée le 22 septembre 1988 et promulguée le 5 octobre 1988, elle consolide la transition démocratique après 24 ans de régime militaire (1964–1985/88) et est reconnue comme une « Constitution citoyenne » pour avoir mis en place des droits fondamentaux et sociaux.

393 *Constitution*, en ligne : http://www.wipo.int/wipolex/fr/text.jsp?file_id=218254.

La Constitution représente un changement de paradigme dans la société brésilienne car, en plus de considérer « l'environnement écologiquement équilibré » comme un droit fondamental (article 225)[394], elle élève la protection des animaux au niveau constitutionnel[395]. En effet, dans le chapitre dédié à l'environnement (titre VII, chapitre VI), la Constitution fédérale impose aux pouvoirs publics l'obligation de protéger la faune et la flore et d'interdire, par l'intermédiaire de lois, les pratiques qui compromettent les fonctions écologiques, provoquent l'extinction d'espèces ou soumettent les animaux à la cruauté (article 225, paragraphe 1, alinéa VII)[396]. L'impératif de la protection des animaux, élevé au rang constitutionnel, apporte explicitement une limite au droit

---

394 Dans les Constitutions brésiliennes précédentes, il n'y a pas eu de mention équivalente à des préoccupations de protection de l'environnement, sauf à propos de l'utilisation des ressources naturelles, telles que l'exploitation minière et hydraulique. Il s'agissait d'une approche plus économique qu'écologique. Sur la protection constitutionnelle de l'environnement, v. Fernanda Medeiros, *Meio ambiente: direito e dever fundamental*, ed. Livraria do Advogado, 2004 ; José Joaquim Gomes Canotilho, José Rubens Morato Leite, *Direito Constitucional Ambiental Brasileiro*, ed. Saraiva, 2015.

395 Letícia Albuquerque, Fernanda Medeiros, "Lei Arouca: Legítima proteção ou falácia que legitima a exploração?", *in* : Maria C. de Souza *et al.* (dir.), *Direito ambiental II*, ed. CONPEDI, 2014, p. 27.

396 L'article 225 dipose : « Tout un chacun a droit à un environnement écologiquement équilibré, bien à l'usage commun du peuple et essentiel à une saine qualité de vie ; le devoir de le défendre et de le préserver au bénéfice des générations présentes et futures s'impose à la puissance publique et à la collectivité.

Paragraphe premier. Pour assurer le caractère effectif de ce droit, il incombe à la puissance publique :

[...] VII – de protéger la faune et la flore ; sont interdites, selon les formes de la loi, les pratiques qui mettent en danger leur fonction écologique, provoquent l'extinction d'espèces ou soumettent les animaux à la cruauté. »

Malgré cette disposition, il y a des interprétations divergentes pour définir ce qui caractérise une cruauté envers un animal. Dès la première version du texte constitutionnel, ce dispositif faisait partie du chapitre concernant la protection de l'environnement. Il a été formulé par la sous-commission de la santé, de la sécurité et de l'environnement de l'Assemblée nationale constitutionnelle, réunie le 7 avril 1987 pour discuter la rédaction de la nouvelle constitution. Pour consulter les notes de la sous-commission v. Brasil, Assembléia Nacional Constituinte, *Ata da 1° Reunião (Instalação) da Subcomissão de Saúde, Seguridade Social e Meio Ambiente*, en ligne : http://www.senado.leg.br/publicacoes/anais/constituinte/7b%20%20SUBCOMISS%C3%83O%20D%20SA%C3%9ADE,%20SEGUR186IDADE%2 0E%20MEIO%20AMBIENTE.pdf.

fondamental à la vie et à la dignité de la personne humaine. Les droits humains à la vie et aussi à un environnement écologiquement équilibré doivent être évalués au regard de l'interdiction de toute cruauté envers les animaux. Par conséquent, la Constitution de 1988 propose une vision nouvelle par rapport à la perspective juridique traditionnelle, qui traitait les animaux comme des biens à protéger en raison de leur pertinence pour l'écosystème, donc en raison de leur fonction écologique. Ce changement de perspective est un objectif essentiel du mouvement qui revendique des droits à accorder aux animaux (*Animal Rights Movement*[397]) et c'est dans ce contexte idéologique que le dispositif constitutionnel en question a suscité un grand débat au Brésil[398]. Lors de l'analyse subséquente de plusieurs demandes judiciaires déposées à des fins de protection des animaux, il faudra garder à l'esprit ce contexte.

Malgré ces changements apportés par la Constitution de 1988, pourquoi faut-il parler de régression ? Alors que l'article 225 de la Constitution a été à l'origine d'une amélioration de certaines pratiques envers les animaux, un amendement constitutionnel récent révise la situation initiale innovatrice. En effet, la proposition de révision constitutionnelle n° 50/2016 a été adoptée par la loi n° 96/2017 du 6 juin 2017 (dans la terminologie brésilienne il s'agit d'un amendement constitutionnel : *Emenda à Constituição* – EC n° 96/2017 »). Concrètement, cet amendement a permis d'ajouter un nouveau paragraphe 7 à l'article 225 de la Constitution fédérale qui se lit de la manière suivante (notre traduction) :

> Paragraphe 7 : Aux fins de ce qui est disposé à la fin de l'alinéa VII du paragraphe premier du présent article ne sont pas considérées comme cruelles les pratiques sportives qui utilisent des animaux tant qu'elles sont des manifestations culturelles conformément au paragraphe premier de

---

[397] D'après les idées défendues dans le cadre de ce mouvement, les êtres humains n'ont notamment pas le droit d'utiliser des animaux pour satisfaire leurs intérêts anthropocentriques. Rappelons-nous que le débat autour de la condition de l'animal est devenu notoire à partir de la publication, en 1975, de l'ouvrage intitulé *Animal Liberation* du philosophe australien Peter Singer (pour la traduction française, v. Peter Singer, *La libération animale*, Payot, 2012). D'autres auteurs ont donné suite au débat, comme par exemple : Tom Regan, *The case of Animal Rights*, University of California Press, 2004 ; Gary Francione, Robert Gardener, *The Animal Rights Debate: Abolition or Regulation? Critical Perspectives on Animals: Theory, Culture, Science, and Law*, Columbia University Press, 2010.

[398] Daniel Lourenço, *Direito dos Animais: fundamentação e novas perspectivas*, ed. Fabris, 2008; Fernanda Medeiros, *Direito dos animais*, ed. Livraria do Advogado, 2013.

l'article 215 de la Constitution fédérale, inscrites comme biens naturels immatériels faisant partie intégrante du patrimoine culturel brésilien, devant être réglementées par une loi spécifique qui garantit le bien-être des animaux concernés[399].

Il résulte de cette révision que les pratiques qui ont pour objet l'utilisation des animaux, mais qui sont reconnues comme faisant partie du patrimoine culturel et qui sont réglementées par la loi, ne sont plus considérées comme étant des pratiques cruelles. Cet amendement est en réalité une réaction à un recours d'inconstitutionnalité (dans la terminologie brésilienne une *Action directe d'Inconstitutionnalité* – ADI) du 6 octobre 2016, déposé devant le Tribunal Fédéral Suprême (ADI n° 4983[400]). Ce recours a été initié par le Bureau du Procureur de la République contre l'État Fédéré du Ceará contre une loi en vigueur uniquement dans cet État autorisant la pratique de la *vaquejada*, une variante de rodéo populaire dans le nord-est du Brésil. La décision du Tribunal Fédéral Suprême a condamné la pratique de la *vaquejada* comme soumettant des animaux à la cruauté et étant, par conséquent, contraire à la Constitution fédérale. Cette décision était fortement contraire aux intérêts des secteurs socio-économiques actifs dans le domaine de la *vaquejada*, comme les éleveurs de chevaux, les propriétaires des arènes où la pratique se déroule, les grandes entreprises diffusant de la publicité lors des rodéos, etc.

Cela a conduit, avec l'appui de parlementaires, à une contre-réaction de la part du Congrès National[401], optant pour la technique du redressement jurisprudentiel par amendement constitutionnel. Il s'agissait de mettre fin à toute remise en question de pratiques utilisant les animaux dans le

---

[399] « § 7º Para fins do disposto na parte final do inciso VII do § 1º deste artigo, não se consideram cruéis as práticas desportivas que utilizem animais, desde que sejam manifestações culturais, conforme o § 1º do art. 215 desta Constituição Federal, registradas como bem de natureza imaterial integrante do patrimônio cultural brasileiro, devendo ser regulamentadas por lei específica que assegure o bem-estar dos animais envolvidos. » Comp. Brasil, Senado, *PECn.50*, en ligne : https://www25.senado.leg.br/web/atividade/materias/-/materia/127262. D'après l'article 215, par. 1, l'État protège les manifestations des cultures populaires, indiennes, afro-brésiliennes et des autres groupes qui participent au processus national de civilisation.

[400] Brasil, Supremo Tribunal Federal, ADI n° 4.983/CE, 2016, en ligne : http://redir.stf.jus.br/paginadorpub/paginador.jsp?docTP=TP&docID=12798874.

[401] Cette contre-réaction est à l'origine de la proposition de révision constitutionnelle n° 50/2016 adoptée par l'amendement constitutionnel EC n° 96/2017 du 6 juin 2017, en ligne : https://www25.senado.leg.br/web/atividade/materias/-/materia/127262.

cadre de la *vaquejada* et d'autres manifestations similaires, comme les rodéos, dans tous les États de la Fédération.

Il a fallu trois décennies d'efforts d'interprétation et de consolidation du texte constitutionnel pour interdire tout type de cruauté envers les animaux et pour affermir le droit à l'environnement écologiquement équilibré en tant que droit fondamental. L'amendement constitutionnel EC n° 96/2017 s'analyse dans ce contexte nettement comme une régression en matière de protection de la faune. Il pourrait préfigurer la neutralisation d'autres droits dits fondamentaux si la société civile ne réagit pas de manière adéquate.

La présente contribution poursuit trois objectifs. D'abord, elle met en relief un aspect actuel du constitutionnalisme environnemental brésilien, à savoir la protection des animaux en tant que partie intégrante de la protection environnementale générale consacrée à l'article 225 de la Constitution brésilienne.

Ensuite, elle alerte contre la régression en matière de protection environnementale qui résulte de la révision constitutionnelle de 2016. Cette dernière conforte une tendance vers la régression manifeste aussi dans d'autres domaines étant donné que le projet écologique du pays adopté dans le cadre de la Constitution de 1988 n'a pas réussi à changer vraiment la société brésilienne, malgré certains progrès législatifs. D'un côté d'importants groupes continuent à exercer des pressions pour rendre la réglementation environnementale moins protectrice, comme l'illustre l'affaire de la *vaquejada*, d'un autre côté des groupes utilisent le droit pour faire régresser la situation des autochtones en matière de démarcation des terres[402].

Elle donne enfin une illustration typiquement brésilienne de résolution d'un conflit environnemental, en l'occurrence régressive au regard de l'acquis constitutionnel. Le Brésil se place effectivement au 3e rang mondial en matière de conflits environnementaux selon une étude publiée en 2014[403] et réalisée dans le cadre d'un projet de l'Université Autonome de

---

402 La dimension environnementale est présente puisque la conservation des ressources naturelles et la garantie des conditions environnementales essentielles à la vie qui en résulte, sur le fondement de l'article 231 de la Constitution, sont directement liées à la préservation des territoires autochtones. À ce propos, v. Adriana B. Aparicio, *O Instituto do Indigenato e Teoria Crítica*, thèse de doctorat, 18 février 2018, Universidade Federal de Santa Catarina.

403 Environmental Justice Organization, *Atlas da injustiça ambiental*, en ligne : http://www.ejolt.org/maps/.

Barcelone. Cette étude apporte le témoignage de 58 différends brésiliens dont des conflits agraires, relatifs aux autochtones, concernant les ressources en eau et les ressources minérales. Ces conflits[404] se perçoivent dans une perspective d'exploitation des ressources naturelles en tant que produits à exporter, conformément au modèle encore prédominant en Amérique latine. D'autres conflits sont liés à la construction d'infrastructures et à la production d'électricité, comme les projets hydroélectriques, thermoélectriques et éoliens[405].

De manière paradigmatique, l'exploitation des animaux s'inscrit dans ce contexte conflictuel. La réduction des zones de protection environnementale, que ce soit en raison de l'expansion agricole ou du développement des grands projets hydroélectriques, touche directement l'habitat de la faune. L'élevage intensif et la réalisation de pratiques dites culturelles, comme la *vaquejada*, mettent en évidence l'exploitation économique des animaux par les secteurs protagonistes liés aux agro-affaires.

Par la suite, le régime de la protection de l'animal en tant que spécialité représentative et intégrante du constitutionnalisme environnemental brésilien sera analysé à la lumière de la révision constitutionnelle du 6 juin 2017. Cela sera fait en présentant la protection de l'animal comme un acquis du constitutionnalisme environnemental brésilien (II), la décision du Tribunal suprême fédéral de 2016 favorable à cette protection (III) et les conséquences de cette décision déclenchant une régression critiquable du constitutionnalisme environnemental brésilien (IV).

II) La protection de l'animal comme acquis du constitutionnalisme environnemental brésilien

En partant des progrès scientifiques récents sur la sensibilité des animaux, comment justifier l'utilisation des animaux pour le plaisir et le divertissement de l'homme, pour ses vêtements et sa nourriture,

---

404 Fiocruz, *Mapa de conflitos envolvendo Justiça Ambiental e Saúde no Brasil*, en ligne : http://www.conflitoambiental.icict.fiocruz.br/index.php.

405 Ces types de projets ont aussi un impact sur la législation de protection de l'environnement. Il existe, par exemple, une autre proposition d'amendement constitutionnel : Brasil, Senado, *PEC* n° 65 de 2012, en ligne : https://www25.senado.leg.br/web/atividade/materias/-/materia/109736). Signalons que cette révision ne respecterait pas l'un des principes du droit de l'environnement, celui de la précaution.

pour ses expériences pédagogiques et scientifiques ? Face à l'évolution de l'opinion publique et de l'éthique animale, le droit s'est saisi de la question, y compris au niveau le plus élevé de la hiérarchie des normes, la constitution. Le cas brésilien est particulièrement remarquable étant donné que la Constitution fédérale pose une obligation de fond, c'est-à-dire l'interdiction de cruauté, alors que dans d'autres constitutions il s'agit simplement d'une réglementation sur la répartition des compétences en la matière[406] ou d'une indication générale adressée aux autorités étatiques[407]. L'état du droit brésilien a été influencé par les écrits philosophiques de la mouvance des « droits des animaux » (*supra* introduction) et cette influence reste importante[408], y compris au sein des facultés de droit de certaines universités brésiliennes[409].

Un antécédent intéressant du dispositif constitutionnel de 1988 se trouve au niveau législatif, tel l'ancien décret-loi n° 24.645 du 10 juillet 1934[410]. Ce décret-loi qui n'est plus en vigueur était important parce qu'il donnait des exemples concrets de pratiques cruelles vers les animaux, qui devaient donc être interdites. Aujourd'hui, la législation parle d'interdiction de cruauté, mais ne définit pas la cruauté, laissant l'interprétation ouverte aux juges.

Postérieurement à 1988, le dispositif constitutionnel est mis en œuvre dans le domaine du droit pénal. À cette fin est adoptée la loi n° 9.605 du 12 février 1998 sur les crimes environnementaux. Son article 32 érige en infraction le fait de commettre des actes et des abus de maltraitance, des blessures ou des mutilations à l'encontre d'animaux sauvages, domestiques ou domestiqués, natifs ou exotiques[411]. Pour le système juridique brésilien,

---

406 P. ex. la Constitution suisse dispose à l'article 80 que « [l]a Confédération légifère sur la protection des animaux » (Constitution fédérale de la Confédération Suisse), en ligne : https://www.admin.ch/opc/fr/classified-compilation/19995395/index.html#a80.

407 P. ex. la Constitution du Luxembourg dispose à l'article 11*bis* que l'État « promeut la protection et le bien-être des animaux » (Constitution du Grand-Duché de Luxembourg), en ligne : http://data.legilux.public.lu/file/eli-etat-leg-recueil-constitution-20161020-fr-pdf.pdf.

408 Carlos Naconecy, *Ética & Animais: um guia de argumentação filosófica*, EDIPUCRS, 2014 ; Luiz Paulo Rouanet *et al.* (dir.), *Ética e direitos dos animais*, ed. UFSC, 2016.

409 P. ex. l'Université Fédérale de Santa Catarina propose un cours de droit des animaux à la Faculté de droit depuis 2013.

410 Brasil, Decreto Lei n. 24645/1934, en ligne : http://www.planalto.gov.br/ccivil_03/decreto/1930-1949/d24645.htm.

411 Brasil, Lei n. 9605/1998, en ligne : http://www.planalto.gov.br/ccivil_03/leis/l9605.htm.

la cruauté est donc synonyme de crime. Ainsi, le système judiciaire a commencé à être sollicité par des associations de protection des animaux afin d'appliquer la loi. Nous avons des décisions importantes qui sont prises par les juridictions sur l'interprétation de ce dispositif constitutionnel concernant la cruauté envers les animaux[412] parmi lesquelles la décision ADI n° 4.983/CE, mais qui est malheureusement à l'origine d'une régression.

III) La décision du Tribunal suprême fédéral de 2016 favorable à la protection de l'animal

La prise de position du Tribunal suprême fédéral contre la pratique de la *vaquejada*, fondée sur une analyse détaillée du contexte factuel, met correctement en œuvre l'esprit du constitutionnalisme environnemental brésilien. Rappelons que, le 6 octobre 2016, la formation plénière du Tribunal suprême fédéral a accueilli la demande en déclaration d'inconstitutionnalité (décision ADI n° 4.983/CE) formulée par le Procureur général de la République de l'époque, Rodrigo Janot, à l'encontre de la loi n° 15.299 du 8 janvier 2013[413]. Cette loi de l'État du Ceará avait réglementé la *vaquejada* comme une pratique sportive et culturelle. La majorité des juges du Tribunal a suivi la position du rapporteur, le juge Marco Aurélio, qui a considéré que la *vaquejada* est une pratique cruelle envers les animaux. Voici la traduction du sommaire officiel de la décision :

> *Vaquejada* – Manifestation – Culture – Animaux – Cruauté explicite – Conservation de la faune et de la flore – Inconstitutionnalité. L'obligation de l'État de garantir à tous le plein exercice des droits culturels, favorisant la valorisation et la diffusion des manifestations, ne le dispense pas du respect des dispositions de l'alinéa VII, paragraphe 1 de l'article 225 de la Charte fédérale, qui interdit toute pratique aboutissant à soumettre les animaux à la cruauté. La pratique de la *vaquejada* est en désaccord avec la norme constitutionnelle[414].

---

[412] Notamment la décision *farra do boi* (en 3.6.1997, RE n° 153.531/SC) et la décision sur le combat de coqs (en 29.6.2005, ADI n° 2.514/SC et 26.5.2011, ADI n° 1.856/RJ), v. *infra*.

[413] Brasil, Ceará, Lei n. 15299/2013, en ligne : https://www.legisweb.com.br/legislacao/?id=250070.

[414] Brasil, Supremo Tribunal Federal, ADI n. 4.983/CE, 2016, en ligne : http://redir.stf.jus.br/paginadorpub/paginador.jsp?docTP=TP&docID=12798874. Traduction de l'auteur.

De manière traditionnelle, la *vaquejada* est une pratique culturellement acceptée dans toute la fédération brésilienne, notamment dans le Nord-Est où deux *cow-boys* (*peão de rodeio* en portugais), montés sur des chevaux, doivent abattre un taureau, en le tirant par la queue. Comme le précise la décision de justice, l'animal est préalablement cloîtré, fouetté et incité à sauter à travers l'ouverture de la porte de la clôture. Une équipe de deux *cow-boys* est formée de compétiteurs qui galopent en entourant le taureau qui fuit. Le but est de conduire l'animal vers une zone délimitée (indiquée par des traits de chaux) et là, de l'attraper par la queue, le faire tomber, et le positionner avec les quatre pattes vers le haut[415]. Si dans le passé, la *vaquejada* était une pratique de gestion du bétail limitée au milieu rural, c'est devenu une activité de masse très rentable à partir de la seconde moitié du siècle dernier[416].

La décision collégiale du Tribunal concernant la déclaration d'inconstitutionnalité présente, au fil de ses 150 pages, le débat autour de la *vaquejada* : s'agit-il d'une pratique culturelle méritant d'être protégée, aux termes de l'article 215 de la Constitution fédérale, ou, au contraire, d'une pratique cruelle qui doit être interdite par application de l'article 225, paragraphe 1, VII, de cette même Constitution ? Malgré les votes divergents au sein du Tribunal suprême fédéral, la majorité des juges a décidé que la *vaquejada* est une pratique cruelle et injustifiable à l'époque actuelle.

Le rapporteur qui a convaincu la majorité du tribunal, le juge Marco Aurélio, rappelle la jurisprudence du Tribunal suprême face à la nécessité de mettre en balance le droit à l'environnement avec les droits individuels. Il estime devoir donner la priorité à l'intérêt collectif de protection de l'environnement en se fondant sur des décisions antérieures d'inconstitutionnalité du Tribunal : a) la décision *farra do boi*[417] (en 3.6.1997, RE n° 153.531/SC) ; b) la décision sur le combat de

---

415 Cette pratique est bien décrite à la p. 5 de la décision ADI n. 4.983/CE, en ligne : http://redir.stf.jus.br/paginadorpub/paginador.jsp?docTP=TP&docID=12798874.

416 Actuellement, 600 événements ont lieu chaque année, avec des arènes remplies et avec une audience moyenne de plus de 80.000 personnes par soirée. De gigantesques récompenses en argent sont distribuées. Eduardo Savanachi, "O milionário mundo da vaquejada", *Revista Dinheiro Rural*, 2016, en ligne : https://www.dinheirorural.com.br/secao/agronegocios/o-milionario-mundo-da-vaquejada.

417 *Farra do Boi* est une pratique courante dans l'État de Santa Catarina. Cette pratique a lieu le long du littoral pendant la période du Carême et consiste à relâcher un bœuf dans l'espace public et ainsi « fêter avec l'animal », en faisant courir le bœuf derrière les personnes qui participent à cette fête. Après le jeu, l'animal retourne

coqs (en 29.6.2005, ADI n° 2.514/SC et 26.5.2011, ADI n° 1.856/RJ)[418]. Le juge Luís Roberto Barroso, à son tour, souligne que l'interdiction des pratiques qui soumettent les animaux à la cruauté constitue une « protection constitutionnelle autonome » et que les animaux doivent être protégés contre les actes cruels, qu'il y ait ou non des conséquences sur l'environnement, sur la fonction écologique de la faune ou sur la préservation des espèces. En revanche, le juge Edson Fachin est parvenu à la conclusion opposée à celle adoptée par le juge Marco Aurélio, ne percevant pas l'existence de cruauté envers les animaux et insistant sur la *vaquejada* en tant que manifestation culturelle à protéger[419]. Les juges Teori Zavascki, Luiz Fux, Dias Toffoli et Gilmar Mendes ont appuyé l'opinion du juge Fachin. Pour le juge Gilmar Mendes, en l'occurrence, l'interdiction de la pratique de la *vaquejada*, ainsi que de pratiques similaires, « rendrait la vie ennuyeuse »[420].

C'est finalement dans une décision serrée (six voix contre cinq, où l'a emporté le vote de la juge Carmen Lúcia) que le Tribunal suprême fédéral s'est prononcé contre la pratique de la *vaquejada* et pour une déclaration d'inconstitutionnalité de la loi 15299 du 8 janvier 2013 de l'État du Ceará. Les juges ont ainsi suivi la politique jurisprudentielle établie[421].

Cette décision du Tribunal suprême fédéral, dans la continuité du constitutionnalisme environnemental brésilien, a eu des répercussions

---

dans les pâturages (d'où il peut à nouveau être emporté pour la *Farra do Boi*) ou est récupéré pour l'abattage. Parfois, il est sacrifié après la fête et la viande est partagée entre les participants. Les partisans de la pratique la justifient comme faisant partie du patrimoine culturel, issue des pêcheurs portugais venus des îles des Açores, alors que les groupes de défense des droits des animaux la considèrent comme cruelle et dégradante.

418 Brasil, Supremo Tribunal Federal, ADI n. 4.983/CE, 2016, p. 5, en ligne : http://redir.stf.jus.br/paginadorpub/paginador.jsp?docTP=TP&docID=12798874. *Farra do boi* jugée le 3.6.1997, RE n. 153.531/SC ; *Rinhas de galo*/Combats de coqs, affaire jugée le 29.6.2005, ADI n. 2.514/SC ; et en 26.5.2011, ADI n. 1.856/RJ. Pour consulter les arrêts, aller sur le site du Tribunal suprême fédéral : http://portal.stf.jus.br.

419 Brasil, Supremo Tribunal Federal, ADI n. 4.983/CE, 2016, p. 15, en ligne : http://redir.stf.jus.br/paginadorpub/paginador.jsp?docTP=TP&docID=12798874.

420 Souligné spécialment par le juge Marco Aurélio dans son vote : Brasil, Supremo Tribunal Federal, ADI n. 4.983/CE, 2016, p. 17, en ligne : http://redir.stf.jus.br/paginadorpub/paginador.jsp?docTP=TP&docID=12798874.

421 Brasil, Supremo Tribunal Federal, ADI n. 4.983/CE, 2016, p. 13, en ligne : http://redir.stf.jus.br/paginadorpub/paginador.jsp?docTP=TP&docID=12798874.

très fortes, notamment au sein du Parlement brésilien, dominé par une majorité d'hommes politiques liés au secteur nommé *BBB*, en allusion aux mots « *biblia* » (bible), « *boi* » (bœuf) et « *bala* » (munitions). Ce sont donc des parlementaires qui représentent les intérêts de groupes très conservateurs de la société, liés à la sphère religieuse (notamment les Églises évangéliques) et à l'exploitation animale et agricole (les grands propriétaires terriens). Financés par l'agro-industrie, ces secteurs ont réussi à imposer une vraie régression en matière environnementale : en effet, l'amendement constitutionnel n° 96/2017 est révélateur de la façon dont le Parlement adopte des lois, voire des révisions de constitution, capables de mettre en danger les progrès en matière de protection de l'environnement et des droits humains durement acquis au cours des trois dernières décennies au Brésil.

IV) La régression critiquable du constitutionnalisme environnemental brésilien suite à la décision du Tribunal suprême fédéral

L'amendement constitutionnel n° 96/2017, rappelons-nous, ajoute un nouveau paragraphe à l'article 225 de la Constitution fédérale. Selon ce nouveau paragraphe, l'utilisation d'animaux pour certaines activités, comme la *vaquejada* par exemple, ne peut être considérée comme étant cruelle lorsque ces pratiques sont reconnues comme partie intégrante du patrimoine culturel brésilien et lorsqu'elles sont réglementées par une loi.

Cette régression, neutralisant l'acquis constitutionnel, viole doublement des principes constitutionnels : celui de la clause *pétrea*[422] et celui de l'interdiction de la régression en matière environnementale.

En ce qui concerne le premier principe, il faut savoir que le droit à un environnement écologiquement équilibré, consacré à l'article 225 de la Constitution brésilienne, est un droit fondamental et ne peut, à ce titre, être l'objet d'une révision par amendement constitutionnel. Ce procédé est effectivement interdit à l'article 60, paragraphe 4, alinéa IV, de cette même Constitution qui n'admet pas de révision pour abolir les droits

---

[422] Dispositif constitutionnel rigide qui ne peut être modifié, même par un amendement proposé à la constitution. Les clauses *pétreas* insérées dans la Constitution brésilienne de 1988 sont énoncées à l'article 60, § 4. Ce sont : la forme fédérative de l'État ; le vote direct, secret, universel et périodique ; la séparation des pouvoirs et les droits et garanties individuels.

collectifs et individuels. Le droit à un environnement écologiquement équilibré est donc fondé sur la solidarité et la fraternité, un droit collectif conçu pour protéger les meilleurs intérêts de l'humanité, des générations actuelles et futures. Comme les autres droits fondamentaux, le droit à un environnement écologiquement équilibré se conçoit comme étant indisponible et inaliénable[423]. À ce propos, Tiago Fensterseifer, examinant le thème de la protection de l'environnement au regard de la théorie des droits fondamentaux, met en évidence la dimension écologique du principe de la dignité humaine qui limite les pouvoirs publics, y compris le pouvoir constituant. Pour cet auteur, la dégradation de l'environnement, ainsi que tous les risques écologiques existants dans le contexte des relations sociales contemporaines, compromettent de manière significative le bien-être individuel et collectif. Dans son ouvrage de référence, il inclut de manière définitive la protection de l'environnement dans le champ normatif des droits fondamentaux[424].

Le principe de l'interdiction de la régression en matière environnementale est également violé par l'amendement constitutionnel n° 96/2017 étant donné que les garanties déjà accordées pour la protection de l'environnement et des animaux contre les pratiques cruelles sont supprimées. Le principe, selon l'interprétation consolidée dans la doctrine au Brésil[425], consiste en un principe constitutionnel implicite, ayant comme base constitutionnelle, entre autres, le principe de l'État démocratique et social de droit, le principe de la dignité de la personne humaine, le principe d'efficacité des normes qui définissent les droits fondamentaux, le principe de sécurité juridique et le devoir qui incombe à l'État de développer les droits sociaux, économiques, culturels et

---

423 Brasil, Ministério Publico Federal, PGR, ADI n° 5772/2017, p. 22–23, en ligne : http://www.mpf.mp.br/pgr/documentos/ADI5772vaquejada.pdf.

424 Tiago Fensterseifer, *Direitos Fundamentais e proteção do ambiente : a dimensão ecológica da dignidade humana no marco jurídico-constitucional do Estado socioambiental de Direito*, ed. Livraria do Advogado, 2008. V. aussi Tiago Fensterseifer, Ingo Wolfgang Sarlet, *Direito Constitucional Ambiental : Constituição, Direitos Fundamentais e Proteção do Ambiente*, ed. RT, 2014.

425 Ingo Wolfgang Sarlet, Tiago Fensterseifer, "Notas sobre a proibição de retrocesso em matéria (sócio) ambiental", *in*: Brasil, Senado Federal, *O principio da proibição de retrocesso*, p. 143, 2012, en ligne : http://www.mma.gov.br/port/conama/processos/93127174/Voto_APROMAC_ANEXO.pdf. Cet ouvrage est le résultat d'un colloque international sur le principe de l'interdiction de la régression. Il a été organisé par le Sénat brésilien avec la participation de juristes brésiliens et étrangers comme, du côté français, Michel Prieur.

environnementaux. À propos de la protection de l'environnement et des animaux contre les pratiques cruelles, le Tribunal suprême fédéral avait donc raisonnablement considéré que les événements culturels et sportifs devaient être garantis et encouragés, à condition qu'ils soient guidés par le droit fondamental à un environnement équilibré. Ceci exclut les activités préjudicielles à l'environnement ainsi que les pratiques soumettant les animaux à la cruauté.

La conséquence de la nouvelle version constitutionnelle va d'après Ingo Sarlet créer un concept normatif de cruauté envers les animaux dans la mesure où des traditions qui, avant l'amendement, étaient considérées comme cruelles, perdent cette qualification lorsqu'un acte normatif autorise leur pratique. Il est aussi incohérent pour cet auteur que des manifestations culturelles, dites « non cruelles », aient besoin d'une réglementation infraconstitutionnelle afin de respecter le bien-être des animaux[426].

La controverse à ce sujet n'est pas close. En effet, le 6 septembre 2017, le Procureur général de l'époque, Rodrigo Janot, a déposé une demande en déclaration d'inconstitutionnalité (action directe d'inconstitutionnalité – ADI n° 5.772) auprès du Tribunal suprême fédéral. Le but de cette demande est de contester la constitutionnalité de l'amendement constitutionnel n° 96/2017 et de la loi n° 13204 du 29 novembre 2016[427], qui a inscrit la pratique de la *vaquejada* sur la liste du patrimoine culturel immatériel du Brésil. Les motifs juridiques de cette action sont précisément la violation de l'article 60, paragraphe 4 de la Constitution fédérale (clause *pétrea*), celle du principe de l'interdiction de la régression en matière environnementale ainsi que celle des articles 1°, al. III (principe de la dignité de la personne humaine) et 225, par. 1, al. VII de la Constitution (interdiction de cruauté). Le Procureur envisage aussi de contester la constitutionnalité de la loi n° 10220 du 11 avril 2001, qui a réglementé l'activité du *peão de rodeio*[428], l'assimilant à un athlète professionnel, et incluant les *vaquejadas* comme modalité de compétition. Malgré le fait que cette loi fédérale a été promulguée, le sujet réglementé ne serait pas compatible avec l'ordre constitutionnel

---

426 Ingo Wolfgang Sarlet, "Novamente a proteção constitucional dos animais no Brasil: o caso da EC 96/2017", Consultor Jurídico, 2017, en ligne : https://www.conjur.com.br/2017-jul-07/direitos-fundamentais-protecao-constitucional-animais-ec-962017.

427 Brasil, Lei n. 13364/2016, en ligne : http://www.planalto.gov.br/ccivil_03/_ato20152018/2016/lei/L13364.htm.

428 Une sorte de cow-boy pour les rodéos.

brésilien. En effet, la *vaquejada*, au-delà de son aspect culturel revendiqué par une partie de la population, soumet inévitablement les animaux à un traitement cruel et violent, raison pour laquelle celle-ci ne doit pas être considérée comme une modalité de compétition ni le *peão de rodeio* considéré comme un athlète[429]. Le sujet sera examiné par le Tribunal suprême fédéral.

V) Conclusion

Cette contribution écrite en juin 2018 sur la condition animale au Brésil présente un aperçu sur un dispositif juridique qui trouve sa source dans la Constitution de la République Fédérative du Brésil et qui, plus précisément, fait explicitement partie du droit constitutionnel de l'environnement. Il a été démontré que, malgré un fort enracinement du droit de l'environnement dans la constitution, le texte de la norme suprême n'est pas à l'abri de révisions qui vont dans un sens restrictif. Cette réalité montre clairement qu'il existe toujours un décalage entre l'acquis constitutionnel et la réalité du pays. La régression représentée par l'adjonction du paragraphe 7 à l'article 225 de la Constitution est aussi le résultat de pressions exercées par le secteur économique et ne relève pas uniquement de la discussion sur l'importance de conserver une pratique dite culturelle.

La régression en matière de droits acquis n'est pas limitée au domaine de la protection des animaux. D'une façon générale, même après la promulgation de la Constitution de 1988, le développement d'une politique environnementale n'a pas été la priorité des différents chefs d'État que le pays a connus[430]. Malgré la participation du Brésil dans les Conférences des Nations unies sur la thématique environnementale,

---

[429] À ce propos v. le texte de l'ADI n. 5772/2017 (action directe d'inconstitutionnalité), p. 2–4, en ligne : http://www.mpf.mp.br/pgr/documentos/ADI5772vaquejada.pdf.

[430] Depuis les 30 ans d'existence de la Constitution citoyenne de 1988, le Brésil a eu sept présidents de la République et est passé par beaucoup de changements sociaux et politiques. Pendant cette période, il y a aussi eu la mise en œuvre de deux procédures d'*impeachment* présidentiel : l'une en 1992 contre le Président Fernando Collor, qui a démissionné avant d'être condamné et, plus récemment, en 2016, contre la Présidente Dilma Roussef, qui a été destituée de ses fonctions présidentielles par le Congrès National. Collor était le premier Président élu démocratiquement par vote direct de la population après la Dictature Militaire. Dilma Roussef était la première femme élue Présidente. Elle était une ancienne combattante contre le

les agendas pour la mise en place d'un vrai changement en faveur de la protection de l'environnement ont souvent été bloqués par le discours du développement économique. Cette dissymétrie met en évidence le danger de régression en matière des droits acquis, telle la question concernant la cruauté animale, spécialité pourtant paradigmatique à l'intérieur du constitutionnalisme environnemental.

---

régime militaire et, à l'époque, a été torturée et incarcérée en raison de ses positions politiques. On s'aperçoit alors que la démocratie au Brésil est encore jeune. Avec les derniers événements, tel l'*impeachment* de Dilma Roussef, le démantèlement des droits sociaux et les assassinats de défenseurs des droits de l'homme, le Brésil est loin de consolider le processus de démocratisation commencé à partir de 1985.

Part 2) Impact of Environmental Constitutionalism beyond Constitutional Law

In this part, impact of environmental constitutionalism is considered beyond constitutional law. Through a first set of papers it gives priority to the typical French system with its different court orders. Simon Jolivet explains how administrative law follows the requirements of the Charter on the Environment, especially through the case law of the *Conseil d'État* (chapter 8). Olivier Cachard deals with the scope of the precautionary principle, codified in the Environmental Charter, in the field of (private) corporate law by focusing on the role of the state as a shareholder (chapter 9). Samuel Ferey provides a practical outsider's perspective on environmental constitutionalism by analyzing how economic compensation methods for environmental harm comply with the polluter-pays-principle under the Environmental Charter (chapter 10).

Secondly, in a wider, international perspective, Sven Kaufmann explores the relationship between environmental constitutionalism and EU Law. It is in a functional sense that the European Union treaties, with their environmental related provisions, act as a Constitution (chapter 11).

Partie 2) L'impact du constitutionnalisme environnemental au-delà du droit constitutionnel

Dans cette partie, l'impact du constitutionnalisme environnemental est mesuré au-delà des normes du droit constitutionnel. Le droit français, comme système typique doté de plusieurs ordres juridictionnels, est privilégié à travers un premier ensemble de contributions. Simon Jolivet explique la mise en œuvre de la Charte de l'environnement en droit administratif, notamment à travers la jurisprudence du Conseil d'État (chapitre 8). Olivier Cachard s'intéresse à la portée du principe de précaution, codifié dans la Charte de l'environnement, dans le domaine du droit (privé) des affaires au regard de l'État comme actionnaire (chapitre 9). Samuel Ferey contribue avec un point de vue non juridique sur le constitutionnalisme environnemental grâce à une analyse économique des méthodes de réparation du dommage écologique en conformité avec le principe constitutionnel de pollueur-payeur (chapitre 10).

Dans un second temps, une perspective plus large et internationale est adoptée. Sven Kaufmann s'intéresse dans la dernière contribution à la relation entre constitutionnalisme environnemental et droit de l'Union européenne. C'est dans un sens fonctionnel que les traités européens, avec leur dispositif environnemental, remplissent un rôle de Constitution (chapitre 11).

Chapitre 8

Le constitutionnalisme environnemental en droit administratif français : progrès et limites

Chapter 8

Environmental Constitutionalism in French Administrative Law: Progress and Limitations

Simon JOLIVET

Maître de conférences en droit public à l'Université de Poitiers, France
Faculté de droit et des sciences sociales
Institut de droit public (IDP) - EA 2623

Résumé : Poser la question du constitutionnalisme environnemental en droit administratif français, revient à se demander de quelle façon et dans quelle mesure la Charte de l'environnement exerce sur lui sa suprématie. Pour y répondre, il faut d'abord s'interroger sur les indicateurs permettant d'évaluer une telle suprématie. Trois indicateurs du constitutionnalisme environnemental en droit administratif sont proposés au fil de la recherche : l'invocabilité de la Charte de l'environnement par les justiciables devant le juge administratif, l'évolution du contenu des normes administratives et la contribution à l'amélioration du niveau de protection de l'environnement. À la lumière de ces indicateurs, on peut d'abord affirmer que les progrès du constitutionnalisme environnemental consistent essentiellement en un respect accru de normes existantes. Ensuite ses limites résident toujours, bien que dans une moindre mesure, dans le phénomène des écrans normatifs, qu'ils soient législatif, conventionnel ou constitutionnel. L'influence de la Charte de l'environnement pour l'évolution du contenu des normes est, enfin, difficile à évaluer.

Abstract: This paper explores how and to what extent the French constitutional Environmental Charter, entered into force in 2005, controls French administrative law. Three indicators of environmental constitutionalism are proposed in order to assess this supremacy: the justiciability of the Environmental Charter before the administrative courts, the evolution of the content of administrative norms since 2005, and the Charter's contribution to improving the level of environmental protection. Progress in environmental constitutionalism since 2005 has come from better compliance with existing norms at the legislative level. However normative "screens" continue to limit environmental constitutionalism. Moreover, it remains difficult to assess the way the Environmental Charter has influenced the evolution of the content of administrative norms.

I) Introduction

L'objet de notre contribution est une réflexion sur ce que peut signifier le constitutionnalisme environnemental[431] en droit administratif français, sur ce qu'ont été ses progrès mais aussi ses limites depuis l'entrée en vigueur de la Charte de l'environnement (1er mars 2005).

Le droit administratif étant notre champ privilégié d'investigation, les normes juridiques infraconstitutionnelles qui nous intéressent sont donc d'abord les actes administratifs pris dans le champ de l'environnement, et au-delà si nécessaire (la Charte a-t-elle un impact sur d'autres secteurs du droit administratif ?). De plus, ce sont aussi les normes juridiques infraconstitutionnelles qui s'interposent entre la Charte et les actes administratifs, mais seulement dans la mesure où elles s'interposent : c'est d'ailleurs le problème central de notre réflexion.

Plus précisément, la question est la suivante : de quelle façon et dans quelle mesure la Charte de l'environnement exerce-t-elle sa suprématie sur le droit administratif ? Pour y répondre, une question liminaire s'impose : comment évalue-t-on cette suprématie, ce qui revient à poser la question des indicateurs du constitutionnalisme environnemental ?

En juriste positiviste, on pense d'abord et avant tout à l'invocabilité de la Charte de l'environnement par les justiciables devant le juge administratif, et corrélativement à la sanction (juridictionnelle) des actes administratifs contraires à la Charte. On y pense d'autant plus naturellement que la Charte reprend, dans une large mesure, des principes législatifs pour les hisser au niveau constitutionnel. Dès lors, un des indicateurs de l'influence de la Charte sur le droit administratif pourrait être de se demander si celle-ci a amélioré le respect des normes environnementales existantes. L'essentiel de notre contribution sera ainsi

---

431 Entendu comme la doctrine fondée sur l'idée de la suprématie de normes environnementales inscrites dans la Constitution sur les normes juridiques infra-constitutionnelles. V. James R. May, Erin Daly, *Global environmental constitutionalism*, Cambridge University Press, 2014.

consacré à cette question, grâce à une analyse du contentieux devant les juridictions administratives et en particulier devant le Conseil d'État.

Toutefois, nous sommes conscients des limites de cette approche : d'une part, le contentieux n'est toujours que la « dimension pathologique du droit », selon la formule de Jean Carbonnier[432] ; d'autre part, pour reprendre les termes de Xavier Bioy, constitutionnaliser consiste certes à « refonder des dispositions existantes et des objets consacrés » mais aussi « à fournir une base, un terreau constitutionnel, sur lequel de nouvelles règles naîtront »[433]. Pour être plus complet dans l'analyse de l'influence de la Charte de l'environnement sur le droit administratif, il faudrait donc aussi s'interroger sur une éventuelle évolution du contenu des normes administratives, de l'écriture du droit administratif suite à l'entrée en vigueur de la Charte, soit par l'adoption de nouveaux textes, soit par la modification de textes existants. Nous y reviendrons en conclusion.

Pour revenir à l'interrogation centrale de notre contribution, il nous semble qu'il y a un paradoxe au cœur du sujet. D'un côté, les normes constitutionnelles étant (en droit interne du moins) au sommet de la hiérarchie des normes, et les actes administratifs au plus bas, c'est bien vis-à-vis de ces derniers que la suprématie de la Constitution devrait en principe s'imposer avec le plus de force. Ce n'est pourtant pas certain. En effet, d'un autre côté, cet écart dans la hiérarchie des normes entre la Constitution et les actes administratifs est tellement grand qu'il est fréquemment comblé par des normes intermédiaires. On veut bien évidemment parler de la loi, à laquelle renvoie précisément un certain nombre d'articles de la charte – c'est d'ailleurs une de ses spécificités. Mais on veut aussi parler des sources externes supra-législatives, que sont les traités internationaux et les instruments de droit dérivé de l'Union européenne. Or, autant la confrontation directe entre les articles de la Charte de l'environnement et les actes administratifs permet à la Charte de déployer ses pleins effets, autant l'interposition de normes intermédiaires entre la Charte et les actes administratifs peut rendre plus incertain l'exercice de sa suprématie. C'est le thème bien connu de l'écran, qu'il soit législatif, conventionnel voire constitutionnel.

---

432 Jean Carbonnier, *Flexible droit. Pour une sociologie du droit sans rigueur*, LGDJ, 10e éd., 2001 (rééd. 2014).

433 Xavier Bioy, « L'environnement, nouvel objet du droit constitutionnel ou : qu'est-ce que "constitutionnaliser" ? », *in* : Henry Roussillon, Xavier Bioy, Stéphane Mouton (dir.), *Les nouveaux objets du droit constitutionnel*, Presses de l'Université des sciences sociales de Toulouse, 2006, p. 25.

Il nous semble précisément que l'appréciation (forcément subjective) de l'influence que la Charte exerce sur le droit administratif de l'environnement varie en fonction de l'absence ou de la présence d'un troisième terme et du troisième terme considéré, loi ou norme externe. Ainsi, on verra dans un premier temps que le principal progrès du constitutionnalisme environnemental consiste dans un respect accru de normes existantes (II), puis que ses principales limites résident – de façon variable, et parfois ambivalente – dans le phénomène des écrans normatifs, qu'ils soient législatif, conventionnel ou constitutionnel (III).

II) Le respect accru de normes existantes, progrès du constitutionnalisme environnemental

La consécration de la Charte de l'environnement comme source de légalité administrative, catalysée par l'arrêt *Commune d'Annecy*[434], a entraîné des effets en cascade ; il s'agit d'une réévaluation multidimensionnelle des normes environnementales (A), dont le décloisonnement des principes du droit de l'environnement est une manifestation particulière (B).

A) Une réévaluation multidimensionnelle des normes environnementales

Nous prendrons ici deux illustrations : celle des procédures d'urgence, et (surtout) celle de l'appréciation de l'utilité publique.

S'agissant d'abord des procédures d'urgence, on ne peut ici passer sous silence la très fameuse ordonnance du tribunal administratif de Châlons-en-Champagne du 29 avril 2005[435] qui, moins de deux mois après l'entrée en vigueur de la Charte, suspend un arrêté préfectoral autorisant un teknival dans un site Natura 2000 en raison de son risque grave d'atteinte au droit à l'environnement. Par la même occasion, le droit à l'environnement est reconnu comme une liberté fondamentale, condition indispensable à l'obtention de la suspension d'un acte administratif dans le cadre du référé-liberté. Or c'est bien parce que le

---

[434] CE, Ass., 3 octobre 2008, n° 297931.

[435] TA Châlons-en-Champagne, 29 avril 2005, *Conservatoire du patrimoine naturel et autres*, n° 0500828.

droit à l'environnement, déjà présent dans la loi depuis 1995[436], a été hissé au niveau constitutionnel par la Charte, que le juge de l'urgence de Châlons-en-Champagne accepte de le faire accéder au niveau d'une liberté fondamentale dans le cadre du contentieux de l'urgence, permettant ainsi la suspension de mesures néfastes à l'environnement. Toutefois, le regard que l'on peut porter, avec le recul, sur cette décision prometteuse est mitigé : même si elle n'a jamais été infirmée par le Conseil d'État, elle apparaît tout de même assez esseulée, cet isolement produisant un curieux décalage par rapport au flot de commentaires dont elle a fait l'objet.

Bien que cela soit moins spectaculaire que la décision du tribunal administratif de Châlons-en-Champagne en matière de référé-liberté, le recours au référé-suspension – et ses chances de succès – ont également été accrus dans le domaine environnemental depuis l'entrée en vigueur de la Charte de l'environnement[437].

S'agissant ensuite de l'appréciation de l'utilité publique, les éléments environnementaux étaient, certes, présents dans le contrôle du bilan opéré par le Conseil d'État en matière de déclaration d'utilité publique, et ce bien avant la Charte de l'environnement. Mais ils ne pesaient traditionnellement pas bien lourds, dans la balance, face aux avantages économiques et sociaux avancés par les porteurs de projet[438].

Au moment de l'entrée en vigueur de la Charte de l'environnement, des auteurs tels que Jean Untermaier avaient prédit, en cas de contentieux, la modification de l'appréciation de l'utilité publique par le juge qui en résulterait : « la reconnaissance du droit à l'environnement devrait se traduire par une réévaluation écologique des éléments du bilan »[439].

---

436 Article L. 110-2 du Code de l'environnement, dans sa rédaction issue de la loi n° 95–101 du 2 février 1995 relative au renforcement de la protection de l'environnement (dite « loi Barnier »), *JORF* du 3 février 1995, p. 1840.

437 Sur ce point, v. Delphine Hédary, « Les effets de la Charte de l'environnement sur le droit de l'environnement », *in* : Carolina Cerda-Guzman, Florian Savonitto (dir.), *Les 10 ans de la Charte de l'environnement 2005–2015*, Institut universitaire Varenne, 2016, p. 198.

438 V. notamment Michel Prieur *et al.*, *Droit de l'environnement*, Précis Dalloz, 7e éd., 2016, p. 81–82.

439 Jean Untermaier, « La Charte de l'environnement face au droit administratif », *in* « La Charte constitutionnelle de l'environnement en vigueur », *Revue juridique de l'environnement*, n° spécial, 2005, p. 159.

C'est ce qui s'est effectivement produit avec l'arrêt d'assemblée du Conseil d'État rendu le 12 avril 2013, *Association coordination interrégionale stop THT*[440]. En l'espèce, c'est le principe de précaution qui était en jeu. Le principe de précaution est classiquement utilisé par le juge dans son contrôle du bilan en matière d'utilité publique, dès avant la constitutionnalisation[441]. Là ne réside donc pas la nouveauté. Ce qui change avec l'arrêt *Stop THT*, c'est que le principe de précaution devient un élément autonome d'appréciation de l'utilité publique par le juge administratif, indépendamment du contrôle du bilan, et préalablement à celui-ci. Dans cet arrêt, le Conseil d'État considère en effet pour la première fois « qu'une opération qui méconnaît les exigences du principe de précaution ne peut légalement être déclarée d'utilité publique ». L'émancipation du principe de précaution par rapport au contrôle du bilan est manifestement le signe que le juge administratif lui accorde une plus grande importance, du fait de sa constitutionnalisation.

Par ailleurs, l'un des effets les plus tangibles de la constitutionnalisation de certains principes du droit de l'environnement est leur décloisonnement, autrement dit leur application à des matières connexes à l'environnement.

B) Un décloisonnement des principes du droit de l'environnement

Ici aussi, c'est le principe de précaution qui peut fournir une illustration de ce décloisonnement, dans ses rapports avec la santé publique et le droit de l'urbanisme. Lorsque le principe de précaution était simplement de niveau législatif, son application en droit de l'urbanisme (notamment vis-à-vis de la délivrance d'autorisations d'urbanisme) se voyait systématiquement opposer le principe prétorien[442] d'indépendance des législations. On rappellera que ce principe interdit en substance d'appliquer à une autorisation relevant d'une législation donnée (en l'espèce l'urbanisme), les dispositions d'une autre législation (en l'espèce l'environnement) dont la mise en œuvre serait susceptible d'en limiter la réalisation. Le refus de contrôler la délivrance d'une

---

[440] N° 342409 : *Actualité juridique de droit administratif (AJDA)*, 2013, p. 1046, note Xavier Domino, Aurélie Bretonneau.

[441] V. par ex. CE, 28 juillet 1999, *Association intercommunale « Morbihan sous très haute tension »*, n° 184268.

[442] CE, 1er juillet 1959, *Sieur Piard*, *Rec.*, p. 513.

autorisation d'urbanisme par rapport au principe de précaution avait été affirmé une fois encore par le Conseil d'État le 20 avril 2005 (soit un peu plus d'un mois après l'entrée en vigueur de la Charte, mais pour des faits antérieurs), dans un arrêt *Société Bouygues télécom*[443].

Attendu, le revirement de jurisprudence s'est finalement produit avec l'arrêt du 19 juillet 2010, *Association du Quartier les Hauts de Choiseul*[444] : pour la première fois, le Conseil d'État reconnaît l'invocabilité du principe de précaution à l'encontre d'une autorisation d'urbanisme. En effet, si le principe d'indépendance des législations – qui concerne les rapports des *législations* entre elles, comme son nom l'indique – peut être opposé à une norme législative, il doit s'incliner devant la norme constitutionnelle que le principe de précaution est entre-temps devenu. La portée de la décision *Association du Quartier les Hauts de Choiseul* va sans doute au-delà du principe de précaution : certains auteurs, tel Philippe Prével, n'hésitent pas à soutenir que le principe d'indépendance des législations est vraisemblablement écarté pour toute la Charte[445].

Cette affirmation mérite toutefois d'être nuancée. En effet, le décloisonnement des principes du droit de l'environnement, du fait de leur constitutionnalisation, n'est pas sans limites.

D'abord, les effets du décloisonnement sont susceptibles d'être relativisés par les conditions imposées à l'application d'un article de la Charte dans un autre domaine que l'environnement[446]. C'est précisément le cas dans les rapports entre le principe de précaution et le droit de l'urbanisme : dans un arrêt *Société Orange France* du 21 octobre 2013[447], le Conseil d'État a précisé dans un sens restrictif l'opposabilité du principe de précaution aux autorisations d'urbanisme. Ainsi, l'article 5 de la Charte ne saurait permettre de « refuser légalement la délivrance d'une autorisation d'urbanisme en l'absence d'éléments circonstanciés

---

443 *AJDA* 2005, p. 1191, concl. Yann Aguila.

444 V. notamment Julien Bétaille, « Le décloisonnement du principe de précaution, un effet de sa constitutionnalisation », *Droit de l'environnement*, n° 182, septembre 2010, p. 278–279.

445 Philippe Prével, « La Charte de l'environnement, l'administration et le Conseil d'État : applicabilité ou invocabilité de la Charte ? », *Revue française de droit administratif*, 2014, p. 773.

446 V. notamment Nicolas Marty, « Les effets de la Charte de l'environnement en droit de l'urbanisme », *in* : Carolina Cerda-Guzman, Florian Savonitto (dir.), *Les 10 ans de la Charte de l'environnement 2005–2015*, cité, p. 211.

447 *RDI*, 2014, p. 61, note Pierre Soler-Couteaux.

sur l'existence, en l'état des connaissances scientifiques, de risques, même incertains, de nature à justifier un tel refus d'autorisation » (considérant 7). Or « la Charte de l'environnement n'habilite pas, par elle-même, le maire d'une commune à exiger la production de documents non prévue par les textes législatifs ou réglementaires en vigueur » (considérant 8).

Ensuite, toutes les normes administratives ne peuvent pas être contrôlées vis-à-vis de la Charte de l'environnement : encore faut-il qu'elles entrent dans son champ d'application *ratione materiae*. Or le Conseil d'État a par exemple une conception restrictive de la notion de décision ayant une incidence sur l'environnement[448], laquelle détermine si une mesure administrative entre ou non dans le champ d'application de l'article 7 sur le droit à l'information et à la participation.

Enfin, il n'est pas possible à une autorité publique d'invoquer la Charte de l'environnement pour adopter un acte administratif dès lors qu'elle ne possède pas de compétences dans le domaine concerné, et ce même si elle a l'intention de prendre une mesure ambitieuse du point de vue de la protection de l'environnement. Le Conseil d'État a ainsi été conduit à préciser la répartition des compétences des autorités publiques pour la mise en œuvre du principe de précaution. Dans un considérant de principe utilisé tant en matière de police des ondes électromagnétiques[449] que de police des organismes génétiquement modifiés (OGM)[450], il a affirmé que « le principe de précaution, s'il est applicable à toute autorité publique dans ses domaines d'attributions, ne saurait avoir ni pour objet ni pour effet de permettre à une autorité publique d'excéder son champ de compétence et d'intervenir en dehors de ses domaines d'attributions ». En conséquence le maire ne pouvait pas, sur le fondement de sa police administrative générale, adopter dans un cas une réglementation limitant l'implantation d'antennes relais, et dans l'autre interdire les OGM sur le territoire de sa commune. En effet, une police spéciale existe dans ces deux domaines, qui a été confiée aux autorités de l'État central.

La relativité du décloisonnement des principes du droit de l'environnement est-elle une première limite du constitutionnalisme environnemental ? On

448 En ce sens, v. notamment Aude Farinetti, « L'utilisation du principe de participation dans le cadre de la QPC : la Charte contre elle-même ? », *Environnement et développement durable*, décembre 2014, étude 17.

449 CE, Ass., 26 octobre 2011, *Commune de Saint-Denis*, n° 326492 : *AJDA*, 2011, p. 2219, chron. Jacques-Henri Stahl, Xavier Domino.

450 CE, 24 septembre 2012, *Commune de Valence*, n° 342990 : *JCP A*, 2013, n° 1, p. 49, note Philippe Billet.

peut l'affirmer dans une certaine mesure, tout en ayant conscience que le respect de la répartition des compétences est une exigence importante dans le cadre d'un État de droit. D'autres limites, au moins aussi sérieuses, pourraient résulter du phénomène des écrans normatifs.

III) Les écrans normatifs, limites du constitutionnalisme environnemental ?

Le phénomène des écrans normatifs est polymorphe dans la jurisprudence administrative ; il peut ainsi concerner les rapports de la Constitution avec la loi, ou avec les normes externes. Or, autant l'écran législatif, en tant qu'obstacle au constitutionnalisme environnemental, semble avoir été partiellement contourné (A), autant la situation paraît plus incertaine s'agissant des conflits avec les normes externes (B).

A) L'écran législatif : un obstacle au constitutionnalisme environnemental partiellement contourné

Identifiée dès le départ comme une limitation potentielle de la portée de la Charte[451], la théorie de l'écran législatif n'est évidemment pas propre à la matière environnementale : c'est potentiellement un obstacle à l'effectivité de la suprématie de l'ensemble des dispositions constitutionnelles par rapport aux actes administratifs, dès lors qu'une loi s'interpose entre ces deux normes. Mais la particularité de la Charte de l'environnement est que certains de ces articles renvoient expressément au législateur le soin de mettre en œuvre la disposition constitutionnelle (articles 3, 4, et 7), alors que d'autres (ceux que l'on n'a pas cités) n'opèrent pas un tel renvoi. Fallait-il alors faire une différence entre ces articles, du point de vue de leur invocabilité à l'encontre d'une décision administrative en présence d'une loi-écran ?

La présentation de la situation actuelle exige de la nuance. Certes, le principe de l'écran législatif est maintenu car en présence d'une loi de mise en œuvre de la Charte de l'environnement, celle-ci n'est en principe pas invocable devant le juge administratif. Ceci vaut pour les articles de la Charte qui renvoient à la loi[452], comme pour ceux qui n'envisagent pas

---

[451] Jean Untermaier, cité, *RJE*, n° spécial 2005, p. 146.

[452] CE, 23 avril 2009, *France nature environnement*, n° 306242 : *AJDA*, 2009, p. 858.

une telle intervention[453]. Toutefois, les méfaits de l'écran législatif pour le respect de la hiérarchie des normes sont atténués, du fait de la convergence de plusieurs phénomènes.

D'abord, grâce à une évolution de la jurisprudence du Conseil d'État, on peut considérer que le constitutionnalisme environnemental a progressé en droit administratif. Ainsi, une nouvelle[454] forme d'écran législatif « transparent » (autrement dit, qui laisse passer la Constitution) a été reconnue, à propos de la Charte de l'environnement, par l'arrêt du 12 juillet 2013 *Fédération nationale de la pêche en France*[455]. Il vise le cas des dispositions réglementaires d'application d'une loi qui ne se bornent pas à tirer les conséquences nécessaires de cette loi. Un contrôle de constitutionnalité de ces dispositions réglementaires est possible dans la mesure où ils ajoutent à la loi. En l'espèce il s'agissait d'une loi de mise en œuvre de l'article 3, lequel renvoie à la loi. Mais selon Philippe Prével, « la possibilité de l'écran-transparent devrait logiquement être *a fortiori* étendue pour les articles de la Charte qui ne comportent pas de renvoi »[456]. L'arrêt *Ban Asbestos France* du 26 février 2014[457] va dans ce sens, en confirmant la solution de *Fédération nationale de la pêche en France* mais pour l'article 1 sur le droit à l'environnement, lequel ne comporte pas de renvoi à la loi.

Rendre l'écran législatif transparent pour censurer les vices propres à l'acte réglementaire d'application d'une loi est un premier moyen, issu de la jurisprudence administrative, de contourner cette théorie jurisprudentielle discutable.

Mais il existe ensuite un autre moyen, potentiellement beaucoup plus important, de contourner l'écran législatif. Il est issu de la révision constitutionnelle du 23 juillet 2008, entrée en vigueur le 1er mars 2010 : on veut bien entendu parler de la possibilité de déposer une question prioritaire de constitutionnalité (QPC) en matière environnementale. La QPC remédie dans une certaine mesure aux inconvénients de la théorie de la loi-écran, car aujourd'hui si un justiciable estime qu'un

---

453 CE, 19 juin 2006, *Assoc. Eau et rivières de Bretagne*, n° 284456.

454 Auparavant, l'écran législatif « transparent » avait été reconnu pour les lois d'habilitation, ne contenant pas de dispositions de fond : CE, 17 mai 1991, *Quintin*, n° 100436.

455 Req. n° 344522.

456 Philippe Prével, cité, *RFDA*, 2014, p. 773.

457 Req. n° 351514.

acte administratif est contraire à la Constitution tout en sachant que celui-ci est conforme à la loi dont il tire son fondement, il peut soulever l'exception d'inconstitutionnalité de la loi au cours du litige. Toutefois, le Conseil constitutionnel, saisi par renvoi du Conseil d'État, n'acceptera de se prononcer que si la QPC porte sur l'atteinte à un « droit » ou une « liberté » que la Constitution garantit[458]. Or tous les articles de la Charte n'entrent pas dans cette catégorie. Ainsi, les juges de la rue Montpensier ont refusé de qualifier de la sorte le principe de conciliation des piliers environnemental, économique et social du développement durable (article 6 de la Charte)[459], et évité pour l'instant de se prononcer à propos du principe de précaution (article 5)[460]. Il reste que l'introduction de la QPC a bel et bien favorisé certains progrès du constitutionnalisme environnemental en droit administratif. Preuve en est l'abondance des QPC déposées devant le juge administratif sur le droit à la participation du public (article 7 de la Charte)[461], et surtout l'effet qu'elles ont eu. Ce sont clairement elles qui ont poussé le législateur à la modernisation du cadre de la participation du public aux décisions réglementaires, avec l'adoption de la loi du 27 décembre 2012[462].

Si, comme nous venons de le voir, les méfaits de l'écran législatif pour le constitutionnalisme environnemental ont été progressivement atténués, qu'en est-il maintenant lorsque c'est une norme externe qui s'interpose entre la Charte de l'environnement et un acte administratif ?

B) Les conflits avec une norme externe : le constitutionnalisme environnemental contre lui-même ?

L'hypothèse visée ici est celle où ce n'est pas (ou pas seulement) une loi qui s'interpose entre la Charte de l'environnement et un acte administratif, mais une norme externe[463]. La question que fait

458 Article 61-1 de la Constitution du 4 octobre 1958 (dans sa version issue de la révision constitutionnelle du 23 juillet 2008).

459 CC, 23 novembre 2012, décision n° 2012-283 QPC.

460 V. notamment CC, 11 octobre 2013, décision n° 2013-346 QPC.

461 V. notamment CC, 13 juillet 2012, décision n° 2012-262 QPC ; CC, 23 novembre 2012, décisions n° 2012-282 et 2012-283 QPC.

462 Loi n° 2012-1460 relative à la mise en œuvre du principe de participation du public défini à l'article 7 de la Charte de l'environnement, *JORF* du 28 décembre 2012.

463 Par norme externe, précisons que nous entendons à la fois une norme relevant du droit international public, mais aussi (sans nier les spécificités) une norme issue du droit de l'Union européenne.

surgir ce conflit de normes, dans la perspective d'une réflexion sur le constitutionnalisme environnemental, est double : premièrement, en cas de conflit entre la Charte de l'environnement et une norme externe, laquelle des deux s'impose en dernier ressort face à un acte administratif ? Deuxièmement, la protection de l'environnement sort-elle nécessairement gagnante d'un progrès du constitutionnalisme environnemental, si la Charte de l'environnement s'avère moins ambitieuse que le texte de droit international ou européen de l'environnement avec lequel elle est susceptible d'être en conflit ?

Il n'y a pas de réponse univoque à ces questions, car deux variables entrent en ligne de compte. La première variable est relative au type d'écran : écran constitutionnel[464] ou écran conventionnel[465]. La deuxième variable est relative au type de norme externe : norme issue du droit international « classique », ou du droit de l'Union européenne.

Les relations entre la Charte de l'environnement et les normes externes ayant déjà été analysées dans leur richesse et leur complexité[466], nous voudrions simplement insister ici sur les deux hypothèses qui, d'un point de vue théorique, sont les plus susceptibles de bousculer nos idées préconçues à propos du constitutionnalisme environnemental. L'alternative, certes caricaturale, est la suivante : faire primer la Charte au risque d'une régression des normes environnementales, ou faire primer la norme externe au détriment du constitutionnalisme environnemental.

La première hypothèse, sans doute la plus problématique, est celle de l'écran constitutionnel[467]. En effet, dans l'arrêt d'assemblée *Sarran et Levacher* du 30 octobre 1998 (qui ne concernait donc pas spécifiquement la Charte)[468], le Conseil d'État procède à une interprétation littérale de l'article 55 de la Constitution (qui n'évoque que la supériorité des traités sur les lois et non sur la Constitution) et refuse de censurer des

---

464 Lorsqu'une loi (et/ou son acte réglementaire d'application), mettant en œuvre une disposition constitutionnelle, risque de contrevenir à une norme externe.

465 Lorsqu'une loi (et/ou son acte réglementaire d'application), mettant en œuvre une norme externe, est susceptible de contrevenir à la Constitution.

466 V. notamment Hubert Delzangles, « La Charte de l'environnement et les normes externes », *in* : Carolina Cerda-Guzman, Florian Savonitto (dir.), *Les 10 ans de la Charte de l'environnement 2005–2015*, cité, p. 153.

467 Le problème avait été perçu précocement par Marie-Anne Cohendet, « Les effets de la réforme », *in* « La Charte constitutionnelle en débat », *RJE*, n° spécial 2003, spécialement p. 154–156.

468 *RFDA* 1998, p. 1081, concl. Christine Maugüé, note Denis Alland.

normes nationales mettant en œuvre la Constitution au nom de leur incompatibilité vis-à-vis d'engagements internationaux[469]. Il n'est donc pas possible, devant le juge administratif, d'invoquer le droit international de l'environnement contre la Charte, ni par extension contre un acte réglementaire d'application de la Charte. Or l'on sait que, par exemple, le droit international peut être plus ambitieux sur le principe de participation[470], ou encore sur celui de précaution[471]. La théorie de l'écran constitutionnel est bien un élément de constitutionnalisme environnemental (au sens formel de la suprématie de la norme environnementale constitutionnelle sur les normes inférieures), mais ne risque-t-elle pas de se traduire par une régression du niveau de protection de l'environnement, si la norme internationale est plus ambitieuse ?

La deuxième hypothèse est spécifique aux rapports entre le droit français et le droit de l'Union européenne : c'est celle de l'écran conventionnel vis-à-vis d'une norme de droit européen dérivé. Dans l'arrêt d'assemblée *Société Arcelor Atlantique et Lorraine* du 8 février 2007[472], le Conseil d'État était saisi de la conformité au principe constitutionnel d'égalité d'un décret de transposition d'une directive sur les quotas d'émission de gaz à effet de serre. Il opère, pour résumer, une conciliation entre l'affirmation de la suprématie de la Constitution sur le droit international (fondée sur l'article 55 de la Constitution) et la spécificité du droit de l'Union (matérialisée notamment par l'exigence de transposition des directives de l'article 88-1 de la Constitution). La haute juridiction indique qu'il faut d'abord rechercher s'il existe une règle ou un principe général du droit communautaire équivalent au principe constitutionnel invoqué. Dans l'affirmative et au cas où un problème sérieux de compatibilité de la directive vis-à-vis du droit primaire se pose, le Conseil renverra la question de la validité de la directive à la Cour de justice de l'Union européenne via le mécanisme du renvoi

---

469 L'affaire concernait certes un traité issu du droit international « classique », mais la solution fut transposée sans surprise à propos du droit de l'Union : CE, 3 décembre 2001, *Syndicat national de l'industrie pharmaceutique*, req. n° 226514.

470 Convention d'Aarhus sur l'accès à l'information, la participation du public au processus décisionnel et l'accès à la justice en matière d'environnement (signée le 25 juin 1998).

471 V. par exemple le Principe 15 de la déclaration de Rio sur l'environnement et le développement (1992), ou le Protocole de Cartagena sur les risques biotechnologiques (signé le 29 janvier 2000).

472 *RFDA* 2007, p. 384, concl. Mattias Guyomar.

préjudiciel (sinon il écartera lui-même le moyen). Dans l'hypothèse inverse, le juge administratif examine directement la constitutionnalité de la disposition réglementaire (et donc indirectement la directive elle-même) et motive ce contrôle par l'appartenance en propre du principe invoqué à l'identité constitutionnelle française. Il y a toutefois peu de chances pour que cette réserve de constitutionnalité s'applique vis-à-vis de la Charte de l'environnement, précisément parce que son contenu est fortement influencé par les sources externes[473]. Dans son arrêt *Confédération paysanne et autres* du 3 octobre 2016, qui actualise la jurisprudence *Arcelor*, le Conseil d'État a d'ailleurs confirmé que le principe de précaution, tel qu'énoncé par l'article 191 du Traité sur le fonctionnement de l'Union européenne et tel qu'interprété par la Cour de justice, a « une portée garantissant l'effectivité du respect » du principe constitutionnel de précaution[474].

L'impact de la Charte de l'environnement sur le droit administratif transposant une directive est donc faible : le constitutionnalisme environnemental s'efface derrière ce que l'on pourrait appeler le « communautarisme environnemental ». La protection de l'environnement y perd-elle ? Ce n'est pas certain car les normes européennes sont souvent ambitieuses en matière environnementale, aussi sinon davantage que la Charte.

En tous cas, pour conclure sur les conflits entre la Charte et les normes externes, il nous semble que la réflexion sur le constitutionnalisme environnemental ne devrait pas considérer la question de la suprématie des dispositions constitutionnelles isolément de la finalité de la norme environnementale, qui est d'aboutir à une meilleure protection de l'environnement. Même en étant positiviste il est difficile d'écarter cette considération, dans la mesure où les auteurs s'accordent pour fonder la définition du droit de l'environnement sur un critère finaliste[475]. De plus, la question de la finalité est inhérente à la notion d'effectivité, comme l'a montré Julien Bétaille, pour qui l'effectivité est « le degré d'influence qu'exerce la norme juridique sur les faits au regard de sa

---

473 En ce sens, Hubert Delzangles, « La Charte de l'environnement et les normes externes », *in* : Carolina Cerda-Guzman, Florian Savonitto (dir.), *Les 10 ans de la Charte de l'environnement 2005–2015*, cité.

474 *AJDA*, 2017, p. 288, note Fanny Tarlet, Guillaume Léonard.

475 V. notamment Michel Prieur *et al.*, *Droit de l'environnement*, cité, p. 8–9.

propre finalité »[476]. Or *in fine* c'est bien l'effectivité de la protection de l'environnement qui nous intéresse, et dont on cherche à savoir si elle est améliorée ou non par le constitutionnalisme environnemental. Après l'invocabilité de la Charte de l'environnement par les justiciables devant le juge administratif, et (avant) l'évolution du contenu des normes administratives (dont nous allons brièvement parler en conclusion), la contribution à l'amélioration du niveau de protection de l'environnement (ou du moins sa non-régression) pourrait être un troisième indicateur du constitutionnalisme environnemental.

IV) Conclusion

Nonobstant les difficultés susmentionnées liées aux écrans normatifs en tous genres (législatif, conventionnel, constitutionnel), il est indéniable que la Charte de l'environnement a permis un respect accru de normes environnementales existantes au niveau législatif, du fait des conséquences tirées par le juge de leur élévation dans la hiérarchie des normes.

Cet élément est important du point de vue du constitutionnalisme environnemental, mais paraît un peu réducteur. D'abord il nous semble, comme nous l'avons indiqué en introduction, qu'il ne faudrait pas réduire la réflexion sur le constitutionnalisme environnemental au seul contentieux. Ensuite, mais les deux éléments sont liés, il nous semble également qu'il ne faudrait pas réduire la réflexion au respect des normes existantes, mais envisager aussi l'évolution de leur contenu pour une meilleure protection de l'environnement.

Pour le dire autrement, qu'en est-il de l'influence de la Charte de l'environnement sur l'écriture des normes, sur leur contenu ? Le droit de l'environnement a incontestablement évolué depuis l'entrée en vigueur de la Charte de l'environnement, avec un certain nombre de lois importantes (loi sur les parcs du 14 avril 2006[477], loi sur la responsabilité environnementale du 1er août 2008[478],

[476] Julien Bétaille, Les conditions juridiques de l'effectivité de la norme en droit public interne : illustrations en droit de l'urbanisme et en droit de l'environnement, Thèse (sous la direction de Michel Prieur), Limoges, 2012, p. 22.

[477] Loi n° 2006-436, *JORF* du 15 avril 2006.

[478] Loi n° 2008-757, *JORF* du 2 août 2008.

lois « Grenelle » 1 et 2 en 2009[479] et 2010[480], loi sur la transition énergétique du 17 août 2015[481], loi « biodiversité » du 8 août 2016[482], etc.), immanquablement suivies de nombreux décrets d'application. Pour autant, quel a été l'impact de la Charte sur cette évolution ? Delphine Hédary, qui fut responsable de la préparation de la Charte, jugeait en 2015 que « la Charte a eu peu d'effets sur le contenu des exigences environnementales »[483]. Pour le dire autrement, on a souvent l'impression que la Charte vient *après* les sources externes en tant que moteur de l'évolution des normes environnementales, même s'il est difficile d'apprécier leurs influences respectives, étant donné l'enchevêtrement particulièrement prégnant des ordres juridiques en droit de l'environnement. L'évolution du droit de la participation du public (surtout la loi du 27 décembre 2012 déjà citée, et l'ordonnance du 5 août 2013[484]) est, certes, directement imputable à la Charte et surtout à son interprétation par les juges. Mais il n'en va pas de même, par exemple, pour la loi sur la responsabilité environnementale du 1er août 2008 : alors que l'article 4 de la Charte porte précisément sur la responsabilité environnementale, c'est bien le droit de l'Union européenne (avec la directive du 21 avril 2004[485]) qui a constitué le chaînon indispensable entre le droit constitutionnel et le régime de police administrative que transpose la loi du 1er août 2008[486].

Que manque-t-il à la Charte pour influencer le contenu des normes, peser réellement sur leur évolution ? Du temps, sans doute (douze ans, c'est court pour juger un texte constitutionnel), et peut-être l'infusion dans les esprits – à défaut de sa constitutionnalisation,

---

479 Loi n° 2009-967 du 3 août 2009, *JORF* du 5 août 2009.

480 Loi n° 2010-788 du 12 juillet 2010, *JORF* du 13 juillet 2010.

481 Loi n° 2015-992, *JORF* du 18 août 2015.

482 Loi n° 2016-1087, *JORF* du 9 août 2016.

483 Delphine Hédary, citée, *in* :: Carolina Cerda-Guzman, Florian Savonitto (dir.), *Les 10 ans de la Charte de l'environnement 2005–2015*, cité, p. 198.

484 Ordonnance n° 2013-714, *JORF* du 6 août 2013.

485 Directive 2004/35/CE du Parlement européen et du Conseil sur la responsabilité environnementale en ce qui concerne la prévention et la réparation des dommages environnementaux, *JOUE*, L 143 du 30 avril 2004, p. 56.

486 Sur cette question, v. plus largement Agathe Van Lang, « L'enracinement constitutionnel de la responsabilité environnementale », *in* : Chantal Cans (dir.),

qui paraît politiquement difficile – du principe de non-régression, cher à Michel Prieur[487] et entendu comme un principe de progrès (continu) du droit de l'environnement[488].

La responsabilité environnementale. Prévention, imputation, réparation, Dalloz, 2009, p. 45.

487 V. notamment Michel Prieur, Gonzalo Sozzo (dir.), *La non-régression en droit de l'environnement*, Bruylant, 2012.

488 C'est d'ailleurs l'interprétation à laquelle invite l'article L. 110-1, II, 9°, du Code de l'environnement, dans sa rédaction issue de la loi « biodiversité », qui définit le principe de non-régression comme celui « selon lequel la protection de l'environnement, assurée par les dispositions législatives et réglementaires relatives à l'environnement, ne peut faire l'objet que d'une amélioration constante, compte tenu des connaissances scientifiques et techniques du moment ».

CHAPITRE 9

L'État actionnaire et le principe constitutionnel de précaution

I) Introduction
II) L'État actionnaire n'est pas un actionnaire comme les autres
 A) Les prérogatives de l'actionnaire ordinaire
 B) Les privilèges de l'actionnaire particulier
III) L'État actionnaire est tenu par le principe de précaution consacré par la Charte de l'environnement
 A) L'État actionnaire directement tenu par le principe de précaution
 B) L'État actionnaire indirectement tenu par le principe de précaution
IV) Conclusion

CHAPTER 9

The State as a Shareholder and the Precautionary Principle Enshrined in the French Environmental Charter

I) Introduction
II) The State as a Shareholder is not an Ordinary Shareholder
 A) The Powers of an Ordinary Shareholder
 B) The Prerogatives of a Privileged Shareholder
III) The State as a Shareholder is Bound by the Precautionary Principle

Olivier CACHARD

Agrégé de droit privé et sciences criminelles, Professeur à l'Université de Lorraine, France
Institut François Gény (EA 7301)
Doyen honoraire de la Faculté de droit de Nancy
Avocat à la Cour

Résumé : L'État actionnaire détient fréquemment un bloc de contrôle ou au moins une minorité de blocage dans des entreprises de premier plan sur les marchés sectoriels de l'énergie ou de l'industrie. Ces anciens champions nationaux, aujourd'hui constitués selon les règles du Code de commerce, exercent des activités ayant une forte empreinte environnementale et sanitaire. Comme n'importe quel opérateur de droit privé, ces entreprises sont assujetties au principe de précaution, selon une jurisprudence en plein essor qui consacre l'invocabilité horizontale des règles constitutionnelles. Cependant, les particularismes découlant du contrôle étatique soulèvent la question originale de l'invocabilité verticale des règles constitutionnelles de protection de l'environnement et de la santé humaine. Cette question doit être appréhendée tant d'un point de vue organique que d'un point de vue fonctionnel.

Summary: The French State has created a set of corporate entities that often have majority shares, or at least a "controlling interest" in major players on the European markets of energy and industry. These former "national champions", now incorporated under the ordinary rules of company law, exert influence that have a strong environmental impact, as well as a public health impact. As any private player, these companies must comply with the precautionary principle following the emerging case law related to the horizontal justiciability. However, the peculiarities of State control raise the specific question of the vertical justiciability of environmental constitutional rules. This question is analyzed under the rubric of the organic influence of the State as well as under the functions of State control and in the light of assets and specific representation rules.

I) Introduction

De l'époque des Manufactures royales à la République numérique, l'État français conserve un engouement particulier pour l'intervention sur le marché et la promotion de l'innovation technique[489]. Certes, « [i]l n'existe pas de recensement exhaustif des participations dans les entreprises détenues par l'État actionnaire, entendu au sens large, ni non plus de valorisation globale de son portefeuille »[490]. Mais, les participations directes de l'État français dans des sociétés de droit privé sont comparativement plus importantes que celles des autres États de l'OCDE. Et en 2017, la Cour des comptes estime que l'État détenait 1 800 participations directes dans des sociétés pour plus de 100 milliards d'euros[491]. Il s'agit souvent de participations majoritaires ou, au moins, de minorités de blocage. L'interventionnisme de l'État est étudié à la loupe en droit de l'Union européenne, notamment sous l'angle des aides d'État[492], tout comme il est étudié en droit du commerce international sous l'angle du droit des investissements et du droit des immunités. Paradoxalement, l'État actionnaire était moins étudié en droit public de l'économie[493] et en droit

---

489 L'auteur remercie Madame Francine Mansuy, maître de conférences HDR à la Faculté de droit de Nancy, Institut François Gény, pour l'échange de vues lors de la préparation de ce colloque et pour la richesse des débats lors du colloque organisé par l'Institut François Gény le 26 mars 2018 à l'occasion de l'anniversaire de la Loi n° 2017-399 du 27 mars 2017 relative au devoir de vigilance des sociétés mères et des entreprises donneuses d'ordre, *JO*, 28 mars 2017.

490 Cour des comptes, *L'État actionnaire. Rapport public thématique*, janvier 2017, p. 19 s.

491 *Ibid.*

492 Par exemple, Martine Lombard, « La parole de l'État actionnaire n'est pas une aide d'État », *Revue juridique de l'économie publique*, n° 678, 2010/8, à propos de TPIUE, 21 mai 2010, aff. T-425/04, *République française/Commission*, au sujet du soutien verbal apporté à France Télécom alors que les agences de notation avaient dégradé sa note.

493 Stéphane Braconnier, *Droit public de l'économie*, PUF (Thémis), 2015, p. 361 s., consacrant plusieurs pages aux « entreprises publiques », sans se pencher cependant sur leur gouvernance sous l'angle du droit des sociétés ; Jean-Bernard Auby, « La doctrine de l'État actionnaire », *Droit administratif*, 2014, n° 10.

des sociétés[494], avant que le « patriotisme économique » ne se manifeste avec la « loi Florange »[495]. L'État actionnaire était alors principalement scruté par l'Agence des participations de l'État[496] et, marginalement, par bpifrance pour les PME. La juridiction financière avait également quelque peu délaissé ce volet de l'action publique jusqu'au rapport thématique de la Cour des comptes sur l'État actionnaire rendu en 2017.

Dans la perspective de protection de l'environnement et de la santé humaine qui traverse le mouvement doctrinal du constitutionnalisme environnemental, l'analyse des devoirs de l'État actionnaire est cruciale. En effet, il détient des participations significatives et exerce une influence déterminante sur des sociétés ou des groupes de sociétés ayant, en France et dans le reste du monde, une forte empreinte sanitaire et environnementale. Il suffit de se référer au secteur des industries extractives, au secteur du nucléaire, au secteur de la fourniture et de la distribution d'énergie, au secteur des télécoms, au secteur manufacturier avec un fort impact environnemental, par exemple dans l'automobile avec le récent *Dieselgate* et au secteur industriel ayant un fort impact sanitaire sur ses salariés, avec notamment l'usage de l'amiante. Or l'État, qu'il intervienne sur le marché domestique ou dans le commerce international, se trouve dans une situation originale. Tout en étant législateur et régulateur, il se trouve simultanément être un opérateur soumis aux règles et aux principes qu'il a adoptés. Du point de vue du droit des sociétés, il faut alors se demander si l'État est un actionnaire comme les autres[497]. Du point de vue du droit de l'environnement, il faut également se demander dans quelle mesure l'État actionnaire est assujetti à la constitutionnalisation du droit de l'environnement.

---

494 Philippe Merle, *Droit des sociétés*, 21e éd., Dalloz, 2017, notamment p. 18 sur les sociétés nationalisées et p. 391 s. sur la loi dite Florange ; Georges Ripert, René Roblot, Louis Vogel, *Traité de droit des affaires*, t. 1, 20e éd, LGDJ, 2016, n° 252 sur les sociétés d'économie mixte ; Catherine Malecki, « L'État actionnaire et la gouvernance des entreprises publiques », *D.*, 2005, p. 1028.

495 Loi n° 2014-384 du 29 mars 2014 visant à reconquérir l'économie réelle, notamment signée par le ministre du Redressement productif.

496 Décret n° 2004-963, 9 septembre 2004 portant création du service à compétence nationale « Agence des participations de l'État », *JORF*, 10 septembre 2004, dont l'annexe, modifiée par le décret n° 2013-946, identifie les sociétés relevant du périmètre de l'agence.

497 Bruno Dondero, « L'État, un actionnaire comme les autres ? », *Gaz. Pal.*, 2/12/2015, p. 3.

La Charte de l'environnement, élevée au rang de norme constitutionnelle par la loi n° 2005-205, fixe un ensemble de droits et de devoirs s'imposant aux pouvoirs publics et aux autorités administratives dans leurs domaines de compétences respectives[498]. Le Conseil d'État devait d'ailleurs ensuite décider que la Charte est opposable dans toutes ses dispositions à tous les types de décisions administratives, notamment en matière d'urbanisme[499], et pas seulement aux décisions relevant de la politique environnementale. Parmi ces principes, nous pensons en particulier au *principe de prévention* et au *principe de précaution*. Le *principe de prévention* trouve à s'appliquer aux risques dont l'existence est connue, y compris lorsque leur incidence et leur prévalence sont faibles ; les activités industrielles impliquant l'usage et la production d'amiante ou de rayonnements ionisants entrent dans le champ d'application matériel du *principe de prévention*. Le *principe de précaution*, pour sa part, trouve à s'appliquer lorsque des risques vraisemblables menacent l'environnement et la population pourvu qu'un seuil minimum de scientificité du risque soit franchi. Par exemple, des études épidémiologiques identifient suffisamment les effets sanitaires directs à long terme des champs électromagnétiques (CEM) dans des contextes d'exposition déterminés, pour que les activités industrielles et de service émettant des CEM soient soumises au *principe de précaution*[500].

La formule de l'article 5 de la Charte selon laquelle « [l]es autorités publiques veillent [...] dans leurs domaines d'attributions » n'a pas pour effet de limiter l'invocabilité du principe de précaution à l'invocabilité verticale, dans les seules relations avec l'administration. En effet, le juge judiciaire est bien une autorité publique, devant donner plein effet aux règles constitutionnelles et donc au principe de précaution. La Cour de cassation a déjà opéré son contrôle au visa de la Charte et du principe de précaution[501].

La perspective aujourd'hui retenue ne consiste pourtant pas à déterminer si les sociétés de droit privé peuvent ou non, comme toute

---

498 Conseil constitutionnel, DC n° 208-564 du 19 juin 2008 ; Michel Prieur, « Promesses et réalisations de la Charte de l'environnement », *Les nouveaux cahiers du Conseil constitutionnel*, 2014, n° 2, p. 5–24.

499 CE, 19 juillet 2010, *Association du quartier des Hauts de Choiseul*, req. n° 328687.

500 Olivier Cachard, « La preuve des risques associés à l'exposition aux champs électromagnétiques », *JCP éd. G*, 2017, étude n° 944.

501 Cass. Civ. 1re, 3 mars 2010, pourvoi n° 08-19.108 ; Cass. civ. 3e, 18 mai 2011, pourvoi n° 10-17.645.

personne de droit privé, se soustraire à l'application horizontale de la Charte. La perspective, à la fois organique et fonctionnelle, consiste à déterminer si l'État actionnaire peut lui-même se soustraire aux principes que le pouvoir constituant a déterminés. D'un point de vue organique, il faut d'abord déterminer, y compris pour le lecteur environnementaliste non spécialiste du droit des sociétés, si l'État est ou non un actionnaire comme les autres, pour reprendre la formule de M. Dondero (II). D'un point de vue fonctionnel, il faut ensuite déterminer si, dans l'exercice de ses fonctions d'actionnaire, l'État peut s'affranchir des principes constitutionnels environnementaux, singulièrement du principe de précaution (III).

II) L'État actionnaire n'est pas un actionnaire comme les autres

Actionnaire dans des sociétés de droit privé régies par le Code de commerce, l'État actionnaire jouit des droits d'un actionnaire ordinaire (A). Toutefois, l'État actionnaire jouit de prérogatives particulières (B).

A) Les prérogatives de l'actionnaire ordinaire

L'État actionnaire jouit de tous les droits attachés à la détention d'un titre de capital. Cela s'entend d'abord du droit à l'information, exercé différemment selon la forme sociale, du droit de concourir à l'exercice du pouvoir délibérant par le vote et du droit à rémunération lors des dividendes. Cela s'entend ensuite des droits nés des éventuels pactes d'actionnaires, pour déterminer notamment les conditions de l'entrée et de la sortie du capital social. Cela s'entend enfin du droit d'agir en justice pour faire anéantir les décisions irrégulières, du droit d'agir contre les administrateurs et du droit d'agir *ut singuli*. Cela s'entend encore du droit à la protection diplomatique contre les atteintes portées à l'étranger aux filiales contrôlées par le groupe.

L'État actionnaire jouit en outre des prérogatives attachées au contrôle ou à la participation dans le cadre de droits attachés à la détention de blocs d'actions. *Stricto sensu*, le contrôle s'entend de la détention de plus de la moitié du capital social, au sens de l'article L 233-1 du Code de commerce. L'article 2 de l'ordonnance du 20 août 2014 vient consacrer une acception élargie de la détention de la majorité du capital en disposant que « [s]ont regardées comme des sociétés dont plus de la moitié du capital est détenue indirectement par l'État ou ses établissements publics, seuls ou conjointement, celles dont plus de la moitié du capital est détenue par des sociétés placées dans une même chaîne ininterrompue de participations majoritaires »[502]. *Lato sensu*, au sens de l'article L 233-3 I du Code de commerce, le contrôle découle d'un faisceau de critères parmi lesquels figurent, outre la détention de titres de capital, la jouissance de droits contractuels, la détention des technologies nécessaires à l'accomplissement de l'activité ou les titres de propriété intellectuelle (enseigne, marques, brevets). Quoi qu'il en soit, le contrôle s'exerce en conformité avec l'intérêt social et sans abus de majorité. En droit commun, la participation s'entend pour sa part de la détention d'une minorité de blocage, étant précisé que l'exercice de la minorité de blocage ne saurait conduire à un abus de minorité. À ces prérogatives déjà significatives vu le niveau important des participations de l'État, il faut ajouter les privilèges conférés à l'État.

B) Les privilèges d'un actionnaire particulier

L'État actionnaire jouit à la fois de privilèges en tant qu'actionnaire, lui donnant un poids déterminant dans l'assemblée générale des actionnaires, et dans les organes de gestion où la désignation, obligatoire ou facultative selon les cas, d'un représentant de l'État et d'un commissaire du Gouvernement lui permet d'influer sur la gestion de la société. Lorsque l'État actionnaire détient plus de 10 % du capital social, des sièges d'administrateur lui sont réservés et sont à pourvoir par l'assemblée générale. L'introduction de ces sièges réservés déroge à la règle de la stricte proportionnalité. Lorsque l'État détient moins de 10 % du capital social, l'assemblée générale dispose encore de la faculté de « nommer l'État ».

La loi n° 2014-384 du 29 mars 2014 visant à reconquérir l'économie réelle, également appelée « Loi Florange », a introduit l'article L 225-13 du Code de commerce généralisant les droits de vote double lorsque les titres de la société sont admis à la cote d'un marché réglementé et que les

[502] Ordonnance n° 2014-948 du 20 août 2014 relative à la gouvernance et aux opérations sur le capital des sociétés à participation publique, *JORF*, 23 août 2014 ; ratifiée par la loi du 6 août 2015, commentée par Matthieu Zolomian, « La gouvernance modernisée des organes collégiaux des sociétés à participation publique », *Revue des sociétés*, 2015, p. 135.

actions sont détenues à titre nominatif pendant au moins deux ans. Si l'État actionnaire n'est pas explicitement mentionné par la loi et s'il n'est pas le seul à se voir attribuer le doublement des droits de vote, il demeure le principal bénéficiaire *de facto* de ce mécanisme. La condition de durée de détention des actions à titre nominatif privilégie l'État et exclut les investisseurs ou spéculateurs réalisant des arbitrages à court terme sur les cours de bourse. Il reste à savoir si ce mécanisme permettra à l'État de renforcer son contrôle à participation constante ou s'il lui permettra plutôt de maintenir son contrôle au niveau existant en diminuant le niveau de ses participations. Toujours est-il que la « Loi Florange » donne à l'État un outil de politique publique.

Lorsque l'État actionnaire est majoritaire, il jouit en outre d'un droit à une représentation spéciale dans les organes collégiaux de gestion, en l'occurrence le conseil d'administration ou le conseil de surveillance dans les sociétés anonymes. Par application de l'article 4 I de l'ordonnance du 20 août 2014 relative à la gouvernance et aux opérations sur le capital des sociétés à participation publique, lorsqu'il est actionnaire majoritaire, l'État désigne par son ministre de l'économie son représentant « dans les conseils d'administration, les conseils de surveillance ou les organes délibérants ». L'emploi du présent de généralité indique qu'il s'agit d'une désignation obligatoire et non d'une simple faculté. Le représentant de l'État bénéficie des prérogatives d'un administrateur, même s'il n'en a pas le titre faute d'avoir été désigné par l'organe collégial lui-même.

La représentation de l'État n'est qu'une faculté lorsque l'État est actionnaire minoritaire détenant à lui seul plus de 10 % des titres de capital. Ici encore par application de l'article 4 I *in fine* de la même ordonnance, c'est l'État lui-même qui, même minoritaire, désigne son représentant dans l'organe collégial de décision. *A fortiori*, la situation de minorité de l'État renforce le caractère exorbitant de cette prérogative.

Par application de l'article 15 de l'ordonnance du 20 août 2014, « l'État peut désigner, dans des conditions fixées par voie réglementaire, un commissaire du Gouvernement » tant dans les sociétés à participation publique majoritaire que dans les sociétés à participation publique minoritaire. « Sans préjudice des dispositions particulières le régissant, le commissaire du Gouvernement assiste, avec voix consultative, aux séances du conseil d'administration, du conseil de surveillance ou de l'organe délibérant en tenant lieu de la société. Le cas échéant, il expose la politique du Gouvernement dans le secteur d'activité de celle-ci ».

L'État jouit enfin du privilège d'information renforcée. Il résulte non de textes spéciaux régissant l'État actionnaire mais de la « capacité cognitive» de l'État qui peut alimenter son information à une multitude de sources : Cour des comptes, Ministère de l'Économie et des Finances, conseillers du commerce extérieur, préfets, autres administrations déconcentrées. Ainsi, les rapports présentés aux organes sociaux (rapport de gestion, rapports spéciaux), préalablement ou postérieurement aux choix de gestion qui y sont recensés ne sont qu'une source d'information parmi d'autres.

III) L'État actionnaire est tenu par le principe de précaution consacré par la Charte de l'environnement

L'État actionnaire jouit à la fois des droits de l'actionnaire ordinaire et de prérogatives exorbitantes du droit commun des sociétés. Lorsqu'il contrôle une société de droit privé ou lorsqu'il détient une participation, l'État actionnaire se trouve en capacité d'orienter les choix stratégiques de la société de façon à l'inscrire dans le respect des politiques publiques et des principes constitutionnels. Mais ne s'agit-il que d'une faculté ou bien d'un devoir ? La question se pose en particulier en ce qui concerne les principes constitutionnels de la Charte de l'environnement, en particulier le principe de précaution. Nous montrerons que l'État actionnaire est tenu par le principe de précaution, aussi bien directement (A) qu'indirectement (B).

A) L'État actionnaire directement tenu par le principe de précaution

En premier lieu, nous ne pensons pas qu'il n'existe de situation intrinsèque de conflit d'intérêts entre l'État actionnaire et l'État régulateur. En réalité, l'État doit faire preuve de cohérence. Si l'on se réfère aux lignes directrices de l'État actionnaire, élaborées par l'Agence des participations de l'État, « [l]'État se comporte en investisseur avisé avec une vision stratégique », mais « [i]l ne saurait être assimilé à un investisseur pour le compte de tiers (fonds de pension, *hedge funds*) »[503]. Cela exclut que l'État actionnaire doive se préoccuper de la valorisation seulement de ses participations, sans considération pour l'intérêt général et pour les principes constitutionnels. Plusieurs éléments fondent cette approche particulière de l'actionnariat. En l'état du droit positif, il suffit de rappeler que l'État actionnaire contrôle le plus souvent des sociétés chargées d'une mission de service public, de sorte que son intérêt d'associé ne s'épuise pas à la réalisation d'un profit. *De lege ferenda*, les préconisations du Rapport Senard-Notat[504] accentuent encore la prise en considération des enjeux environnementaux pour les sociétés commerciales, et donc *a fortiori* pour les sociétés dont l'État est actionnaire. Le rapport propose ainsi l'adjonction d'un alinéa à l'article 1833 du Code civil disposant que « [l]a société doit être gérée dans son intérêt propre en considérant les enjeux sociaux et environnementaux de son activité ». Ajoutons encore que la conciliation de la poursuite de l'intérêt social et de la poursuite de l'intérêt général ne crée aucun conflit d'intérêts au sens de ce terme en droit positif. En effet, les fonctions financières et les fonctions de régulation sont dévolues par l'État à des représentants différents, respectivement le représentant de l'État et le commissaire du Gouvernement. De la sorte, par la division des rôles de ses représentants, l'État échappe au conflit d'intérêts au sens de la loi n° 2013-907 du 11 octobre 2013 relative à la transparence de la vie publique.

L'institution du commissaire du Gouvernement au sein des sociétés ayant l'État pour l'actionnaire doit être présentée plus en détail, en identifiant d'abord ses prérogatives puis ses missions. S'agissant de ses prérogatives, le commissaire du Gouvernement peut se faire communiquer tout document, demander l'inscription d'un point à l'ordre du jour, parfois demander une deuxième délibération et même demander une nouvelle réunion de l'organe collégial. S'agissant de ses missions, elles ne sont pas énoncées explicitement dans la loi, raison pour laquelle le Conseil d'État a auditionné les commissaires du Gouvernement désignés par l'État dans différentes sociétés afin d'identifier les rôles assumés et afin de formuler des propositions dans le rapport. Le Conseil d'État conclut de ces entretiens sur la pratique des commissaires du Gouvernement « qu'il est le porteur de l'intérêt général défini par le Gouvernement pour le secteur d'activité

---

503 Agence des participations, *Rapport d'activité*, 2015–2016.

504 Jean-Dominique Senart, Nicole Notat, *L'entreprise, objet d'intérêt collectif*, Rapport remis le 9 mars 2018 à M. Bruno Le Maire, ministre de l'Économie et des Finances, M. Nicolas Hulot, ministre de la Transition écologique et solidaire, Mme Muriel Pénicaud, ministre du Travail et Mme Nicole Beloubet, garde des Sceaux.

dans lequel l'entreprise intervient ». La proposition n° 1 du Conseil d'État est de « [r]egarder la fonction du commissaire du Gouvernement comme un moyen pour l'État de s'assurer, selon les cas, de la mise en cohérence ou en compatibilité, voire en conformité, de l'activité de certaines entreprises avec des objectifs de politique publique »[505]. La proposition n° 3 insiste pour sa part sur l'utilité du commissaire du Gouvernement lorsque l'activité de la société a un impact notamment sanitaire : « Ne permettre la présence d'un commissaire du Gouvernement au sein d'une société commerciale que si l'entreprise ou le secteur d'activité peut être regardé comme essentiel à la protection des intérêts du pays en matière d'ordre public, de santé publique, de sécurité publique ou de défense nationale ». Assurément, les sociétés produisant, stockant ou distribuant de l'énergie satisfont cumulativement ces critères qui ne sont qu'alternatifs et indicatifs… Et quoi qu'il en soit du commissaire du Gouvernement, le Conseil d'État recommande dans sa proposition n° 10 de « [c]onserver dans tous les cas le principe d'une présence au conseil d'administration ». Directement tenu par le principe de précaution, l'État actionnaire l'est encore indirectement, notamment au titre de la responsabilité sociale des entreprises (RSE) et du devoir de vigilance des sociétés mères.

B) L'État actionnaire est indirectement tenu par le principe de précaution

Parce qu'il est un actionnaire de référence, investi d'une mission d'exemplarité, l'État actionnaire est usuellement considéré comme devant donner l'exemple en matière de RSE. Ainsi, selon le Rapport 2016 de l'Agence des participations de l'État, « [e]n actionnaire de référence, patient mais exigeant, et en administrateur responsable, accompagner les entreprises dans leur développement, en veillant à la cohérence de leur stratégie, à la qualité de la gouvernance et au respect des meilleures pratiques en matière de responsabilité sociale et environnementale »[506]. Le décret du 9 août 2017 est venu remplacer le rapport RSE par une déclaration de performance non financière[507] qui étend les obligations

---

505 Conseil d'État, *Les commissaires du gouvernement dans les entreprises*, La Documentation française, 2015, p. 31.

506 Agence des participations, *Rapport d'activité*, 2015–2016.

507 Art. L 225-101-1 du Code de commerce et Art. L 225-102-4 du Code de commerce, sur lesquels, Thierry Bonneau, « Réflexions sur la porosité du droit financier aux enjeux de la RSE », *Énergie – Env – Infrastructure*, 2018, Études, n° 4.

déclaratives à divers aspects tels que les conséquences sur le changement climatique, les engagements sociétaux en faveur du développement durable ou en faveur des conditions de travail des salariés.

À ces obligations, il faut ajouter les obligations nouvelles liées au devoir de vigilance, dont on doit considérer qu'il s'agit, en droit international privé, d'une loi de police[508]. Ainsi doivent publier un plan de vigilance les sociétés employant plus de 5 000 salariés en France ou plus de 10 000 dans le monde, plan de vigilance de nature à identifier et prévenir « les atteintes graves envers les droits humains et les libertés fondamentales, la santé et la sécurité des personnes ainsi que l'environnement »[509]. Une injonction de publier le plan de vigilance peut être prononcée par les juridictions judiciaires saisies en référé[510]. La responsabilité civile de la société peut également être engagée sur le fondement de la faute[511], sans toutefois qu'une amende civile puisse venir sanctionner la carence des sociétés[512].

IV) Conclusion

À l'issue de ce voyage le long de la ligne de crête entre le droit des sociétés et le droit public, il faut conclure moins sur la normativité et l'impérativité du principe de précaution déjà acquises que sur les voies de son efficacité qui restent à tracer.

Empruntons d'abord, témérairement pour un privatiste, le versant publiciste de la montagne. Qu'advient-il d'abord si l'État actionnaire majoritaire ou disposant d'une minorité de blocage ne s'est pas opposé à une délibération sociétaire violant ou ratifiant la violation par les dirigeants sociaux du *principe de précaution*, par exemple sur la base de la décision ou de l'instruction d'un ministre ? Qu'advient-il plus

---

508 Horatia Muir-Watt, « Devoir de vigilance et droit international privé. Le symbole et le procédé de la loi du 27 mars 2017, note sous Loi n° 2017-399 du 27 mars 2017 relative au devoir de vigilance des sociétés mères et des entreprises donneuses d'ordre, *JORF*, 28 mars 2017 », *Revue internationale de la compliance et de l'éthique des affaires*, 2017, p. 48–53 ; Constantin Ringot-Nammer, « Le champ d'application international de la loi n° 2017-399 sur le devoir de vigilance », Communication présentée à Nancy le 26 mars 2018, actes à paraître.

509 Art. L 225-1044, I, al. 3 nouveau, Code de commerce.

510 Art. L 225-105, II, nouveau, Code de commerce.

511 Art. 1240 et 1241 Code civil.

512 Conseil constitutionnel, DC n° 2017-750, cons. n° 13.

simplement si le commissaire du Gouvernement a omis de mettre en œuvre ses prérogatives et de faire connaître aux organes sociétaires la position du Gouvernement eu égard à la mise en œuvre du principe de précaution ? Même si la décision sociétaire relève du droit privé et donc de la compétence naturelle du juge judiciaire, il n'est pas exclu que le juge administratif puisse être saisi d'un recours en excès de pouvoir, sur la base de la théorie de l'acte détachable. L'affaire de l'arbitrage Tapie illustre qu'une telle hypothèse ne relève pas du cas d'école[513]. En l'espèce, le juge administratif avait bien été saisi d'un recours en annulation contre la décision d'un ministre de ne pas s'opposer au compromis d'arbitrage conclu avec M. Tapie, puis de ne pas exercer de voie de recours contre la sentence issue de cet arbitrage. On retrouvait dans cette affaire une interpénétration entre l'État et une société de droit privé, la structure de défaisance des actifs toxiques de la banque consistant en une société de droit privé (le CDR ou consortium de réalisation des créances) et un établissement public la contrôlant (l'EPFR). Le recours en annulation n'a pas prospéré pour des raisons de recevabilité *ratione personae* : les contribuables ont été jugés irrecevables en raison de la prohibition de l'action populaire tandis qu'un administrateur de l'EPFR s'est vu opposer la règle de la connaissance acquise. Sur ce dernier point, la décision du Conseil d'État est vivement critiquée par la doctrine. Qu'en serait-il d'un recours en annulation contre une décision administrative conduisant à une délibération sociétaire violant le principe de précaution ? Faudrait-il que le requérant soit un actionnaire petit-porteur ?

Empruntons ensuite, rapidement, le versant privatiste de la montagne, pour nous situer en aval de la décision administrative. Une piste déjà explorée consiste à vérifier si la société ayant méconnu le principe de précaution engage sa responsabilité civile. Une autre piste consisterait à se placer dans la perspective du contrôle de la gouvernance de l'entreprise. Serait-il possible d'introduire une action en nullité de la délibération d'une assemblée générale ordinaire ou extraordinaire, à condition de vérifier l'une des causes de nullité expressément prévues par le Code de commerce ? S'agissant des sociétés anonymes qui représentent 70 % du portefeuille de l'Agence de participation de

---

[513] TA Paris, 8 octobre 2009, v. note Jean-David Dreyfus, « L'arbitrage Tapie et le Crédit Lyonnais devant le Tribunal administratif », *Actualités juridiques de droit administratif*, 2009, p. 2350 ; CE, 26 juillet 2011, v. note Paul Cassia, « Irrecevabilité des recours formés contre la décision administrative de recourir à l'arbitrage dans l'affaire Tapie c. CDR », *AJDA*, 2011, p. 1959.

l'État, il faudrait par exemple, en application de l'article L 235-1, al. 2, du Code de commerce, que la délibération ait été prise « en violation des lois qui régissent les contrats ». La doctrine, soulignant la rareté de telles actions, en déduit qu'« une délibération peut être annulée pour incapacité, défaut ou vice du consentement des participants, objet illicite »[514]. Le silence du commissaire du Gouvernement sur la violation du principe de précaution ou de la RSE entachant une résolution caractériserait-il un vice du consentement des actionnaires par réticence dolosive ? L'adoption d'une résolution aboutissant à la violation du *principe de précaution* ou des obligations de RSE de la société caractérise-t-elle le contenu illicite d'une résolution au sens de l'article 1128 du Code civil ? Rien ne permet de l'exclure, au stade de ces réflexions prospectives. En tout cas, la porosité du droit des sociétés à la RSE et au principe de précaution mérite d'être mieux étudiée…

[514] Michel Germain, *Traité de droit commercial*, t. I, vol. 2, 19e éd., LGDJ, n° 1585, p. 396.

Chapitre 10

Qu'est-ce que l'économiste peut apporter à l'interprétation de la Charte de l'environnement ? L'exemple de l'article 4 et des dommages causés à l'environnement

Chapter 10

How to Use Economics to Better Understand Constitutional Law? The Case of Article 4 of the French Environmental Charter and Environmental Harm

Samuel FEREY

Professeur d'économie à l'Université de Lorraine, France
Faculté de droit, sciences économiques et gestion de Nancy
CNRS, BETA (UMR 7522-1443)

Résumé : Si l'article 4 de la Charte ouvre la voie à une réparation du dommage écologique, ses modalités pratiques restent sujettes à débat, notamment chez les économistes. Dès lors que l'on identifie le dommage écologique à un préjudice subi, *in fine*, par des humains, les outils traditionnels des économistes du droit trouvent assez facilement à s'appliquer : c'est parce que certaines utilités individuelles ont été affectées par la destruction de l'environnement que l'on pourra définir puis mesurer le dommage. Cependant, ces méthodes ne disent rien pour le préjudice écologique « pur », là où aucun humain n'est affecté par le dommage. On touche alors aux limites conceptuelles de la théorie économique, fondée sur une approche subjective de l'utilité et du bien-être. Les méthodes existantes contournent la difficulté autour d'évaluations en termes quasi physiques impliquant une absence de substituabilité économique des services écologiques rendus. Elles rejoignent alors les développements de philosophie morale et politique sur les limites normatives du marché.

Abstract: Article 4 of the French Environmental Charter is an important step in assuring compensation for environmental harm. But methodologies for evaluating compensation for ecological loss is still an ongoing discussion, especially among economists. An economic approach may be useful. Traditional law and economics for torts is easy enough to apply when the ecological harm is considered as a "human" loss. But these methods are not readily applicable when the ecological loss is considered as a "pure" harm – that is, when no human private interests or rights have been infringed. New methods to overcome this problem are being proposed which principally use local evaluations of destroyed environment and depart from general theories of substitutability. Rather, they join some of recent theories on the moral and political boundaries of markets.

I) Introduction

Dans son article 4, la Charte de l'environnement dispose que « toute personne doit contribuer à la réparation des dommages qu'elle cause à l'environnement, dans les conditions définies par la loi ». Pour un économiste, la lecture de cet article 4 est à la fois simple et complexe. Simple car l'article semble affirmer plusieurs principes bien connus des économistes du droit. D'une part, un critère de causalité qui relie un comportement et la survenance du dommage ; d'autre part, un principe de contribution selon lequel les dommages et intérêts payés doivent être dans une proportion avec l'évaluation du dommage causé et enfin, l'affirmation que les dommages en question sont des dommages à l'environnement. Complexe aussi car, au-delà de la simplicité de l'énoncé, il n'est pas sûr que l'économiste puisse réellement s'y retrouver dans cette formulation si jamais il devait prendre position sur la meilleure manière d'évaluer un tel dommage.

En effet, l'article 4 précise bien qu'il s'agit d'un dommage *à l'environnement* sans réellement préciser ce qu'il faut entendre par là et renvoyant aux conditions posées par le législateur pour organiser une telle réparation. Et un certain nombre de textes législatifs, dont la loi du 1er juillet 2008 et la loi du 8 août 2016[515], est venu préciser ce que l'on devait entendre par réparation d'un dommage à l'environnement. L'économie peut-elle aider à définir et à évaluer un tel dommage à l'environnement ? Gageons, sans en être sûr, que ce soit le cas. *A priori*, l'économiste peut apporter sa pierre à l'édifice des régimes de réparation du dommage à l'environnement de deux manières : soit comme interprète des textes juridiques en général, et de cet article 4 de la Charte en particulier, afin de définir les contours conceptuels de ce qui pourrait être, pour lui et sa discipline, la réparation d'un dommage à l'environnement ; soit comme un expert chargé de fournir des outils d'évaluation. Dans le premier cas, l'économiste siégerait à côté du juriste afin de participer au travail doctrinal ; dans le second, il siégerait plutôt à côté des écologues, des ingénieurs ou des spécialistes de la faune et de la flore comme disposant

---

515 Cette dernière loi ajoute un chapitre sur la réparation du préjudice écologique au Code civil : Art. 1246 : « Toute personne responsable d'un préjudice écologique est tenue de le réparer » et art. 1247 : « Est réparable, dans les conditions prévues au présent titre, le préjudice écologique consistant en une atteinte non négligeable aux éléments ou aux fonctions des écosystèmes ou aux bénéfices collectifs tirés par l'homme de l'environnement. »

d'un ensemble d'outils opérationnels que le juriste pourrait mobiliser le cas échéant[516].

Il nous semble qu'une perspective économique peut être pertinente mais, et ce sera l'objet de cette contribution de le montrer, qu'elle ne peut être que partielle dans la mesure où la théorie économique ne peut correctement envisager le dommage écologique « pur ». Cette difficulté relève en fait des fondements mêmes de la théorie économique contemporaine qui définit la valeur des biens et services en termes d'utilité subjective humaine. Dans ce cadre, il est complexe de définir une valeur intrinsèque à l'environnement.

Dans un premier temps, nous étudierons la manière dont le dommage à l'environnement peut être défini en économie (II). Dans une seconde partie, nous traiterons des méthodes d'évaluation utilisées en économie pour évaluer les dommages écologiques (III). La difficulté opérationnelle porte sur le fait que ces dommages sont le plus souvent non marchands et que l'on ne peut se fonder sur l'existence d'un prix de marché pour les évaluer. Ces méthodes peuvent cependant fournir une évaluation économique du dommage. En revanche, l'évaluation d'un dommage écologique « pur » ne peut être résolue par ces méthodes. Ceci nous amènera à considérer des méthodes d'évaluation intermédiaires entre méthodes scientifiques et méthodes économiques dont il est intéressant de comprendre les caractéristiques. L'enjeu est alors de définir des sphères d'activité et de comportements sociaux indépendants les uns des autres permettant ce que l'on pourrait appeler un calcul économique « local ».

II) Définir économiquement le dommage écologique

Contrairement à ce que l'on pourrait penser, et à ce que certains affirment, l'approche économique du droit de la réparation est relativement cohérente avec une approche strictement juridique[517]. Dès lors, les questions

---

516 Ainsi, aux États-Unis par exemple, on a plusieurs exemples d'affaires emblématiques illustrant la pertinence et la fécondité de ce travail interdisciplinaire d'évaluation (mise au point des méthodes « services-services », « ressources-ressources ») qui sont parfois reprises dans les textes communautaires. Pour une analyse de certains de ces cas, v. Adeline Bas, Pascale Gastineau, Julien Hay, Harold Levrel, « Méthodes d'équivalence et compensation du dommage environnemental », *Revue d'économie politique*, 2013, p. 127–157.

517 Pour une critique radicale de l'approche économique du droit qui, cependant, manque à notre avis sa cible, v. Alain Supiot, *La Gouvernance par les nombres*, Seuil, 2015.

qui se posent, en droit, sur la définition du dommage à l'environnement posent également question pour les économistes. Dans un premier temps, on insistera sur la convergence de vues relativement profonde entre économie et droit concernant la réparation des dommages en droit commun (A). Ceci permettra alors, dans un second temps, de considérer les questions que pose la réparation du dommage à l'environnement et de voir si le droit n'est pas plus armé que l'économie pour y faire face. Il faudra notamment s'interroger si le dommage à l'environnement est forcément un dommage « humain » (B).

A) L'économie du droit des dommages

Tout étudiant de deuxième année de droit sait que le droit commun de la réparation impose l'existence d'un dommage comme condition de la mise en œuvre des régimes de responsabilité civile. Ce dommage étant lui-même défini comme devant être direct et certain ouvrant à la victime un droit à agir. Par ailleurs, le principe général de réparation intégrale impose que la victime doit être remise dans l'état initial précédant l'événement qui a causé le dommage à l'aide d'une reconstruction contre-factuelle du passé[518]. De manière générale, les juges considèrent traditionnellement que la réparation en monnaie est une modalité adéquate de réparation et n'impose pas la réparation en nature. Ces dommages et intérêts ne sont d'ailleurs pas affectés à certains usages, mais peuvent être utilisés librement et souverainement par la victime.

Très brièvement rappelés, ces quelques principes fondamentaux sont facilement interprétables par la théorie économique et notamment par l'économie du droit qui, depuis les années 1950, s'est largement développée à l'intersection des sciences juridiques et des sciences économiques. En effet, les concepts fondamentaux des économistes paraissent assez cohérents avec ces principes juridiques[519]. Pour la micro-économie,

---

[518] Pour une discussion de cette notion de causalité juridique et contrefactuelle d'un point de vue interdisciplinaire, v. Samuel Ferey, Florence G'sell (dir.), *Causalité, responsabilité et répartition de la charge de la dette*, Bruylant, 2018.

[519] Pour une présentation de l'économie du droit des dommages, v. Steven Shavell, *Economic Analysis of Accident Law*, Harvard University Press, 2009. Par économie, nous entendons essentiellement l'analyse microéconomique qui étudie les comportements économiques d'affectations de ressources rares à usage alternatif. Le cœur de cette théorie est de considérer que les agents économiques sont rationnels en ce qu'ils cherchent à maximiser leur utilité. Dès lors, les biens et services ont une valeur aux yeux des acteurs en tant qu'ils leur permettent d'atteindre des niveaux

les individus sont analysés comme porteurs de préférences : ils sont capables de classer (du moins préféré au plus préféré) les différents états qui peuvent être les leurs en termes de consommation, de production ou de ressources. Parmi tous les états possibles, il en existe un certain nombre pour lequel les individus peuvent se déclarer indifférents. On résume le plus souvent ces préférences par une fonction d'utilité qui, à chaque situation, associe un indicateur de bien-être, un niveau d'utilité. Deux situations classées de manière indifférente apporteront à l'acteur la même utilité et seront donc indexées par le même nombre. Ces éléments fondamentaux s'ouvrent alors sur les concepts fondamentaux des économistes, à savoir la possible substitution entre biens et services consommés permettant à l'individu de rester au même niveau d'utilité[520].

Dans ce cadre économique, un événement dommageable est simplement un événement qui a eu un impact, non désiré et non volontairement accepté par une victime. L'utilité de la victime ayant diminué du fait d'une cause extérieure à son comportement, il est légitime que cette victime demande une compensation qui, par le principe de substitution, pourra se faire en monnaie. Là où le juriste parlera de dommage direct et certain, l'économiste y verra une variation effective d'utilité ; là où le juriste considérera que l'on doit remettre l'acteur dans son état initial par le biais d'une compensation monétaire, l'économiste considérera que la compensation payée permet à la victime de retrouver son niveau d'utilité initiale.

Cela étant, si les deux disciplines semblent assez proches en termes de principes généraux, on doit noter quelques éléments saillants en ce

de bien-être. Cette théorie micro-économique ne défend pas nécessairement les marchés comme seule modalité institutionnelle d'affectation des ressources, mais met en évidence des échecs de marché ouvrant la réflexion sur le rôle de l'État ou du droit dans la résolution de ces imperfections. Plus fondamentalement, la théorie de la valeur défendue en économie reconnaît le principe de souveraineté des consommateurs – ils sont libres de leurs préférences et de leur rapport du bien-être – qui peut alors être vu comme une volonté d'éviter tout paternalisme où un agent imposerait aux autres ce qu'ils doivent faire ou consommer. De plus, le principe fondamental des comportements économiques reposera sur la substitution : maximiser son bien-être sous contrainte de revenu passe par la possibilité de substituer certains biens, moins chers, à d'autres plus chers pour atteindre un même niveau d'utilité.

520 C'est le cas classique des *textbooks* de microéconomie lorsque l'agent étudié se déclare indifférent entre consommer deux cafés et un chocolat chaud ou un café et demi et un chocolat chaud et demi.

qui concerne la définition économique. D'abord, celle-ci n'a de sens que par rapport à des préférences ou des utilités individuelles et l'on voit mal comment il pourrait y avoir de dommage sans victimes humaines car seuls les agents économiques sont porteurs de préférences et d'utilité[521]. Ensuite, le principe de substitution est crucial puisque c'est lui qui assure que la compensation permet de retrouver un état initial, défini en l'occurrence comme un niveau d'utilité.

B) Dommage à l'environnement, dommage « humain » ?

Appliqués au dommage environnemental, ces principes économiques pour analyser la réparation peuvent facilement se décliner dès lors que l'on peut passer, plus ou moins facilement, d'un dommage à l'environnement à un dommage ayant un sens en termes d'utilités individuelles. On pourrait d'abord penser aux cas évidents où la pollution d'un milieu a des conséquences immédiates sur l'activité économique telle que la pollution d'une rivière entraînant la mort des poissons pêchés et vendus, encore que, dans ce cas, le dommage qui se réalise n'a rien de proprement environnemental et peut être facilement couvert par les principes du droit commun.

On peut cependant penser à d'autres scénarios envisagés explicitement par les textes. Ainsi, dans la loi du 1er juillet 2008, l'article L. 161-1.-I. précise que

> Constituent des dommages causés à l'environnement au sens du présent titre les détériorations directes ou indirectes mesurables de l'environnement qui : 1° Créent un risque d'atteinte grave à la santé humaine du fait de la contamination des sols résultant de l'introduction directe ou indirecte, en surface ou dans le sol, de substances, préparations, organismes ou micro-organismes […] 4° Affectent les services écologiques, c'est-à-dire les fonctions assurées par les sols, les eaux et les espèces et habitats mentionnés au 3° au bénéfice d'une de ces ressources naturelles ou au bénéfice du public.

La référence à la santé humaine ou encore au bénéfice du public illustre bien cette première définition du dommage à l'environnement où celui-ci existe dès lors qu'il possède des conséquences indirectes sur le bien-être

---

521 Cette position, héritée de l'utilitarisme, est parfois discutée et critiquée par les philosophes moraux, y compris ceux de tradition utilitariste. V. notamment Peter Singer, *Animal Liberation : A New Ethics for our Treatment of Animals*, New York Review/Random House, 1975. Peter Singer cherche dans cet ouvrage à fonder une position éthique où les animaux seraient reconnus comme porteurs d'intérêts.

humain. En le rattachant à des bénéfices économiques explicites – la santé, le bénéfice récréatif ou autres – l'environnement devient porteur de « services » dont certains, pas nécessairement tous, ont d'emblée un sens économique sous la forme de la fourniture de bien-être à certains individus. Ceux-ci se trouvent donc dans une situation de victime de préjudice dès lors que ces services sont détruits. On doit ici ajouter que ces bénéfices n'ont pas, pour l'économiste, à être actuels au sens d'existants au temps présent. Ainsi, on peut imaginer que la biodiversité est porteuse de bénéfices futurs de l'humanité, non encore découverts, mais qui pourrait avoir une valeur dans le futur. On raisonnera alors de manière probabilisée en imaginant qu'avec une certaine probabilité, la destruction de la biodiversité se traduira par un coût pour la communauté humaine dans le futur à la faveur d'une sorte de perte de chance si l'on voulait utiliser un terme juridique.

Enfin, on peut également, à la suite de la jurisprudence, évoquer des cas plus complexes tels que le préjudice moral. Dans ce cas, le dommage à l'environnement est réparable car il pourrait porter préjudice à certains individus mais de manière non matérielle. C'est, par exemple, la voie suivie lorsque l'on argumente sur le fondement du préjudice moral, par exemple le préjudice moral d'une association de défense des animaux ou des oiseaux. Une approche économique stricte peut tout à fait justifier ce fondement et lui donner un sens. Il est possible que les préférences de certains acteurs soient fortement dépendantes de l'état de la faune et de la flore et qu'ils retirent une utilité à voir l'environnement naturel préservé.

La source de l'utilité individuelle (ou des utilités collectives) n'est plus liée à des éléments physiques tels que la consommation de biens matériels, mais est purement subjective et morale[522]. De nombreux travaux d'économie partent d'ailleurs de cette idée en mettant en avant le fait qu'il existe des préférences pouvant porter sur des éléments purement sociaux ou moraux de la vie en société[523].

Dans tous ces cas, si le dommage causé à l'environnement ne pose pas de questions conceptuelles particulièrement épineuses à l'économiste, c'est parce que, comme nous l'avons vu, il est possible de ramener ce

---

522 Nous nous plaçons, on l'aura compris, sur un terrain purement conceptuel sans préjuger de la possibilité ou non pour des juges d'accéder de manière objective à cette préférence ou d'évaluer cette utilité qui est purement morale et subjective.

523 Pour un exemple d'usages de ce type de modèles introduisant des préférences sociales, v. Timur Kuran, *Private Truths, Public Lies*, Harvard University Press, 1995 ou Ernst Fehr, Klaus M. Schmidt, « A Theory of Fairness, Competition and Cooperation », *Quaterly Journal of Economics*, 1999, p. 817–868.

dommage à un dommage subjectif impliquant des intérêts humains et des préférences individuelles. Mais est-il possible d'aller plus loin et de donner un sens *économique* au préjudice écologique « pur », celui qui aurait lieu même si aucun humain n'était là pour en subir les conséquences ? Les choses nous paraissent ici plus complexes et impliquent en fait des ontologies différentes entre le droit et l'économie[524].

Concernant le droit, on pourrait considérer qu'il est une pratique sociale particulière qui lui permet de construire ses propres objets d'étude et ses propres concepts. Dans cette vision, la nature et l'environnement pourraient tout à fait être constitués juridiquement sans nécessairement avoir de contreparties empiriques ou matérielles[525]. Il pourrait en être de même pour le dommage pur à l'environnement. En revanche, on ne voit pas comment l'économiste pourrait participer à cette discussion tant ses concepts fondamentaux – préférences, utilité, bien-être – sont étroitement liés à la notion d'individu ou de groupe d'individus. Dans ce cadre, la nature ou l'environnement sera essentiellement vu comme un capital, une source de services, un bien économique ou encore un objet de consommation, mais ne sera jamais considéré en lui-même comme une chose ayant une valeur *indépendamment* de l'utilité indirecte qu'elle fournit. L'ontologie économique est trop étroite pour ouvrir sur ce type de questionnement et les concepts économiques risquent de tomber à plat par rapport au problème à résoudre.

III) Évaluer le dommage à l'environnement

On a montré précédemment les limites conceptuelles d'une approche économique appliquée à la définition du préjudice écologique, au moins en ce qui concerne le dommage écologique « pur ». Cependant, il est possible que le versant d'expertise de l'économie puisse tout de même être utile. Nous verrons ici les méthodes développées en économie

---

524 Sur une (trop) brève comparaison des ontologies économiques et juridiques, voir Samuel Ferey, « Quel avenir pour l'économie du droit ? », *in* : Thomas Clay, Ariane Clement, Bénédicte Fauvarque-Cosson, Françoise Renucci, Sandrine Zientara, *États généraux de la recherche sur le droit et la justice*, Lexisnexis, 2018, p. 131–140.

525 Il ne serait pas impossible par exemple que le système juridique décide de reconnaître l'environnement ou la nature comme un sujet de droit. Certains philosophes ont, par exemple, déjà proposé que les objets naturels puissent être représentés politiquement (v. Bruno Latour, *Politiques de la nature. Comment faire entrer les sciences en démocratie*, La Découverte, 1999).

pour mesurer et évaluer les dommages écologiques. D'abord, les cas les plus simples conceptuellement seront présentés, à savoir ceux où l'on peut ramener le dommage à des préjudices humains indirects qui correspondent aux méthodes économiques traditionnelles (A). Puis nous considérerons le cas plus aigu d'un dommage écologique pur (B).

A) Les méthodes économiques traditionnelles appliquées au dommage écologique

Dès lors que l'on rattache le dommage à l'environnement à une perte d'utilité et de valeur subjective – donc liée aux individus –, les concepts d'évaluation économique peuvent trouver à s'appliquer. La première voie, la plus simple, est lorsque des prix de marché sont disponibles. Ils fournissent une évaluation de la valeur du bien environnemental détruit. Les économistes considèrent que les prix de marché sont une bonne évaluation de la valeur d'un bien qui indiquent à la fois le coût marginal de production du bien ou du service et l'utilité marginale qu'elle rapporte aux individus. Ainsi, une plage souillée de pétrole peut mener à des pertes d'exploitation des installations touristiques facilement évaluables en termes de prix de marché.

Cette méthode peut se généraliser à des phénomènes plus complexes lorsque l'actif environnemental est porteur d'utilité directement économique mais dans le futur. Dans ce cadre, on raisonnera principalement par le biais d'une valeur d'option. Pour reprendre un exemple précité, la biodiversité peut tout à fait n'avoir aucune valeur présente – car les connaissances humaines sont insuffisantes dans leur état actuel pour l'exploiter – mais avoir une valeur future car elle est porteuse d'innovation. On peut en effet imaginer que l'évolution des connaissances humaines permettra, un jour, d'en tirer profit (par exemple par le biais de l'usage de molécules inconnues ou de possibilité d'extraire de certaines plantes de nouveaux médicaments). Ainsi, on peut lui attribuer une valeur d'option aujourd'hui.

La temporalité peut aussi présenter un autre visage bien connu des économistes, celui de l'actualisation future des pertes économiques (considérées ici comme certaines). Si l'environnement est détruit sur un nombre donné de périodes futures, il conviendra d'actualiser les pertes futures pour les comparer aux pertes d'aujourd'hui. Le choix du taux auquel on actualise les pertes futures pour les ramener à une mesure monétaire de pertes aujourd'hui est crucial et peut avoir des conséquences importantes sur le calcul. C'est ce taux qui indiquera si une perte de service environnemental de 100 euros dans 50 ans doit être comptée comme 20 euros, comme 5 euros ou comme 1 euro aujourd'hui !

Mais ce cas simple ne couvre évidemment pas toutes les situations. Le plus souvent, on ne peut disposer de tels prix de marché : les services fournis par l'environnement relèvent souvent du non-marchand. Ainsi, si la pollution d'un cours d'eau conduit à la suppression, pendant une certaine période de temps, de toutes activités de pèches récréatives, comment évaluer cette conséquence ? Utiliser le prix de marché de la truite n'a que peu d'intérêt car l'activité de pêche récréative n'a pas pour but essentiel de produire une truite : elle possède une utilité en elle-même, quelle que soit l'issue de la pêche. C'est pourquoi les économistes ont cherché à développer des méthodologies alternatives permettant d'avoir une certaine idée de la valeur à attribuer à ces services perdus. Citons parmi ces méthodes, la méthode par les coûts de déplacement, la méthode des prix hédoniques ou la méthode des évaluations contingentes. Dans tous ces cas, il s'agit de remonter de l'observable vers l'inobservable, à savoir la valorisation que les individus font des biens, services ou actifs naturels.

La première méthode, celle des coûts de déplacement, est particulièrement bien adaptée lorsque l'actif naturel ou environnemental, dont on cherche à estimer la valeur, donne lieu à des coûts indirects subis par les agents venus en profiter. Estimer la valeur d'une plage ne peut pas passer par des prix de marché (il n'existe pas un prix de marché pour pouvoir accéder à cette plage), mais, en revanche, on peut constater que les individus sont prêts à subir des coûts importants (transports, logements) pour en profiter. Dès lors, l'idée de cette méthode est d'utiliser ces données pour en faire le support de l'estimation.

La seconde méthode, celle des prix hédoniques, part d'un point de départ quelque peu différent en considérant que l'on ne consomme pas des biens pour eux-mêmes, mais pour les caractéristiques qu'ils intègrent[526]. Ainsi, une maison au bord de la mer présente à la fois des caractéristiques de confort, de métrage, mais aussi une dimension de proximité au littoral[527]. Dès lors, même s'il n'existe pas un prix de

---

[526] L'approche par les caractéristiques a été initialement développée par Kelvin John Lancaster et Sherwin Rosen.

[527] Pour un exemple d'application de cette méthodologie des prix hédonique au cas du littoral, v. François Bonnieux, Gildas Appere, Abdelhak Nassiri, Muriel Travers, *Évaluation des bénéfices environnementaux par la méthode des prix hédonistes : une application au cas du littoral*, Économie et Prévision, 2008, p. 47–62.

marché de la vue sur mer ou du fait de profiter du littoral, il est tout de même possible d'estimer le poids de chacune de ces caractéristiques dans les prix de marché des maisons vendues. On décomposera le prix en différentes composantes et l'analyse économétrique peut permettre d'estimer l'effet de chacune de ces composantes sur le prix final. On dispose alors d'une estimation indirecte de la manière dont les individus évaluent monétairement une caractéristique, en l'occurrence pour ce qui nous intéresse, une caractéristique environnementale comme disposer d'un littoral naturel.

Enfin, on trouve une troisième méthode qui a retenu l'attention des économistes, celle des évaluations contingentes[528]. Proche d'une méthodologie expérimentale, cette méthode cherche à faire révéler directement ou indirectement les consentements à payer des individus pour bénéficier de services environnementaux. C'est alors une méthodologie d'enquête sur échantillon représentatif qui est utilisée. L'enquêteur construit des scénarios pour faire révéler aux acteurs leurs préférences et leur consentement à payer pour des services écologiques non marchands. Ces consentements à payer sont des indicateurs de la valeur de ces services. Sans traiter de toutes les limites de cette approche (construction de l'échantillon, représentativité), notons cependant qu'il peut être parfois difficile d'obtenir une révélation de ces préférences. D'abord, l'enquête est souvent sensible au fait que l'on place l'acteur dans une situation où il devrait acheter le service (consentement à payer) ou à le vendre (consentement à vendre). Ces deux indicateurs devraient être égaux (la valeur étant la même à l'achat ou à la vente), or on remarque souvent des différences liées à un effet de dotation. Ensuite, la littérature met en garde contre de nombreux biais possibles lors des réponses comme le fait du biais hypothétique, le scénario étant par nature hypothétique et ne portant pas conséquence pour l'individu interrogé. Ces biais peuvent être minimisés en recourant à des approches proprement expérimentales comme des procédures d'enchères.

---

528 Comme le rappellent Adeline Bas, Pascale Gastineau, Julien Hay et Harold Levrel, cette méthode a été utilisée aux États-Unis devant les tribunaux dans le cadre du procès Exxon-Valdes. Un groupe d'experts pilotés par Kenneth J. Arrow et Robert Solow avaient eu à indiquer les canons méthodologiques que devait respecter cette méthode pour être fiable (Adeline Bas, Pascale Gastineau, Julien Hay, Harold Levrel, « Méthodes d'équivalence et compensation du dommage environnemental », *Revue d'économie politique*, 2013, p. 127–157).

B) Les méthodes d'évaluation du préjudice écologique pur

Si l'on peut mobiliser des méthodes indirectes pour estimer la valeur de services écologiques en l'absence de prix de marché, cela ne résout qu'imparfaitement le problème conceptuel que nous soulevions en première partie en ce qui concerne le dommage écologique « pur ». Toutes les méthodes exposées précédemment ont vocation à chercher à ramener l'évaluation du dommage écologique à des préférences individuelles. Or, nous l'avons vu, on pourrait vouloir disposer d'estimations indépendantes de toute subjectivité humaine et reconnaissant une valeur intrinsèque à l'environnement. Ce sont notamment les approches « services-services » et « ressources-ressources » qui sont alors mobilisées[529]. Elles ont pour caractéristique d'être fondamentalement des estimations *physiques* ne permettant pas de substitution entre les biens.

Plus précisément, les méthodes d'équivalence de services cherchent à construire des indicateurs de qualité des services écologiques rendus par un milieu naturel[530]. Elles nécessitent donc bien l'utilisation d'une unité de mesure commune aux différents aspects du dommage. Mais elles le font sans que cette unité soit une unité monétaire impliquant une substitution entre services écologiques et autres services économiques. Ainsi, pour une surface de milieu endommagé, cette méthode construit une unité de services/hectare/an. Le dommage est alors considéré comme la somme des destructions de ces services sur une période de temps et sur une surface donnée exprimée dans cette unité de mesure. Un exemple simple illustrera cette méthode. Imaginons qu'une pollution touche un milieu naturel aquatique et détruise l'ensemble des services écologiques fournis par ce milieu sur une zone A de 10 hectares et qu'elle détruise la moitié de ces services écologiques sur une zone B de 20 hectares. Dans ce cas, la destruction du milieu sera estimée à 10*100 % + 20*50 % soit 20 hectares de service/an. On complétera ce raisonnement en prenant en compte les périodes de temps futurs et la régénération naturelle éventuelle qui fera que, en période 2, une partie des services écologiques sera naturellement reconstituée. Imaginons que par régénération

---

529 Aux États-Unis, on nomme ces méthodes HEA et REA pour *Habitat Equivalency Analysis* et *Resources Equivalency Analysis*.

530 On trouvera un guide méthodologique de l'application de ces méthodes dans le cadre français *in* : Commissariat général au développement durable, *La Loi responsabilité environnementale et ses méthodes d'équivalence : guide méthodologique*, CGDD, 2012, 128 p.

naturelle, la zone B fournit, en période 2, 100 % de services écologiques et la zone A, 50 % de services écologiques et qu'à la période 3, la régénération naturelle permet à la zone A de retrouver l'ensemble de ses caractéristiques environnementales. Dans ce cas, le nombre de services écologiques perdus en période 2 est de 10*50 % et de 0 en période 3. Le dommage à l'environnement total sur les trois périodes sera donc de 25.

Cette méthode est en fait un intermédiaire entre une évaluation purement technique et une évaluation économique. Elle est avant tout technique et nécessite à ce titre une solide expertise d'ingénieurs ou d'écologues, dans la mesure où elle ne monétise pas et s'en tient à une estimation physique mesurée dans une unité de services fournis par hectare. Elle est cependant économique dans la mesure où l'on aura besoin d'actualiser les pertes futures (exprimées en unités physiques) à un certain taux fourni par les économistes.

La réparation du dommage va alors être considérée comme le fait de rendre équivalents les pertes des services écologiques rendus par le milieu et les gains liés aux mesures de restauration proposées par l'agent qui a causé le dommage. Les méthodes d'équivalence sont donc propres à rendre opérationnelle l'obligation de réparation en nature. Ce point est important et mérite d'être examiné plus précisément car derrière une *technique* se cache une *représentation* sociale du monde et de l'environnement.

On l'a vu, utiliser des méthodes d'évaluation qui choisissent une mesure partagée par de nombreuses activités humaines – comme la monnaie par exemple – permet aux individus de substituer une somme d'argent à la destruction d'un milieu. Définir au contraire une mesure purement physique du dommage à l'environnement supprime cette possibilité et impose une réparation en nature. Non pas que l'auteur du dommage devra nécessairement restaurer le milieu, mais qu'il devra prendre des mesures qui permettront de restaurer autant de services écologiques qu'il en a détruit. On peut autoriser, dans certaines limites, une substitution entre qualité et quantité des mesures de restauration ou encore, si le coût est prohibitif, que les mesures prises portent sur un autre milieu que le milieu ayant subi le dommage. Mais l'important est que l'on considère alors que le monde juridique et social est segmenté. Les débats d'analyse économique de l'environnement retrouvent alors des débats normatifs fondamentaux qui, dans d'autres domaines, partent également de ce point de départ d'interdire la substitution totale et complète entre différentes activités humaines ou différentes sphères. Les travaux, anciens mais encore d'actualité de Michael Walzer ou, plus récents, de Debra Satz partagent ce point de vue d'une substituabilité limitée entre les différents domaines d'action sociale afin de préserver certains domaines d'un calcul économique global. Ces méthodes ouvrent donc la voie à un calcul que l'on pourrait appeler « local » où des tentatives d'optimisation et de maximisation ont un sens – allié d'ailleurs à une substituabilité limitée –, mais en évitant une substitution globale avec l'ensemble des biens économiques[531].

IV) Conclusion

L'objet de cette contribution était de voir ce que les économistes pouvaient apporter à la définition et à l'évaluation des dommages à l'environnement conçues par les juristes, notamment dans le cadre de l'article 4 de la Charte de l'environnement. Comme nous l'avons vu, la théorie économique dispose de solides outils d'évaluation et de définition dès lors que l'on peut rattacher le dommage à des utilités individuelles indirectes. En revanche, dès lors que l'on essaye de définir un dommage écologique pur, la théorie économique semble démunie car il ne peut exister de valeur économique indépendamment d'agents porteurs de préférences ou d'utilité. La nature n'étant pas un agent économique, elle ne saurait voir ses intérêts pris en compte dans le calcul économique. Pourtant, les méthodes plus récentes d'équivalence de service sont une voie intermédiaire – entre sciences, ingénierie et économie – qui ouvrent une voie à une réparation en nature impliquant la définition du dommage économique en terme physique. C'est alors la possibilité d'un calcul économique « local », indépendant des autres biens et services économiques, qui se trouve posée.

---

531 Sur les approches normatives insistant sur l'autonomie des sphères sociales afin d'éviter que tous les domaines d'activités humaines soient contaminés par la sphère économique, voir Michael Walzer, *Spheres of Justice*, Basic Books, 1983 et Debra Satz, *Why Some Things Should Not Be For Sale: The Moral Limits of Markets*, Oxford University Press, 2010.

Chapter 11

Environmental Constitutionalism and EU Law

I) Introduction
II) Preliminary Considerations: Constitutionalism and EU Law?
   A) Constitutional Functions of EU Primary Law
   B) The Supremacy of EU Law over National Legal Systems
III) Environmental Constitutionalism within the EU Legal Order
   A) The Constitutional Scope of the Union Policy on the Environment
   B) The Impact of Title XX TFEU beyond EU Environmental Policy: The Horizontal Clause in Article 11 TFEU
   C) The Fundamental Rights Dimension of Environmental Protection
IV) Environmental Constitutionalism and the Relationship between EU Law and National Legal Systems
V) Conclusion

Chapitre 11

Constitutionnalisme environnemental et droit de l'Union européenne

I) Introduction
II) Considérations préliminaires : constitutionnalisme et droit de l'UE ?
   A) Fonctions constitutionnelles du droit primaire de l'UE
   B) La suprématie du droit de l'UE sur les systèmes juridiques nationaux

Sven KAUFMANN

Lawyer, Court of Justice of the European Union, Luxembourg Research and Documentation Directorate[532]

Abstract: This contribution seeks to analyse EU law from the point of view of environmental constitutionalism and to assess to what extent environmental provisions of EU law may be regarded as enabling or constraining the creation and application of legal standards. One impact of environmental constitutionalism may be found with regard to primary law where it lays down common environmental standards for EU regulatory activities. This is however not the case as regards the relationship between EU law and national legal orders, since primacy and the direct effect of EU law do not amount to supremacy within the meaning of constitutionalism.

Résumé : La présente contribution propose d'analyser le droit de l'UE en termes de constitutionnalisme environnemental et d'apprécier dans quelle mesure les normes environnementales de l'UE peuvent être qualifiées comme habilitant ou restreignant la création et l'application de normes juridiques. Un impact certain du constitutionnalisme environnemental peut être constaté au regard du droit primaire dans la mesure où celui-ci établit des règles environnementales communes applicables à l'ensemble de l'activité régulatrice de l'Union. Tel n'est cependant pas le cas au regard de la relation entre le droit de l'UE et les

[532] This contribution reflects solely the opinion of the author.

ordres juridiques nationaux, la primauté et l'effet direct du droit de l'UE ne pouvant s'assimiler à la suprématie au sens du constitutionnalisme.

I) Introduction

Since the 1980s, environmental protection has been considered as "one of the Community's essential objectives"[533] and is referred to today in Article 3(3) TEU (Treaty on European Union), which states that the Union "shall [...] work for the sustainable development of Europe based on balanced economic growth and [...] a high level of protection and improvement of the quality of the environment [...]". In the light of this strong commitment, the question arises whether European Union law (EU law), a sophisticated legal order featuring an ever more increasing level of regulation based on a consensus on common and fundamental values[534], may be assessed in terms of environmental constitutionalism.

In order to examine whether environmental constitutionalism may have an impact on EU 'constitutional' law, this contribution draws on the assumption that environmental constitutionalism may be defined as the idea of supremacy of environmental constitutional norms over infra-constitutional norms. Without entering the broader discussion of constitutionalism in international law, and more specifically in international environmental law[535], it relies on a functional approach and therefore essentially focuses on the question to what extent environmental provisions of EU law may be regarded as enabling or constraining the creation and application of legal standards[536].

After some preliminary considerations on the scope of environmental constitutionalism in EU law (II), the analysis focuses on environmental constitutionalism within the EU legal order (III) before turning to the relationship between EU law and national legal systems (IV).

---

533 Judgment of 7 February 1985, *ADBHU* (240/83), para. 13.

534 Articles 2 and 3(1) TEU.

535 See e.g. Alexandre Kiss, "The Legal Ordering of Environmental Protection", *in*: Ronald St. John Macdonald, Douglas M. Johnston (eds.), *Towards World Constitutionalism. Issues in the Legal Ordering of the World Community*, Martinus Nijhoff, 2005, p. 567–584, at 568 *et seq.*

536 See Jeffrey L. Dunoff, Joel P. Trachtman, "What is Constitutionalization beyond the State?", *in*: Jeffrey L. Dunoff, Joel P. Trachtman (eds.), *Ruling the World?: Constitutionalism, International Law, and Global Governance*, CUP, 2009, p. 9 *et seq.*

II) Preliminary Considerations: Constitutionalism and EU Law?

Prior to assessing EU law in terms of environmental constitutionalism, two issues should be highlighted, first whether EU primary law may be considered as a "constitution" within the meaning of constitutionalism (A), and second whether constitutionalism may be applied with respect to the relationship between EU law and national legal systems (B).

A) Constitutional Functions of EU Primary Law

As opposed to national legal systems featuring constitutions in the classic sense, it does not seem clear from the outset whether EU law itself may be considered as comprising a 'constitution' or as having 'constitutional effects'. With numerous aspects of this issue having been recurrently discussed following the failure of the Treaty establishing a Constitution for Europe in 2005, EU primary law undoubtedly presents core elements commonly associated with constitutionalism[537].

EU primary law establishes a single and comprehensive set of rules defining the competences of EU institutions, hence binding and directing the latters' scope of action, and provides for strict revision procedures for primary law[538]. In line with the provisions of the Treaty on the Functioning of the European Union (TFEU), the EU may adopt binding norms, such as regulations having direct effect, a standard decision-making process by majority vote, and a complete system of legal remedies and procedures. It also features the Charter of Fundamental Rights of the European Union (the Charter), which has the same legal value as the Treaties[539]. In addition, the European Court of Justice (ECJ) has repeatedly interpreted primary law in a manner similar to a constitution, making references to "constitutional principles stemming from the Treaties"[540], underlining

---

[537] See Louis J. Kotzé, "Arguing Global Environmental Constitutionalism", Transnational Environmental Law 2012, p. 199–233, at 203 *et seq.*, in particular the idea of supreme norms, the existence of provisions curtailing political power and (state) authority, fundamental rights and "higher values", and the existence of judicial review and checks and balances.

[538] Article 48 TEU, which interestingly involves the EU institutions themselves.

[539] Article 6(1) TEU.

[540] Opinion of the Court 1/15 of 26 July 2017, para. 67.

that the EU legal order features its "own constitutional framework and founding principles"[541] and that the Treaties constitute a "basic constitutional charter"[542]. In fact, the ECJ has stressed the existence in EU law of a hierarchy of norms in that sense that EU acts must respect certain rules embodied in primary law as a condition of their lawfulness, notably fundamental rights, which it is for the ECJ to review in the framework of the complete system of legal remedies established by primary law[543]. It has further accepted the existence of general principles of EU law[544] and recognized the principles of primacy and direct effect of EU law[545]. Consequently, there would appear to be no barrier to assessing EU primary law in terms of constitutionalism[546].

B) The Supremacy of EU Law over National Legal Systems

The issue whether EU law itself may be considered as having supremacy over national legal systems within the meaning of constitutionalism seems to be more delicate. It is however the ECJ's settled case-law that "in accordance with the principle of the primacy of EU law, rules of national law, even of a constitutional order, cannot be allowed to undermine the unity and effectiveness of European Union law"[547]. As a consequence, a national court which is called upon to apply provisions of EU law is bound, if necessary, to refuse of its own motion to apply any conflicting

---

541 Opinion of the Court 2/13 of 18 December 2014, para. 158.

542 *Ibid.*, para. 163.

543 Judgment of 3 September 2008, *Kadi v Council and Commission* (C-402/05 P and C-415/05 P), para. 285. A hierarchy of norms also exists within EU secondary legislation, for instance as regards basic and implementing regulations, e.g. Judgment of 19 January 2017, *Schaefer Kalk* (C-460/15).

544 See also General Court, Judgment of 12 September 2007, *Prym and Prym Consumer v Commission* (T-30/05), para. 226, which emphasized the higher legal value ("valeur juridique supérieure") of the proportionality principle as a general principle of EC law over a regulation.

545 See below I, B.

546 See also AG Jääskinen's Opinion of 26 April 2012, *Compass-Datenbank* (C-138/11), para. 37, who considers the European Union a "polity based on the principles of constitutionalism".

547 Judgment of 26 May 2016, *Ezernieki* (C-273/15), para. 53. See also Judgments of 26 February 2013, *Melloni* (C-399/11), para. 59, and 8 September 2010, *Winner Wetten* (C-409/06), para. 61.

provision of national law, even if adopted subsequently[548]. On numerous occasions, the Court has also recognised the direct effect of provisions of both primary law and secondary legislation, thus permitting the application of EU law notwithstanding conflicting national law[549].

If EU law is therefore characterised by its supremacy over the laws of the Member States and also by the direct effect of a range of provisions[550], it may appear at least conceivable to consider the process of constitutionalism, in the sense of supremacy of not only a norm over another but also of a legal system over another, with respect to the relation between EU law and national legal orders.

III) Environmental Constitutionalism within the EU Legal Order

This contribution will examine, first, the constitutional scope of primary law provisions relating to the Union policy on the environment (A), and second, their impact on other fields of EU policy (B). Third, the inclusion of environmental protection in the Charter will be examined in the light of environmental constitutionalism (C).

A) The Constitutional Scope of the Union Policy on the Environment

Environmental norms in primary law are mainly set out in Title XX TFEU relating to the Union policy on the environment and effectively determine the scope and limits of legislative activity in this field (1), as highlighted in relevant case-law in this respect (2).

1) The legal context of Union policy on the environment: Title XX of the TFEU defines the substantial framework of EU legislative action in the field of environmental protection. Under Article 191(1) TFEU, Union policy on the environment shall contribute to pursuit of the objectives of preserving,

---

548 E.g. Judgment of 4 June 2015, *Kernkraftwerke Lippe-Ems* (C-5/14), para. 32.

549 More generally, see the landmark judgments of 5 February 1963, *van Gend & Loos* (26/62), 15 July 1964, *Costa* (6/64), and 17 December 1970, *Internationale Handelsgesellschaft* (11/70).

550 AG Wathelet's Opinion of 19 September 2017, *Achmea* (C-284/16), para. 231. See also Summary No. 2 of Judgment of 17 May 1972, *Leonesio* (93/71): "Supremacy over national law".

protecting and improving the quality of the environment, protecting human health, prudent and rational utilisation of natural resources, and promoting measures at international level to deal with regional or worldwide environmental problems, and in particular combating climate change.

In addition to these objectives, Article 191(2) TFEU establishes a number of principles underlying the Union policy on the environment insofar as the latter shall

- Aim at a high level of protection taking into account the diversity of situations in the various regions of the Union, and
- Be based on: the precautionary principle; the principle that preventive action should be taken; the principle that environmental damage should as a priority be rectified at source; the principle that the polluter should pay.

Although these principles may not necessarily qualify as "constitutional principles" within the meaning of the Court's above-mentioned jurisprudence, which has so far referred to principles of a more general scope such as proportionality, legal certainty, and respect of fundamental rights, they amount to "environmental principles"[551] of EU law establishing substantial criteria for the lawfulness of secondary legislation adopted on the basis of Title XX of the TFEU, breach of which would render the act concerned invalid[552]. In the same way national law would have to be compatible with substantial constitutional requirements of the national legal system, Article 191 TFEU lays out relevant criteria for the lawfulness of secondary legislation adopted on grounds of the Union policy on the environment[553]. Therefore, Title XX of the TFEU may be considered as

---

551 AG Kokott's Opinion of 20 November 2014, *Fipa Group and Others* (C-534/13), para. 3.

552 Given the complexity of the implementation of the objectives and principles mentioned in Article 191 TFEU, judicial review is limited to the question whether the EU legislature has committed a manifest error of appraisal, see judgments of 21 December 2016, *Associazione Italia Nostra Onlus* (C-444/15), para. 46, and 15 December 2005, *Greece v Commission* (C-86/03), para. 88.

553 In addition, Article 191(3) TFEU sets out requirements which shall be taken account of for the preparation of the Union policy on the environment, i.e. available scientific and technical data, environmental conditions in the various regions of the Union, the potential benefits and costs of action or lack of action, and the economic and social development of the Union as a whole and the balanced development of its regions.

having a constitutional scope inasmuch as it both enables and constrains the creation of EU secondary legislation in the field of the environment.

2) Case-law on the compatibility of environmental secondary legislation with EU environmental principles: Relatively little case-law on the validity of secondary legislation adopted on the basis of Title XX TFEU with regard to the environmental principles in Article 191(2) TFEU may be cited in support of the abovementioned findings, as existing jurisprudence relating to the compatibility of environmental secondary legislation with primary law focuses rather on more general principles such as proportionality[554] or equal treatment[555]. Regarding the high level of the protection principle, two cases may however be mentioned.

First, the ECJ disposed of a case concerning the validity of the general prohibition on hydrochlorofluorocarbons (HCFCs) contained in Council Regulation (EC) No. 3093/94 of 15 December 1994 on substances that deplete the ozone layer. The Court held *inter alia* that by adopting a more stringent measure than that deriving from its international obligations under the Vienna Convention of 22 March 1985 for the Protection of the Ozone Layer, the Community legislature did not infringe the requirement of a high level of protection laid down in what is now Article 191(2) TFEU[556].

Second, the ECJ examined the validity of Directive 2001/42/EC of the European Parliament and of the Council of 27 June 2001 on the assessment of the effects of certain plans and programmes on the environment, inasmuch as it provided that the plans and programmes which determine the use of small areas at local level and minor modifications to plans and programmes are to require an environmental assessment only where the Member States determine that they are likely to have significant effects on the environment. The requirement of "significant effects on the environment" in order to trigger the obligation to conduct an environmental assessment was deemed compatible with Article 191 TFEU, as the Court distinguished

---

[554] E.g. Judgment of 15 December 2005, *Greece v Commission* (C-86/03).

[555] E.g. Judgment of 16 December 2008, *Arcelor Atlantique and Lorraine and Others* (C-127/07).

[556] Judgment of 14 July 1998, *Safety Hi-Tech / S. & T.* (C-284/95), para. 48. The appellant in the main proceedings had argued that the Regulation failed to ensure a high level of environmental protection by authorising certain halons which displayed a higher ozone depletion potential and were more damaging to the environment than the substance at stake. The Court also rejected the argument that available scientific and technical data had not been taken into account (paras. 51 *et seq.*).

this situation from that in which a purely quantitative threshold would lead, in practice, to an entire class of plans or programmes being exempted in advance from the requirement of environmental assessment under Directive 2001/42/EC, even if those plans or programmes were likely to have significant effects on the environment. By doing so, the ECJ rejected the referring court's reasoning based on the mere risk that the national authorities, through their conduct, could circumvent the application of Directive 2001/42/EC[557].

In addition, attention should be drawn to the pending case *Blaise and Others* (C-616/17), concerning the validity, in the light of the precautionary principle enshrined in Article 191 TFEU, of Regulation (EC) No. 1107/2009 of the European Parliament and of the Council of 21 October 2009 concerning the placing of plant protection products on the market. The referring French court has raised doubts as to the reliability and impartiality of the evaluation process in the context of the authorisation procedure of plant protection products.

B) The Impact of Title XX TFEU beyond EU Environmental Policy: The Horizontal Clause in Article 11 TFEU

Due to the broadly competency-based structure of the TFEU as regards EU policies, environmental provisions in Title XX of the TFEU are primarily relevant in respect of EU acts adopted on the basis of this specific policy. However, these provisions acquire further relevance by means of the horizontal clause provided for in Article 11 TFUE, according to which environmental protection requirements must be integrated into the definition and implementation of Union policies and activities, in particular with a view to promoting sustainable development[558].

Article 11 TFEU creates an integration obligation requiring the application of the sector-specific environmental principles in Title XX of the TFEU to measures adopted on the basis of other EU policies, and further entitles the Union legislature to promote environmental protection

---

557 Judgment of 21 December 2016, *Associazione Italia Nostra Onlus* (C-444/15), para. 45 *et seq.*

558 A provision with a similar wording was first included in primary law in 1986 by the Single European Act with Article 130r(2) second phrase of the Treaty of the European Communities, which later became Article 3c and then Article 6 of said Treaty.

by adopting measures based on a rule of competence outside the Union policy on the environment[559]. As regards the constitutional aspects of this provision, the possibility to draw on environmental objectives and principles in interpreting both primary law and EU secondary legislation as highlighted by the ECJ's case-law may be of particular interest.

Concerning the interpretation of primary law outside the Union policy on the environment, the ECJ has stated that Article 11 TFEU "emphasises the fundamental nature of that objective and its extension across the range of those policies and activities"[560]. It can therefore be relied on for the interpretation of provisions of primary law in the light of, and ultimately in favour of, environmental protection[561]. In fact, regarding the scope of EU competencies in the field of environmental protection, the Court *inter alia* relied on the horizontal environmental clause as a basis for the former Community's competence in the field of criminal law relating to the environment[562] as well as the inclusion of the protection of the marine environment against ship-source pollution as part of the common transport policy[563].

It has further repeatedly held that national measures that are capable of hindering intra-Union trade may *inter alia* be justified by overriding requirements relating to protection of the environment. Although not always making a direct reference to Article 11 TFEU, the ECJ has done so on a number of occasions in the context of the free movement of goods, for instance in respect of national support mechanisms for the production of green energy[564] and sectoral traffic prohibition for lorries of over a certain weight carrying certain goods[565]. Furthermore, while assessing

[559] For a deeper analysis of Article 11 TFEU, see Julian Nowag, *Environmental Integration in Competition and Free-movement Laws*, OUP, 2016, p. 15 *et seq.*

[560] Judgment of 13 September 2005, *Commission v Council* (C-176/03), para. 42.

[561] Internal market rules themselves include references to environmental protection. In fact, according to Article 114(3) TFEU, harmonisation measures with the aim of establishing or ensuring the functioning of the internal market concerning *inter alia* environmental protection will take as a base a high level of protection, taking account in particular of any new development based on scientific facts.

[562] Judgment of 13 September 2006, *Commission v Council* (C-176/03), paras. 42 and 48.

[563] Judgment of 23 October 2007, *Commission v Council* (C-440/05), paras. 52 *et seq.*

[564] Judgments of 29 September 2016, *Essent Belgium* (C 492/14), of 1 July 2014, *Ålands Vindkraft* (C-573/12), and 13 March 2001, *PreußenElektra* (C-379/98).

[565] Judgments of 21 December 2011, *Commission v Austria* (C-28/09), and 15 November 2005, *Commission v Austria* (C-320/03).

the validity of Directive 2009/28/EC of the European Parliament and of the Council of 23 April 2009 on the promotion of the use of energy from renewable sources, the ECJ drew *inter alia* on Article 11 TFEU in order to interpret the free movement of goods under Article 34 TFEU. It held that the provision in the Directive which had the effect of restricting trade in sustainable biogas was justified on grounds of protection of the environment[566].

Concerning secondary legislation, Article 11 TFEU is considered a provision which "expresses the principle that all [Union] measures must satisfy the requirements of environmental protection"[567], regardless of their legal basis. Hence this provision allows for the horizontal application of sector-specific environmental principles with a view to assessing EU regulatory activity outside the Union policy on the environment[568].

This finding first applies to legal acts adopted on grounds of approximation of laws within the meaning of Article 114 TFEU. Although not expressly referring to the horizontal clause, the ECJ has examined the validity, with regard to the precautionary and high level of protection principles, of Regulation (EC) No. 258/97 of the European Parliament and of the Council of 27 January 1997 concerning novel foods and novel food ingredients, insofar as it provided for a simplified safety assessment procedure for food products substantially equivalent to existing foods which had been applied to foods produced from genetically modified maize[569].

The ECJ has also taken into account the protection of human health and the precautionary principle in order to assess the proportionality of protective measures in the context of the 'Mad cow disease' adopted on the legal basis relating to the common agricultural policy. Notwithstanding the great uncertainty as to the risks posed by live animals, bovine meat and derived products at the time the measures were adopted, the Court dismissed the action brought by the United Kingdom against the ban

---

566 Judgment of 22 June 2017, *E.ON Biofor Sverige* (C-549/15), paras. 44 *et seq*, spec. 48. The relevant provision was adopted on the basis of Article 114 TFEU.

567 Judgments of 29 March 1990, *Greece v Council* (C-62/88), para. 20, and 24 November 1993, *Mondiet* (C-405/92), para. 27.

568 As regards the relationship between two acts of secondary legislation in the light of the horizontal clause in Article 13 TFEU (animal welfare), see Judgment of 26 February 2019, *Œuvre d'assistance aux bêtes d'abattoirs* (C-497/17).

569 Judgment of 9 September 2003, *Monsanto Agricoltura Italia and Others* (C-236/01), paras. 128 *et seq*.

on the export of live bovine animals, permitting EU institutions to act without having to wait until the reality and seriousness of those risks become fully apparent[570].

Environmental principles are also relevant with respect to direct support schemes established within the common agricultural policy, the Court having stated that a Member State may include requirements relating to the maintenance of visible public rights of way in its good agricultural and environmental condition standards under Council Regulation No. 1782/2003 of 29 September 2003 establishing common rules for direct support schemes under the common agricultural policy and establishing certain support schemes for farmers, insofar as those requirements contribute to the retention of those rights of way as landscape features or, as the case may be, the avoidance of the deterioration of habitats[571]. The Court further allowed for an extensive interpretation of secondary legislation in the field of public procurement when stating that Member States may take into account ecological criteria in order to determine the economically most advantageous tender, noting that in the light of the horizontal clause the secondary legislation in question did not exclude the possibility for the contracting authority to use criteria relating to the protection of the environment when assessing the economically most advantageous tender[572].

The abovementioned case-law illustrates the particular importance of Article 11 TFEU as it puts the Union legislator in a position to promote environmental protection in all areas of EU law and, as the case may be, to erect substantial thresholds for the lawfulness of EU acts. It establishes an obligation to (actively) integrate environmental protection into all Union policies and activities and therefore both enables and constrains the creation of secondary legislation. It should however be noted that it does not necessarily have any implications for the actual 'value' of environmental protection when compared with the other interests at stake.

---

570 Judgment of 5 May 1998, *United Kingdom v Commission* (C-180/96), paras. 98 *et seq.* At the time of the proceedings, Article 130r(2) EC only referred to the preventive action principle. See also Judgment of 19 September 2002, *Huber* (C-336/00).

571 Judgment of 16 July 2009, *Horvath* (C-428/07), paras. 25 *et seq.*

572 Judgments of 17 September 2002, *Concordia Bus Finland* (C-513/99), para. 57, and 4 December 2003, *EVN and Wienstrom* (C-448/01), para. 33.

C) The Fundamental Rights Dimension of Environmental Protection

According to Article 37 of the Charter, a high level of environmental protection and the improvement of the quality of the environment must be integrated into the policies of the Union and ensured in accordance with the principle of sustainable development. Although mentioning environmental protection in the context of fundamental rights seems of particular interest while assessing environmental constitutionalism under EU law, a closer examination of the scope of this provision proves to be rather disappointing, since it may be seen from the Explanations relating to the Charter that it merely reflects the content of Article 3(3) TEU, Article 11 TFEU and the objectives and principles enshrined in Article 191 TFEU[573]. In the light of these explanations and recent case-law, Article 37 of the Charter does not seem to have an autonomous substantial or procedural significance of its own.

Indeed, in a case concerning the validity of an environmental directive, the ECJ held that Article 37 of the Charter does not lay down more extensive requirements than those enshrined in Article 191 TFEU[574]. Furthermore, the General Court dismissed an action for annulment, brought by two environmental protection organisations against the Commission's decision to approve an active substance under Regulation (EC) No. 1107/2009 of the European Parliament and of the Council of 21 October 2009 concerning the placing of plant protection products on the market, as inadmissible for lack of standing to bring proceedings and rejected the applicants' arguments based *inter alia* on Article 37 of the Charter in order to challenge the interpretation of the fourth paragraph of Article 263 TFEU and, in particular, the criterion of direct concern. To that effect, it stated that Article 37 of the Charter only contains a principle providing for a general obligation on the European Union in respect of the objectives to be pursued in the framework of its

---

573 Explanations relating to the Charter of Fundamental Rights, *OJ* 2007 C 303, p. 17, at 27. The rather obscure statement that Article 37 "also draws on the provisions of some national constitutions" could however – at least in theory – leave some room for an innovative interpretation in the future.

574 Judgment of 21 December 2016, *Associazione Italia Nostra Onlus* (C-444/15), para. 63: "Since [...] Directive 2001/42 has revealed nothing which could affect its validity in the light of Article 191 TFEU, it follows that that provision also reveals nothing which could affect its validity in the light of Article 37 of the Charter".

policies, and not a right to bring actions in environmental matters before the Courts of the European Union[575].

Although it does not entail an actual 'constitutional upgrading' as far as substantial or procedural rights are concerned, Article 37 of the Charter is not deprived of any significance whatsoever. In fact, it underlines the importance of environmental protection within EU legislative action and, in particular, the necessity of not only maintaining but also improving the quality of the environment, thereby 'greening' EU policy and the EU legal order as a whole[576] and underlining the obligation of the EU legislator to actively pursue an effective environmental policy. With regard to environmental constitutionalism, the provision may actually serve as an "enabling rule of constitutional nature"[577] for the EU legislator, insofar as it could have an impact on the proportionality assessment of EU acts entailing an interference with fundamental rights of economic actors by allowing for a shift in favour of environmental protection in respect to a measure interfering, for instance, with the right to property or the freedom to conduct a business[578]. In addition, the provision could also be relevant in the context of fundamental rights based environmental issues created by economic activities, allowing to tip the balance in favour of effective protection of the environment or human health within the scope of, for instance, the right to life, the right to the integrity of the person, or the right to respect for private and family life. More generally, with reference to this provision, EU law as well as national implementing legislation may be interpreted in a way that could be more consistent with the goal of effective environmental protection.

---

575 General Court, Order of 28 September 2016, *PAN Europe and Others v Commission* (T-600/15), para. 47.

576 See Judgment of 21 December 2011, *Commission v Austria* (C-28/09), para. 121: "The transversal and fundamental nature of [the requirement of environmental protection] is also reaffirmed in [Article 37] of the Charter".

577 See Bernhard Wegener, *in*: Hans Von Der Groeben, Jürgen Schwarze, Armin Hatje, *Europäisches Unionsrecht*, C.H. Beck, 7th ed. 2015, GRC Artikel 37, at 2: "verfassungsrechtliche Ermächtigungsnorm".

578 See, to that effect, General Court, Judgment of 26 September 2014, *Romonta v Commission* (T-614/13), paras. 74 *et seq.*, spec. 76: "[…] the Commission had to balance the fundamental rights of operators of installations that are subject to the emission allowance trading scheme and environmental protection as provided for in Article 37 of the Charter […], the first subparagraph of Article 3(3) TEU and Articles 11 and 191 TFEU".

In short, Article 37 of the Charter certainly has a positive impact on administrative and legislative processes at the EU level, on EU legal methodology, and the role of environmental protection within the EU legal order. In the light of environmental constitutionalism, it is therefore relevant in the same way as Article 11 TFEU, in respect of its impact on both the interpretation of primary law and secondary legislation.

IV) Environmental Constitutionalism and the Relationship between EU Law and National Legal Systems

As stated above, it could prove tempting to analyse the supremacy of EU law over the laws of the Member States, deriving from the principle of primacy without having regard to the national hierarchy of norms, and the direct effect of certain provisions of primary law and secondary legislation, in terms of environmental constitutionalism.

Concerning the relationship between environmental norms in primary law and national law, in particular as regards the applicability of Article 191(2) TFEU, the issue is mitigated since the ECJ has repeatedly recalled that the principles set out in this provision are directed at action at EU level. It has therefore concluded that, first, Article 191(2) TFEU cannot be relied on as such by individuals in order to preclude the application of national legislation in an area covered by environmental policy for which no EU legislation has been adopted on the basis of Article 192 TFEU that specifically covers the situation in question, and, second, competent environmental authorities cannot rely on Article 191(2) TFEU in the absence of any national legal basis for the purposes of imposing preventive and remedial measures[579]. The concept of environmental constitutionalism may therefore not prove useful in this respect.

However, the ECJ also underlined that a principle enshrined in Article 191(2) TFEU would be capable of applying in the main proceedings to the extent that it is implemented by secondary legislation[580]. In this context, Article 11 TFEU and Article 37 of the Charter should allow and require the observation of environmental principles set out in

---

579 Judgment of 4 March 2015, *Fipa Group and Others* (C-534/13), paras. 40 and 41.

580 *Ibid.*, para. 42: "[…] the 'polluter pays' principle is capable of applying in the main proceedings to the extent that it is implemented by Directive 2004/35".

Article 191(2) TFEU by any national legislation which falls within the scope of EU secondary legislation or which implements that law[581]. More generally, any assessment provided for by an act of secondary environmental legislation may take precedence over any rule of national law. The idea of environmental constitutionalism in respect of EU law and national legal systems might hence be pursued in respect of the relation between secondary legislation and national law by recognising that secondary legislation has a constitutional effect as regards the creation and application of national law.

Although EU law does have, unlike more classical regional international law regimes, specific features that could be drawn on to that effect[582], such an understanding of the concepts of primacy and direct effect of EU law seems however to go far beyond the scope of one of constitutionalism's main features, namely, considering certain basic rights and values as inviolable[583]. In fact, the relation between EU law and national legal systems is an issue concerning the relationship between separate legal orders. It is of course settled ECJ case-law that the concept of primacy in EU law derives from EU law itself, but primacy may be effectively applied only because it is also embedded in the national legal orders[584]. Equating primacy with the idea of supremacy in the sense of constitutionalism, which is ultimately based on a value decision, would overstretch primacy as a conflict of law mechanism and also cast strong doubts on the legitimacy of EU law. Eventually, the question of the relationship between EU law and national law is not an

---

581 Similarly, for instance, the ECJ's findings with regard to the principle of proportionality, see e.g. Judgment of 6 March 2014, *Siragusa* (C-206/13), para. 34.

582 See René Barents, *The Autonomy of Community Law*, Kluwer Law International, 2004, spec. p. 189: "The purpose of the doctrine of Community law as a 'legal order' [...] is to establish the autonomy of Community law, or, in other words, its constitutional character".

583 On this aspect of constitutionalism, see, for instance, Michel Rosenfeld, Andras Sajó, "Constitutionalism: Foundations for the New Millenium", *in*: Michel Rosenfeld, Gagik Garushevich Aruntiunian (eds.), *New Millenium Constitutionalism: Paradigms of Reality and Challenges*, Njhar, 2013, p. 11–28, at p. 22.

584 Under German constitutional law, for instance, the primacy of EU law derives from the national ratification law of the EU Treaties. On theoretical aspects of this issue, see Anne Peters, "Rechtsordnungen und Konstitutionalisierung: Zur Neubestimmung der Verhältnisse", *Zeitschrift für öffentliches Recht (ZöR)*, 2010, p. 3–63, at 33 *et seq.*

issue of supremacy aiming to uphold certain values, but of the necessity to strike a balance based *inter alia* on the principle of loyalty and not least on effective cooperation between European and national courts[585].

V) Conclusion

Environmental constitutionalism does have an impact on EU law insofar as environmental standards in primary law, i.e. Title XX of the TFEU, Article 11 TFEU, and Article 37 of the Charter, enable and oblige the EU legislature to pursue an effective environmental policy and to integrate environmental protection requirements into all the Union policies and activities, and also set out specific criteria which have to be taken into account in interpreting both primary law and secondary legislation, regardless of the legal basis upon which an act has been adopted. Even though the inclusion of environmental protection in the Charter does not improve substantial and procedural environmental rights, it has an impact on administrative and legislative processes at EU level in the field of the environment. These provisions, and in particular the environmental principles enshrined in Article 191(2) TFEU, lay down common standards for EU regulatory activity as a whole. They thus have a constitutional function within the EU legal order, both enabling and constraining the creation and/or application of norms of EU law, and may therefore even be described as the EU's "environmental constitution".

Environmental principles enshrined in primary law have, as such, no direct effect in national legal systems. In the light of the principles of primacy and direct effect, environmental constitutionalism could however also be relevant as regards the relationship between EU secondary legislation and the national legal orders. Such an understanding of said principles and, more generally, of the relationship between EU law and national law, would however overstretch both these principles as well as environmental constitutionalism as a concept based on the assumption that certain basic rights and values are considered inviolable.

---

585 See also Paul Kirchhof, "Die Gewaltenbalance zwischen staatlichen und europäischen Organen", *JuristenZeitung*, 1998, p. 965–974, at 973.

Conclusions générales
General conclusions

Jochen SOHNLE

Professeur de droit public à l'Université de Lorraine, France
Faculté de droit, sciences économiques et gestion de Nancy
IRENEE/UL (EA 7303)

Toutes les contributions réunies dans le présent ouvrage cernent *l'impact* du constitutionnalisme environnemental sur les différents systèmes juridiques. Comme il est précisé dans la contribution introductive (chapitre 1), le terme « impact » est utilisé *lato sensu*, dans le sens d'influence ou d'effet. Dans le présent ouvrage bilingue, ce néologisme français permet de couvrir un champ sémantique identique à la langue anglaise.

Cet impact sur les ordres juridiques se mesure par rapport au *constitutionnalisme environnemental*. La contribution introductive apporte aussi un positionnement méthodologique par rapport à une terminologie devenue à la mode, mais peu conceptualisée. Or le constitutionnalisme environnemental indique principalement quatre directions définitionnelles. Il s'agit :

1) d'une idéologie consistant à intégrer dans la Constitution à la fois le libéralisme politique et l'écologisme (constitutionnalisme environnemental au sens d'environnementalisme constitutionnel) ;
2) de normes à valeur constitutionnelle dont le contenu est la protection de l'environnement (constitutionnalisme environnemental au sens de droit constitutionnel de l'environnement) ;
3) de principes juridiques dégagés à partir de méthodes spécifiques du droit comparé (constitutionnalisme environnemental au sens de principes génériques du droit de l'environnement, conformément à la démarche du *tertium comparationis*) ainsi que, grâce à ces méthodes ;

4) de potentiels principes généraux du droit international public susceptibles de s'imposer comme normes de rang supérieur dans les systèmes juridiques nationaux qui présentent encore des lacunes dans ce domaine.

Gitanjali N. Gill insiste dans sa contribution sur l'Inde sur le « mouvement de la gouvernance environnementale » (*environmental governance movement*) et accepte l'idée du constitutionnalisme environnemental dans sa première signification. Il se construit dans ce pays aussi sur un fondement religieux tiré des anciens écrits hindous (comme la *Bhagavad Gita*). L'idéologie se perçoit ainsi au-delà des seules mouvances occidentales. Si le ton de Marie-Anne Cohendet est également engagé sur le plan des valeurs de liberté et d'écologie, il suit la voie laïque conformément à la tradition républicaine française. Le contexte idéologique et militant est présent de manière particulièrement explicite dans la contribution de Letícia Albuquerque sur les droits des animaux au Brésil. Dans ce pays, l'idéologie de l'*Animal Rights Movement* se voit effectivement consacrée par le pouvoir constituant de 1988.

La deuxième signification se reflète dans la contribution de Simon Jolivet sur le volet administratif du constitutionnalisme environnemental français ainsi que dans celle d'Olivier Cachard sur la précaution environnementale de l'État actionnaire. Elle domine aussi les contributions de Marie-Anne Cohendet, d'Anne-Christine Favre et d'Alexander Proelß. Ce dernier choisit explicitement la terminologie de droit constitutionnel de l'environnement dès l'intitulé de sa contribution. Toutefois, comme représentant de la doctrine allemande, il recourt également à la notion d'État environnemental (*Umweltstaat*) qui cristallise l'approche environnementaliste du constitutionnalisme (signification 1). Et c'est dans le sens générique (signification 3) qu'est mis en relief ce que cet auteur appelle le principe de la protection de l'environnement. Ce principe, susceptible de former le noyau d'un constitutionnalisme environnemental régional au niveau de l'Union européenne (UE), irrigue d'après lui tout le système juridique allemand. Sur ce dernier aspect, la démarche adoptée par Anne-Christine Favre autour du droit suisse est différente. Elle analyse l'impact concret des différents principes environnementaux en matière de durabilité, de prévention, de précaution et de payement par le pollueur. Cela la mène à s'interroger non pas sur l'existence d'un principe générique, mais sans détour de *tertium comparationis*, sur celle d'autres principes constitutionnels non écrits en matière environnementale, comme l'obligation de trouver des solutions de substitution avant d'épuiser une ressource rare ou le principe de non-régression.

Pour Erin Daly et James R. May, il s'agit d'intégrer dans la Constitution et de mettre en œuvre sur le plan législatif et judiciaire des droits, devoirs, procédures, politiques et d'autres dispositifs qui visent à promouvoir la protection de l'environnement. Leur approche se situe également à cheval entre les significations 1 et 2. Ils intègrent par ailleurs la signification 3 dans la mesure où la portée transnationale est inhérente au constitutionnalisme environnemental. Cela se reflète dans l'expression *« global » environmental constitutionalism* utilisée par ces deux auteurs états-uniens et qui correspond au titre même de leur livre paru en 2015. Ils actualisent ici leur projet comparatif en mettant en relief les tendances d'évolution au regard de six thèmes (changement climatique, personnalisation juridique de la nature, dignité humaine environnementale, durabilité, normes adoptées au niveau des entités fédérées, droits procéduraux).

Le positionnement de Sven Kaufmann mobilise toutes les quatre dimensions du constitutionnalisme environnemental. Par rapport au droit de l'UE il place d'emblée sa contribution dans le contexte de valeurs communes et fondamentales (signification 1). Dans un contexte non étatique, il doit opter pour une approche fonctionnelle du droit constitutionnel au sens du principe de suprématie des normes constitutionnelles environnementales sur les normes infraconstitutionnelles (signification 2) et l'applique à un contexte systématique supranational, à la fois à l'intérieur de l'ordre de l'UE et dans ses relations avec les ordres nationaux. Il décrit ce phénomène comme la « constitution environnementale » de l'UE (*the EU's "environmental constitution"*). Par ailleurs, dans cet ordre supranational, les juges dégagent des principes généraux, conformément à la démarche de généralisation inhérente au droit comparé (signification 3), qu'ils font primer sur les normes nationales (signification 4). Le droit environnemental primaire n'est cependant pas invocable par les particuliers aussi longtemps qu'il n'y a pas eu de mise en œuvre au niveau de l'UE ou des États membres.

Un *système juridique* peut être appréhendé par rapport aux niveaux décisionnels et les règles de répartition des compétences y relatives. Il se conçoit aussi par rapport à son contenu. Enfin, il peut être compris par rapport à ses procédures contentieuses ou non qui garantissent la mise en œuvre et le respect des normes matérielles et organiques. Or, les contributions réunies ici témoignent de l'impact du constitutionnalisme environnemental sur les systèmes juridiques sur trois plans : organique (1), matériel (2) et procédural (3).

1) Sur le plan organique, on distingue les différents niveaux institutionnels où s'adoptent les normes environnementales à valeur constitutionnelle, à savoir celui des entités fédérées, celui des États souverains et, *mutatis mutandis*, celui des institutions supra-étatiques. À ces relations s'ajoutent celles qui s'établissent entre l'échelon constitutionnel (fédéral ou fédérée) et les systèmes normatifs infraconstitutionnels (de type administratif ou judiciaire).

Notamment les normes constitutionnelles adoptées au niveau des États fédérés ne sont pas à négliger. Erin Daly et James R. May nous rappellent au titre du *subnational environmental constitutionalism* que les premières normes constitutionnelles à vocation environnementale ont été insérées dans les constitutions d'États fédérés (notamment aux États-Unis) et que la tendance de promouvoir le constitutionnalisme environnemental par cette voie reste de toute actualité. La contribution d'Alexander Proelß confirme ce constat pour l'Allemagne. Cette portée du fédéralisme environnemental est approfondie pour d'autres fédérations : Suisse (Anne-Christine Favre), Inde (Gitanjali N. Gill) et Brésil (Letícia Albuquerque).

L'impact du constitutionnalisme environnemental est également énorme sur les systèmes normatifs infraconstitutionnels. Il est exploré par Simon Jolivet (droit administratif français de l'environnement) et Olivier Cachard (droit des affaires et rôle de l'État actionnaire sous l'angle du principe de précaution)[586]. L'impact du principe constitutionnel du pollueur-payeur se mesure également au regard de l'économie (Samuel Ferey).

Au niveau supranational il n'existe pas de Constitution au sens formel. C'est pourquoi pour Simon Jolivet le constitutionnalisme environnemental doit parfois s'effacer derrière ce qu'il appelle le « communautarisme environnemental » de l'UE. La valeur supérieure des normes internationales permet cependant un rapprochement avec les normes constitutionnelles nationales, d'autant plus que cette valeur est le plus souvent inscrite dans la Constitution nationale. À ce titre, la Convention européenne des droits de l'homme et la jurisprudence

---

586 Dans ce contexte manque malheureusement ici la contribution sur le droit civil de l'environnement et la Cour de cassation présentée par Émilie Gaillard lors du colloque à l'origine du présent ouvrage.

environnementale qui en résulte ont un impact considérable dans les systèmes juridiques des États ayant ratifié ce texte. Marie-Anne Cohendet et Anne-Christine Favre se réfèrent à cet instrument respectivement pour la France et la Suisse. Quant à l'étude fournie par Sven Kaufmann, elle porte dans son ensemble un regard au-delà du contexte national et rend féconde la notion de constitutionnalisme environnemental dans le contexte de l'UE.

2) Sur le plan matériel, la consécration constitutionnelle de la protection environnementale peut avoir plusieurs degrés de contrainte normative. Il peut s'agir :

- d'une simple recommandation à portée morale,
- d'un objectif obligatoire adressé à l'État : en ce sens se perçoivent la Loi fondamentale allemande, où l'article 20a vise à la fois le législateur fédéral et les législateurs fédérés, et certaines constitutions de Land (Alexander Proelß) ainsi que la Constitution de l'Inde, art. 48 A et partiellement art. 51 A g (Gitanjali N. Gill),
- de droits subjectifs, invocables par les citoyens : c'est le cas en France, explicitement grâce à la Charte (Marie-Anne Cohendet) et en Inde, grâce à la jurisprudence de la Cour suprême qui déduit, à partir d'obligations constitutionnelles imposées aux citoyens ainsi que du droit général à la vie, des droits individuels environnementaux (Gitanjali N. Gill).

En droit suisse, la situation est plus oscillante. Anne-Christine Favre souligne que la distinction peut être ténue entre un objectif constitutionnel qui oriente l'interprétation du juge et un principe pleinement justiciable. Seul le caractère indéterminé du principe fait barrage à une pleine justiciabilité, un caractère qui peut évoluer suite à des mises en œuvre législatives.

Sur le plan matériel intervient la pondération par le juge constitutionnel des intérêts environnementaux lorsqu'ils sont en conflit avec d'autres intérêts constitutionnels. Alexander Proelß l'évoque à propos de l'Allemagne. Quant à la primauté d'intérêts consacrés par une norme constitutionnelle sur des intérêts infraconstitutionnels, Anne-Christine Favre met en relief la singularité suisse qui, par le jeu des initiatives populaires, permet l'ancrage constitutionnel de textes directement applicables et suite auxquels l'intérêt environnemental s'impose, ne permettant plus une pesée des intérêts en présence par l'autorité d'exécution.

Les différents auteurs soulignent certaines idées-forces du constitutionnalisme environnemental. La reconnaissance de la personnalité juridique de la nature attire l'attention de Marie-Anne Cohendet et est soulignée par Erin Daly et James R. May. Ces derniers distinguent les droits qui en découlent pour la nature, y compris pour les fleuves[587], d'un côté, et les droits reconnus au profit des personnes morales (*corporations*) et des animaux, de l'autre côté. Seulement ces derniers droits sont classés dans la catégorie des droits humains. Si pour Samuel Ferey la personnalisation d'éléments de la nature est compatible avec l'approche non empirique du droit (le droit a effectivement recours à la technique de la fiction[588]), il a des difficultés d'appliquer ses conséquences en économie qui ontologiquement est focalisée sur les utilités humaines matérielles.

Parmi les éléments de la nature, une importance particulière peut être accordée aux animaux dont le régime juridique entre dans le domaine du constitutionnalisme environnemental. Alexander Proelß analyse ce processus de constitutionnalisation et sa portée, explicitement présent dans la Loi fondamentale allemande, notamment par rapport à la sensibilité animale. Letícia Albuquerque consacre l'ensemble de sa contribution à la protection des animaux au Brésil. Il s'agit effectivement, à l'intérieur du dispositif constitutionnel protecteur de l'environnement, d'une dimension peu connue en Europe. Le point de départ est une décision du Tribunal suprême fédéral qui applique à une loi fédérée l'interdiction constitutionnelle de la cruauté envers les animaux et invalide une pratique spécifique de rodéo. Le pouvoir constituant fédéral s'est inscrit en contre-courant à cette évolution, en cassant cette décision au moyen d'une révision constitutionnelle. Par conséquent, l'acquis environnemental a été neutralisé puisque des pratiques cruelles sont désormais admises lorsqu'elles font partie du patrimoine culturel du pays. Nous sommes en présence d'une régression

---

587 V. à ce propos l'étude fondamentale de Catherine J. Iorns Magallanes, « Nature as an Ancestor: Two Examples of Legal Personality for Nature in New Zealand », *in* : Marie-Pierre Camproux Duffrene, Jochen Sohnle (dir.), *La représentation de la nature devant le juge : approches comparative et prospective*, Les Éditions en environnement VertigO, Montréal, Canada, 2015, p. 83–103 et publication parallèle en ligne : https://journals.openedition.org/vertigo/16199.

588 Jochen Sohnle, « La représentation de la nature devant le juge : Plaidoyer pour une épistémologie juridique du fictif », *ibid.*, p. 329–363 et https://journals.openedition.org/vertigo/16343.

criante du constitutionnalisme environnemental, contraire, comme le démontre Letícia Albuquerque, au noyau dur de la Constitution brésilienne, y compris la dignité humaine.

Ce sont des considérations de dignité qui permettent, pour Erin Daly et James R. May, de mettre au premier plan le dommage environnemental qui potentiellement affecte les personnes dans les aspects essentiels de leur vie (alimentation, eau potable, air respirable). De même, Alexander Proelß analyse le principe de protection de l'environnement en relation avec le respect de la dignité humaine, étant donné que la Loi fondamentale est construite en 1949 entièrement autour de cette idée-force. Cette vision est inhérente aussi à l'interprétation environnementaliste donnée par la Cour suprême de l'Inde au droit fondamental à la vie selon Gitanjali N. Gill.

Le constitutionnalisme de la durabilité (*sustainability constitutionalism*) fait également partie, d'après Erin Daly et James R. May, des nouvelles tendances. Ils constatent cependant à ce propos une certaine dichotomie : alors que des constitutions se réfèrent régulièrement à la durabilité, les auteurs et les praticiens du droit y voient seulement un principe directeur silencieux (*silent guiding principle*) et sont lents à le promouvoir. Alexander Proelß, au contraire, donne des arguments convaincants, y compris fondés sur la jurisprudence, que la consécration constitutionnelle du principe de développement durable appuie le caractère contraignant du principe de précaution. Le constat d'Anne-Christine Favre à propos du droit constitutionnel suisse va dans le même sens. À travers une analyse jurisprudentielle, elle constate, sur le fondement de l'invitation constitutionnelle adressée à la Confédération et aux cantons d'œuvrer à l'établissement d'un équilibre durable, une constitutionnalisation non seulement du principe de précaution, mais aussi de celui qui impose une certaine gestion des ressources naturelles (concrètement l'obligation de trouver des solutions de substitution avant d'épuiser une ressource rare) et des cours d'eau.

L'évaluation du dommage à l'environnement, dont la réparation s'impose en vertu de l'article 4 de la Charte française de l'environnement, exige l'intervention de l'économiste. Pour Samuel Ferey, il peut intervenir doublement. D'abord comme interprète de l'article 4 afin de définir pour sa discipline les contours conceptuels de la réparation, avec les limites déjà mentionnées lorsqu'il s'agit de considérer la nature comme agent (personne). Ensuite comme expert chargé de fournir des outils d'évaluation pour mettre en œuvre l'article 4. À cet égard, l'économie est particulièrement féconde. Elle fournit toute une panoplie de techniques d'évaluation, non seulement pour réparer le préjudice matériel et moral classique, mais aussi le préjudice écologique « pur ». L'auteur apporte aux juristes environnementalistes un éclaircissement précieux sur les méthodes récentes d'équivalence de service qui, méthodologiquement à cheval entre sciences naturelles, ingénierie et économie, ouvrent la voie à une réparation en nature, conformément au constitutionnalisme environnemental.

Si le dispositif matériel protecteur de l'environnement se reflète, d'après Marie-Anne Cohendet, dans la Charte de l'environnement d'une manière particulièrement complète, elle propose toutefois, à l'intérieur de la systématique constitutionnelle française, de rehausser la valeur de certains de ses principes fondamentaux en les juxtaposant à la garantie de l'égalité, de la laïcité et de l'indivisibilité de la République mentionnée à l'article 1er de la Constitution qui représentent les principales obligations qui s'imposent à tous. Comme le constate et l'illustre Sven Kaufmann à travers la jurisprudence, un rehaussement de ce type existe déjà en droit de l'UE à travers le principe d'intégration de la protection environnementale (TFUE, art. 11) qui joue comme clause horizontale pour toutes les politiques sectorielles ainsi que les libertés fondamentales. Ce principe est ainsi mobilisable au-delà des seules compétences transférées au titre de la politique environnementale et cela pour interpréter à la fois le droit primaire et le droit dérivé. En revanche, à côté de l'article 11 (TFUE), l'article 37 de la Charte des droits fondamentaux de l'UE ne déploie pas d'effets autonomes et ne réalise pas véritablement un « rehaussement constitutionnel » (*constitutional upgrading*). Sven Kaufmann perçoit cependant un certain potentiel dans cette disposition susceptible d'affecter dans un sens environnemental l'interprétation d'autres principes et droits fondamentaux.

Marie-Anne Cohendet regrette aussi la formulation restrictive des principes de précaution et pollueur-payeur dans la Charte française. Mais elle souligne surtout qu'on devrait élever au rang constitutionnel d'autres aspects comme le principe de respect des limites planétaires et le principe de non-régression. Dans le contexte allemand, Alexander Proelß propose de déduire ce dernier de l'article 20a de la loi fondamentale alors que pour la Suisse, Anne-Christine Favre le déduit des principes de prévention et précaution, avec des indices de comportement du législateur à l'appui. Lorsque le principe de non-régression existe seulement sur le plan international, il peut être neutralisé suite au jeu des relations entre droit constitutionnel et droit international : même si ce dernier est plus favorable à la protection de l'environnement, c'est la Constitution qui prime pour le juge national. Ce phénomène est bien analysé par Simon Jolivet à propos de la doctrine jurisprudentielle française de l'écran conventionnel. Enfin, le principe de non-régression peut subir une attaque frontale, comme au Brésil à propos de l'interdiction de cruauté envers les animaux, d'après le témoignage de Letícia Albuquerque.

Le rehaussement de principes environnementaux au rang des normes constitutionnelles impacte très fortement les systèmes normatifs infraconstitutionnels. Le principe de précaution a ainsi pu devenir un élément autonome d'appréciation de l'utilité publique par le juge administratif français, indépendamment du contrôle du bilan, et préalablement à celui-ci, comme le précise Simon Jolivet. Cet auteur met également en évidence le décloisonnement, même si c'est de manière seulement relative, de ce principe appliqué désormais au-delà du droit de l'environnement par exemple en droit de l'urbanisme, affaiblissant ainsi la doctrine prétorienne d'indépendance des législations.

3) Sur le plan procédural, il y a non seulement le respect de certaines procédures non contentieuses représentées par les deux premiers piliers de la Convention d'Aarhus (1998), à savoir l'accès à l'information environnementale et la participation aux décisions environnementales. Il y a aussi les procédures contentieuses, conformément au troisième pilier de cette convention, sous forme d'un droit d'accès à la justice.

Olivier Cachard envisage ces piliers sous un angle inhabituel. Il interpelle non seulement le juge judiciaire français par rapport à l'application du principe constitutionnel de précaution, mais également les procédures du droit des sociétés qui attribuent à l'État actionnaire un rôle particulier en matière d'information et de participation. L'État se trouve effectivement en capacité d'orienter les choix stratégiques d'une société commerciale de façon à l'inscrire non seulement dans le respect des politiques publiques, mais également des principes constitutionnels. À propos de cet enjeu fondamental pour la politique environnementale, mais peu familier aux juristes environnementalistes, l'auteur explique avec pédagogie dans quelle mesure l'État actionnaire est tenu par le principe de précaution : directement, au moyen du rôle du commissaire du Gouvernement, représentant de l'État dans la société, et indirectement, au moyen de la responsabilité sociale des entreprises et du devoir de vigilance des sociétés mères.

Dans les systèmes juridiques qui s'inscrivent dans la tradition de la *common law* le rôle du juge est consubstantiel dans l'élaboration des normes constitutionnelles protectrices de l'environnement. La contribution de Gitanjali N. Gill en donne une excellente illustration sur la Cour suprême de l'Inde qui, pour lutter contre la pollution et les inégalités sociales, interprète la Constitution de manière extensive, aussi grâce à une formation spécialement créée (*Social Justice Bench*). Même si l'auteure témoigne aussi des lenteurs et des problèmes de mise en œuvre des décisions de justice en Inde, l'appareil juridictionnel contribue à contrebalancer l'ineffectivité de l'action gouvernementale, l'insuffisance de l'action législative et la corruptibilité du secteur public.

Toujours sur le plan du contentieux, Erin Daly et James R. May analysent le lien fécond entre constitutionnalisme environnemental et un nombre croissant de procès nationaux déclenchés par des individus, des groupes d'individus ou des associations de défense de l'environnement pour reprocher aux autorités étatiques leur inaction en matière de lutte contre le changement climatique. Anne-Christine Favre rapporte sur l'une de ces affaires devant les juridictions suisses (affaire de l'association *KlimaSeniorinnen*), susceptible de tracer la voie vers la reconnaissance d'un droit fondamental à un environnement sain.

Si en France, des droits environnementaux individuels sont garantis, Marie-Anne Cohendet attire de manière critique l'attention sur la jurisprudence du Conseil constitutionnel à propos du contentieux *a posteriori* de la question prioritaire de constitutionnalité (article 61-1 de la Constitution) qui admet seulement l'invocabilité des quatre premiers articles et de l'article 7 de la Charte, à l'exclusion des autres, y compris les considérants du préambule. Quant à Anne-Christine Favre, elle insiste sur le fait que l'absence de mise en œuvre d'un principe constitutionnel environnemental par le législateur rend le tribunal constitutionnel impuissant, en l'occurrence en ce qui concerne le principe pollueur-payeur. Cette difficulté est bien évidemment pertinente au-delà du seul droit suisse. Elle est problématisée par Simon Jolivet qui démontre que les normes à valeur constitutionnelle (la Charte française) ne s'imposent pas toujours au pouvoir administratif comme elles devraient le faire d'après le principe de constitutionnalité inhérent au constitutionnalisme. Notamment les écrans législatif et conventionnel peuvent s'y opposer en droit français. Cet auteur illustre cependant de quelle manière la doctrine, critiquable, de l'écran législatif a été affaiblie grâce au recours offert dans le cadre de la question prioritaire de constitutionnalité.

Quant à l'intérêt à agir devant les tribunaux[589], Gitanjali N. Gill souligne pour l'Inde que les droits environnementaux du citoyen s'étendent d'après la jurisprudence à tous les citoyens défendant la cause publique, aux institutions intéressées et aux associations (*public-spirited citizens, interested institutions and NGOs*). L'intérêt pour agir est en effet conçu de manière large dans le domaine des droits sociaux collectifs et diffus au titre d'une politique judiciaire spécifique (*Environmental Public Interest Litigation).* Le juge accepte de remédier à un manque d'expertise juridique dans le cadre d'une requête qui serait rejetée dans d'autres situations socialement moins sensibles. L'auteure s'interroge cependant sur les standards applicables pour atteindre un environnement sain : ces standards doivent-ils consister dans des « transplantations juridiques » occidentales ou être déduits de la situation de l'Inde ?

Si les droits environnementaux procéduraux peuvent être perçus de manière fragmentée (les trois piliers de la Convention d'Aarhus : information, participation, accès à la justice), Erin Daly et James R. May nous font part de la tendance des juges à les concevoir de manière holistique : l'information est nécessaire pour la participation et l'accès à la justice est nécessaire pour revendiquer le droit à l'information et à la participation.

En définitive, pour reprendre une idée de Gitanjali N. Gill, il convient d'évoluer vers un constitutionnalisme transformatif à travers une approche polycentrique, participative et démocratique (*a transformative environmental constitutionalism approach being polycentric, participatory and democratic*). Afin que les juges et les autres acteurs deviennent sensibles à cette approche, il faut soutenir l'appel impérieux de Marie-Anne Cohendet à une formation adéquate des juristes en droit de l'environnement et cela à la fois dans les universités et les grandes écoles ainsi que lors de la formation initiale et continue des avocats, des juges et des autres professionnels appliquant le droit.

---

589 Pour aller plus loin sur cet aspect : Marie-Pierre Camproux Duffrene, « La représentation de l'intérêt collectif environnemental devant le juge civil : après l'affaire Erika et avant l'introduction dans le Code civil du dommage causé à l'environnement », *ibid.*, p. 265–292 et en ligne : https://journals.openedition.org/vertigo/16320 ; Véronique Jaworski, « Les représentations multiples de l'environnement devant le juge pénal : entre intérêts général, individuel et collectif », *ibid.*, p. 205–222 et en ligne : https://journals.openedition.org/vertigo/16272 ; Alexandra Aragão, « Les intérêts diffus, instruments pour la justice et la démocratie environnementale », *ibid.*, p. 225–240 et en ligne : https://journals.openedition.org/vertigo/16284.

ÉcoPolis

La collection ÉcoPolis est dédiée à l'analyse des changements qui se produisent simultanément dans la société et dans l'environnement quand celui-ci devient une préoccupation centrale.

L'environnement a longtemps été défini comme l'extérieur de la société, comme ce monde de la nature et des écosystèmes qui sert de soubassement matériel à la vie sociale. Les politiques d'environnement avaient alors pour but de « préserver », « protéger », voire « gérer » ce qui était pensé comme une sorte d'infrastructure de nos sociétés. Après quelques décennies de politique d'environnement, la nature et l'environnement sont devenus des objets de l'action publique et il apparaît que c'est dans un même mouvement que chaque société modèle son environnement et se construit elle-même. Cette dialectique sera au centre de la collection.

Directeur de collection : Marc Mormont,
Professeur à la Fondation universitaire luxembourgeoise
(Université de Liège, Belgique)

Dans la collection

N° 31 – Cécilia Claeys (ed.), *Mosquitoes management. Between environmental and health issues*, 2019.

N° 30 – Sylvain Guyot, *La nature, l'autre frontière. Fronts écologiques au Sud (Afrique du Sud, Argentine, Chili)*, 2017.

N° 29 – Divya Leducq, Helga-Jane Scarwell et Patrizia Ingallina (dir.), *Modèles de la ville durable en Asie. Utopies, circulation des pratiques, gouvernance*, 2017.

N° 28 – Ludovic Ginelli, *Jeux de nature, natures en jeu. Des loisirs aux prises avec l'écologisation des sociétés*, 2016, 240 pages. N° 27 – Xavier Arnauld de Sartre, *Agriculture et changements globaux. Expertises globales et situations locales*, 2016, 204 pages.

N° 26 – Bernard Hubert et Nicole Mathieu (dir.), *Interdisciplinarités entre Natures et Sociétés. Colloque de Cerisy*, 2016, 396 pages.

N° 25 – Arnaud Buchs, *La pénurie en eau est-elle inéluctable ? Une approche institutionnaliste de l'évolution du mode d'usage de l'eau en Espagne et au Maroc,* 2016, 331 pages.

N° 24 – Valérie Deldrève, *Pour une sociologie des inégalités environnementales,* 2015, 243 pages.

N° 23 –Zhour Bouzidi, *Se coordonner dans un périmètre irrigué public au Maroc.* Contradictio in terminis ?, 2015, 373 pages.

N° 22 – Laura Silva-Castañeda, Étienne Verhaegen, Sophie Charlier, An Ansoms (dir.), *Au-delà de l'accaparement. Ruptures et continuités dans l'accès aux ressources naturelles,* 2014, 244 p.

N° 21 – Xavier Arnauld de Sartre, Monica Castro, Simon Dufour, Johan Oszwald (dir.), Political ecology *des services écosystémiques*, 2014, 288 pages.

N° 20 – Céline Granjou, *Micropolitiques de la biodiversité. Experts et professionnels de la nature*, 2013, 202 pages.

N° 19 – Corinne Larrue (dir.), *Le régime institutionnel d'une nouvelle ruralité. Analyses à partir des cas de la France, des Pays-Bas et de la Suisse,* 2013, 214 pages.

N° 18 – François Bertrand et Laurence Rocher (dir.), *Les territoires face aux changements climatiques. Une première génération d'initiatives locales,* 2013, 269 pages.

N° 17 – Véronique Ancey, Isabelle Avelange, Benoît Dedieu (dir.), *Agir en situation d'incertitude en agriculture. Regards pluridisciplinaires au Nord et au Sud,* 2013, 419 pages.

N° 16 – N° 16 – Cécilia Claeys and Marie Jacqué (eds.), *Environmental Democracy Facing Uncertainty*, 2012, 185 pages.

N° 15 – Josiane Stoessel-Ritz, Maurice Blanc, Nicole Mathieu (dir.), *Développement durable, communautés et sociétés. Dynamiques socio-anthropologiques*, 2012, 230 pages.

N° 14 – Philippe Hamman, Christine Blanc et Cécile Frank, *La négociation dans les projets urbains de tramway. Éléments pour une sociologie de la « ville durable »*, 2011, 246 pages.

N° 13 – Denise Van Dam, Michel Streith et Jean Nizet (dir.), *L'agriculture bio en devenir. Le cas alsacien*, 2011, 140 pages.

N° 12 – Philippe Hamman et Jean-Yves Causer (dir.), *Ville, environnement et transactions démocratiques. Hommage au Professeur Maurice Blanc*, 2011, 291 pages.

N° 11 – Géraldine Froger (dir.), *Tourisme durable dans les Suds ?*, 2010, 316 pages.

N° 10 – Muriel Maillefert, Olivier Petit et Sandrine Rousseau (dir.), *Ressources, patrimoine, territoires et développement durable*, 2010, 283 pages.

N° 9 – Philippe Hamman et Christine Blanc, *Sociologie du développement durable urbain. Projets et stratégies métropolitaines françaises*, 2009, 260 pages.

N° 8 – François Mélard (dir.), *Écologisation. Objets et concepts intermédiaires*, 2008, 214 pages.

N° 7 – David Aubin, *L'eau en partage. L'activation des règles dans les rivalités d'usages en Belgique et en Suisse*, 2007, 247 pages.

N° 6 – Géraldine Froger (dir.), *La mondialisation contre le développement durable ?*, 2006, 315 pages.

N° 5 – Laurent Mermet (dir.), *Étudier des écologies futures. Un chantier ouvert pour les recherches prospectives environnementales*, 2005, 411 pages.

N° 4 – Jean-Baptiste Narcy, *Pour une gestion spatiale de l'eau. Comment sortir du tuyau ?*, 2004, 342 pages.

N° 3 – Pierre Stassart, *Produits fermiers : entre qualification et identité*, 2003, 424 pages.

N° 2 – Cécilia Claeys-Mekdade, *Le lien politique à l'épreuve de l'environnement. Expériences camarguaises*, 2003, 245 pages.

N° 1 – Edwin Zaccaï, *Le développement durable. Dynamique et constitution d'un projet*, 2002 (2e tirage 2003), 358 pages.

www.peterlang.com